THE
WORD
EXCHANGE

THE
WORD
EXCHANGE

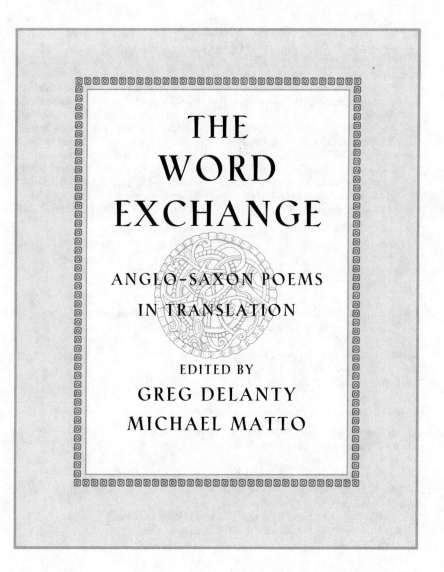

ANGLO-SAXON POEMS
IN TRANSLATION

EDITED BY

GREG DELANTY
MICHAEL MATTO

W. W. NORTON & COMPANY

New York London

For information about special discounts for bulk purchases, please contact
W. W. Norton Special Sales at specialsales@wwnorton.com or 800-233-4830

Manufacturing by RR Donnelley Harrisonburg
Book design by JAM Design
Production manager: Julia Druskin

Library of Congress Cataloging-in-Publication Data

The word exchange : Anglo-Saxon poems in translation /
edited by Greg Delanty, Michael Matto.
p. cm.
In Old English with English translations.
Includes bibliographical references and index.
ISBN 978-0-393-07901-2 (hardcover)
1. English poetry—Old English, ca. 450–1100—Modernized versions.
2. English poetry—Old English, ca. 450–1100. I. Delanty, Greg, 1958–
II. Matto, Michael.
PR1508.W67 2010
829'.108—dc22

                                                    2010028560

W. W. Norton & Company, Inc.
500 Fifth Avenue, New York, N.Y. 10110
www.wwnorton.com

W. W. Norton & Company Ltd.
Castle House, 75/76 Wells Street, London W1T 3QT

1 2 3 4 5 6 7 8 9 0

CONTENTS

POEMS ABOUT HISTORICAL BATTLES, PEOPLE, AND PLACES

SECOND RIDDLE-HOARD

POEMS ABOUT LIVING

FOREWORD

THE BATTLE OF MALDON, A WORK COMMEMORATING THE DOOMED
stand of a troop of East Anglian warriors against a band of Norse raid-
ers, is one of the glories of Anglo-Saxon poetry. The poem is swift,
succinct, unified in tone and effect, a tale of exemplary loyalty and
heartfelt loss, yet for all its emotional and stylistic coherence, it is
incomplete as a text. The manuscript begins with two words—*brocen
wurde*—which have stayed with me from the moment I first read
them in Sweet's *Anglo-Saxon Reader,* a prescribed book when I was
studying for a degree in English fifty years ago. The words form the
conclusion of a sentence now lost forever, but they lead into a poem
which might nevertheless have pleased Aristotle: even without its
beginning *The Battle of Maldon* has a completeness to it. It observes
the classical unities, being the imitation of an action that occurs in the
same place in the course of a single day, although that coincidence
meant little to me as an undergraduate. What pleased me then and
stamped itself indelibly on my memory was the head-on, plainspoken
force of that truncated phrase: "*brocen wurde.*" "[It] was broken."

The words could almost function as a very condensed history of
Anglo-Saxon poetry: it was too broken like the shield wall at Maldon,
not by Norse raiders in 991 but by Norman invaders in 1066 when a
legendary arrow—a "battle-adder" as the native *scop* or poem-shaper
or word-hoarder might have called it—pierced King Harold's eye at
the Battle of Hastings, and the followers of William the Conqueror
arrived in force to change the laws and language and ultimately the
literature of England.

This anthology contains translations of the finest poetry that has
survived from that Anglo-Saxon period of English history, the six

hundred years from the middle of the fifth to the middle of the eleventh century. The only significant absence is the heroic narrative we know as *Beowulf,* that complete work whose 3,182 lines comprise 10 percent of the total corpus of Old English verse. Yet it could be argued that *Beowulf* is nevertheless in some sense present since much of the work included here gives expression to codes of behavior and attitudes of mind that are fundamental to the world depicted in the epic, a world where the ethic of an older warrior culture underlies and coexists with but has not yet been entirely co-opted by the new Christian faith. The note in many of the famous shorter poems—*The Wanderer* and *The Seafarer,* for example—is audible throughout *Beowulf,* a note that manages to combine resolution and resignation, to be heroic yet homiletic, to acknowledge the virtue of a thane's fidelity to his warrior lord in the mead hall but to recognize also the warrior lord's dependence for salvation on an eternal lord in the heavens.

The anthology, however, is a reminder that Anglo-Saxon poetry isn't all stoicism and melancholy, isn't all about battle and exile and a gray dawn breaking: it can be unexpectedly rapturous as in *The Vision of the Cross* and happily didactic as in the allegory of *Whale.* It can be intimate and domestic, and take us to places far behind the shield wall, as in the love poems of the opening section and the remedies and charms included toward the end. And everywhere, as is evident in the riddles interspersed throughout the book, it rejoices in its own wordcraft, its inventiveness, its appositive imagining and fundamental awareness of itself as a play of language.

This play of language is resumed by the poets who have translated the work included here, proof that the lifeline to and from this poetry has not been broken, that all language is an entry to further language. Reading these old poems voiced in new ways by contemporary poets reminded me of something I read years ago in the foreword to a different collection of Anglo-Saxon poetry where the editor said that he preferred the term "rendered" to the term "translated." This does seem a wise preference, since it allows for a truce of sorts between the "free" and the "faithful" or "obedient" schools of translators. Consider, for example, just a few of the primary meanings of "render," to be found in *The Shorter Oxford Dictionary:* "to repeat (something learned); to say over; to give in return, give back, restore; to submit to, or lay before, another for consideration or approval; to obtain or extract by melting."

Each of these definitions applies to a greater or lesser extent to the work done by the editors and contributors to *The Word Exchange.* Essentially they are involved in what I once called "the redress of poetry" where "redress" meant "to set upright again, to raise again to an erect position. Also figuratively to restore, reestablish." So instead of *"brocen wurde"* with its suggestions of defeat and lost tradition, the epigraph to this book could be *"wæs ic aræred,"* a proud phrase from *The Vision of the Cross* meaning "I was raised up" and signifying the ongoing vitality of Anglo-Saxon poetry a millennium after its demise might have been expected.

—Seamus Heaney

PREFACE

WE TEND TO THINK OF ANGLO-SAXON POETRY AS ISSUING FROM the uniform voice of the great poet Anonywulf, especially once the poems are translated by the learned Master Olde English. This uniform voice, of course, is an illusion created by the way Anglo-Saxon poetry has been presented down through modern times. As Michael Matto explains in the introduction, the poetry of the Anglo-Saxon period came from many different poets. The identities of those poets are now lost, but to those who can read Anglo-Saxon poetry in the original, the diverse registers, personalities, and backgrounds of the poems are apparent. *The Word Exchange* is intended to give readers, not just those who are able to read Old English, a vivid sense of that diversity. To accomplish this we invited over seventy poets to translate the poems anew. The outcome is a book unique among collections of Old English poetry in translation.

The guidelines that Michael Matto and I sent to the contributing poets, adapted from my friend Katharine Washburn's introduction in another anthology called *World Poetry,* were "to translate in whatever way you are comfortable with while remaining true to the original. What we have in mind are the second and third categories of John Dryden's taxonomy in his *Preface to Ovid's Epistles* where he reduced translations to three 'heads.' The first, which he called 'metaphrase,' we would call a humble crib—the turning of a poem word by word and line by line from one language to another. The second head he termed a 'paraphrase' or 'translation with latitude,' allowing the translator to keep the author in view while altering words, but not sense. The third embraced the possibilities of 'imitation,' a translation in which the poet works from the original text but departs from words and sense, sometimes writing as the author would have done had she or he lived in the time and place of the reader. We would not want an imitation to stray so far from the original that it becomes unrecognizable, but a fair amount of latitude is possible." It seems most of the translations fall into Dryden's second category, though many ventured into his third category also. The readers can judge for themselves which translations fall where.

Many of the poets are not well versed in Old English. As A. E. Stallings says in her commentary, "I have no Anglo-Saxon, except inasmuch as I speak English." We thought it would be an informative addition to have a dozen poets comment on Old English poetry and on the process of translating it. We believed the poets—rather than translators who were not poets—could lift the poems from mere translations to poems in themselves, thus matching the original spirit-energy as well as content. The reader can see, for instance, how successful the translations are in A. E. Stallings tour de force *The Riming Poem*. Many of the translators worked with Michael Matto who gave the individual poets cribs, glossaries, and interpretive direction. For those who weren't expert in Old English, David Slavitt's words are true in his prose note about translating *The Battle of Maldon*: "What the translator needs is accurate information from a sympathetic guide and a competence in the target language." Others were at home in Anglo-Saxon poetry in their own right, poets such as Bernard O'Donoghue, who teaches Old English himself at Oxford University.

The Anglo-Saxon poems resonate in different ways with our times. Eavan Boland remarks, "Texts like *The Seafarer* and *The Wanderer* and *The Battle of Maldon* now seemed urgent, contemporary, and necessary." It is the parallel to our war-torn world and how we are destroying it environmentally that lead me to translate *The Wanderer* and Yusef Komunyakaa to translate *The Ruin*. Some of the more intriguing lesser-known poems such as Kelly Cherry's *The Fortunes of Men* also ring true today, and a modern sensibility is evident in the playfulness of the riddles translated by Edwin Morgan, Gerry Murphy, Marcia Karp, Neil Rollinson, David Barber, and many others.

The invitation to translators had as much to do with serendipity as it did with intention, but once they were invited the poets chose which Old English texts to take on. We assigned one translator per poem, but in the case of *Riddle 43* and *Riddle 80* two poets simultaneously translated the same riddle, and we decided to include both, if only to show how translations can vary. Many of the translators I know as poets and as friends; poets I believe in, and who I believed would relish a renewing exchange with poems from over a thousand years ago, worthily matching that word-hoard with a word-hoard of our times.

—Greg Delanty

THE
WORD
EXCHANGE

INTRODUCTION

THE GREAT MAJORITY OF OLD ENGLISH POEMS ARE ANONYMOUS. Without authors' names or even titles in the manuscripts, we easily forget that any two Old English poems might have been composed hundreds of years as well as hundreds of miles apart. (Titles for these poems are the inventions of editors and translators.) We tend to imagine they speak with one voice—that they are all simply "Old English." Anthologies inadvertently reinforce this impression when a single writer does all the translating, whether he or she chooses a good prose style for greater accuracy or a single metrical approach for poetic resonance. In this collection the panoply of voices is meant to return a sense of individuality to each text, allowing those who cannot read Old English to experience the poems as a collection of diverse authorial viewpoints instead of as a homogeneous, and dead, corpus.

The Old English phrase *wordum wrixlan* (meaning "to exchange words") had great currency in Anglo-Saxon England. Unlike a person's *wordhord*—one's personal storehouse of language from which poetic utterances might be drawn—*wordum wrixlan* is language's participation in an economy of exchange as we trade words or weave them into stories. The writer of the poem *Maxims I* uses a variation on this phrase, *gieddum wrixlan* (a *gied* is a song or story), to demand his reader's engagement in the play of ideas (here expressed in David Curzon's translation):

> I won't speak my spirit   if you hide your heart.
> Those who know   must traffic their maxims.

The title of this book, *The Word Exchange,* honors this notion of trafficking in words. Certainly the contemporary poets in this collection have exchanged the words of one language for another while translating; but beyond that all poets weave words to exchange ideas, a process that links writers in English across a span of over a thousand years as they practice their shared craft. How might the poems of this distant past speak to us today—to poets and readers alike? Like the *Maxims* poet, we have called on "those who know" to traffic in stories within the economy of cultural touchstones.

Our hope is that each poem can stand on its own as a poem, with a minimum of introduction. Still, these works are products of their own time and culture: the six-hundred-year stretch we call "Anglo-Saxon England." This general introduction therefore offers the reader unfamiliar with that period a brief overview of its culture, its language, and its literary history, followed by some specific suggestions about how to approach reading this collection.

THE ANGLO-SAXONS

At the start of the fifth century, the southern half of the island then known as "Britannia" was peopled primarily by Celts (called "Britons") who were subjects of the Roman Empire. The previous few decades had witnessed a steady withdrawal of Roman garrisons that were needed to defend lands closer to Rome. This left the inhabitants of Brittania to fend largely for themselves against invaders—no idle concern for the Britons who, with no real centralized government or organized defense, suffered assault from all sides: the Picts from the north, the Irish from the west, and Germanic raiders all along the east coast.

Between the years 450 and 600, demographics on the island shifted as invaders and settlers of Germanic origin (Angles, Saxons, and Jutes) supplanted the Britons linguistically and culturally in the east and south, areas that would come to be known as "Angle-land." Whether by driving the Celtic population out or by subsuming them within the transplanted Germanic culture, they initiated what we now call the Anglo-Saxon period in England, which lasted until the Norman invasion of 1066. The Angles provided the eponym for "England" and "English," while the Saxons left their mark in regional names still in use, such as Essex, Wessex, and Sussex (that is, the lands of the East-, West-, and South-Saxons).

Such times of demographic and social upheaval are prime occasions for storytelling. This period of British resistance to the Anglo-Saxons provides the backdrop for the earliest tales of King Arthur as a Celtic freedom fighter battling the continental invaders. But a lesser-known myth about this era involves two Germanic mercenary brothers, Hengest and Horsa. As the story goes, around the year 449 a British leader named Vortigern (who, in Arthurian myth, usurps the throne of Uther Pendragon's family) saw that he needed help defending his lands against Picts. Vortigern invited Hengest and Horsa from the Jutland peninsula (modern Denmark) to settle on the island of Thanet in return for military service. The brothers drove back the Picts, and Horsa was killed in battle. But afterward the agreement apparently did not satisfy Hengest, and he soon forced Vortigern to install him as ruler in Kent. More elaborate versions of the story have Vortigern marrying Hengest's daughter, allowing Hengest to use Vortigern as a puppet king, opening the door to further Saxon incursions into Britannia.

The Saxon brothers may well be a mythopoetic invention or exaggeration repeated by later historians of early England; they remind us of such other foundation-myth pairings as Romulus and Remus, or Amphion and Zethus; further, their names, meaning "stallion" and "horse," echo other divine twins with equine associations, such as the Greek Castor and Pollux and the Vedic Ashvins. The appeal of this foundation myth has remained so strong that Thomas Jefferson suggested the Saxon brothers might provide a fitting iconography for the seal of the United States (opposite an image of the Israelites following the pillars of fire and cloud out of captivity), claiming that the roots of the American principles of government and desire for self-determination could be found in the jurisprudence of these sea cross-ers. In any case, the brothers' historicity notwithstanding, their story offers a fitting example of the prevailing Anglo-Saxon ethos: pride in military conquest and loyalty coupled with a dedicated pragmatism.

Though we often refer to "Anglo-Saxon England" as a single period, its six hundred years saw an immense amount of political and cultural change. Governmental organization moved in fits and starts from localized clans and warring small kingdoms to a centralized English authority, adopting law codes and procedures of justice along the way that do in fact remain at the root of modern English jurisprudence. The descendents of those first migratory Angles and Saxons adopted Christianity as their religion, with England quickly becoming a center of Christian learning. Their metalwork and craftsmanship in jewelry rivaled that of the Celts. And they produced one of the earliest and most extensive records of vernacular literature in Europe. Hardly a representative of a dark age, Anglo-Saxon England is a cultural bright spot in the European world in the centuries following the sack of Rome.

OLD ENGLISH LANGUAGE AND WRITING

The languages of the Angles, Saxons, and their continental cousins were mutually intelligible Germanic dialects. Once transplanted to England, however, they followed their own courses. "Old English" is an umbrella term that covers all these dialects as they diverged and merged across the island. Old English reminds the modern eye and ear more of German than of modern English, largely because after the Norman Conquest of 1066, English was profoundly influenced by the French spoken by the expatriate Normans. Still, at its core modern English remains a Germanic language. For instance, though only some 25 percent of the average English speaker's vocabulary is of Old English origin, by one count 97 of the 100 most commonly used words are from Old English. These include pronouns, articles, the verb "to be," and other common verbs, and a handful of nouns and adjectives. Also, much of Old English grammar remains, and even accounts for many apparent oddities in modern English. The "s" that signals the plural for nouns comes from Old English, but so do the words that do not use the "s," such as "men" and "feet," or more strangely "deer" and "sheep." The two competing ways to mark the past tense of verbs are both found in Old English; thus we have "drink"/"drank" and "sink"/"sank," but "link"/"linked" instead of "link"/"lank." Such similarities in vocabulary and grammar allow us to read some Old English sentences with ease; others have been obscured by significant changes in pronunciation, spelling, and grammar. Compare the opening line of an Old English translation of the Lord's Prayer:

> Fæder ure þu þe eart on heofonum
> Father our, you who are in heaven

with the sixth line:

> Urne gedæghwamlican hlaf syle us todæg
> Our   daily   bread give us today

"Father," "our," and "heaven" are easy to spot; "daily," "bread" (as *hlaf*, "loaf"), and "give" (as *syle*, in which we can recognize the ancestor of "sell") are less so.

Unfortunately, we cannot hear firsthand how Old English was spoken either in conversation or in formal artistic performances, but the written record gives us many clues. Old English is preserved in an alphabet nearly identical to our own, copied in manuscript codices. In edited texts, the only unusual characters are þ and ð, both of which sound like modern "th," and æ, which is the vowel sound of "cat." (Other differences in pronunciation can be found in the "Guide to Reading Aloud" after this introduction.) But early Old English writing is also found in stone engravings that use not the Roman alphabet but rather the runes of the *fuþorc,* an alphabet designed explicitly for carving. Each runic character had a common name that started with its sound, such as *þorn* (thorn) for "th," *hægl* (hail) for "h," *ac* (oak) for "a." (Many of these runes can be found in James Harpur's version of *The Rune Poem* in this collection.) Runes are written into a number of Old English poems to stand in for whole words, not unlike modern textese, where "see you later" is written "c u l8r." They can also help create puzzles or word games, such as in Marcia Karp's riddle in this collection that begins "I saw, at foreplaying, two wondrous ones"— here, the runes in the original are to be read as full words within the text, but they also provide the solution if their initial sounds are reordered to spell new words.

A great deal of Old English prose writing survives—mostly in sermons and translations of Latin texts, but also in the monumental *Anglo-Saxon Chronicle,* which tells the (sometimes apocryphal) history of England from the year 1 until 1154.

Of Anglo-Saxon poetry about thirty thousand total verse lines have survived the fires and other vicissitudes of history. Fully 10 percent of that total is *Beowulf.* The total number of poems is approximately one hundred (depending on what we count as a poem), plus another ninety-five or so verse riddles, as well as a number of verse translations of biblical Psalms and of passages from Boethius's *Consolation of Philosophy.* All but a small number of the poems and riddles are collected in four major manuscripts known as the Exeter Book, the Nowell Codex, the Vercelli Book, and the Junius Manuscript. All were produced between 950 and 1025, though the texts they record were composed throughout the preceding three hundred years. Each manuscript has a colorful history:

The Exeter Book is the largest compendium of Old English poetry, containing some 130 poems including *The Wanderer, The Seafarer,* and virtually all the riddles. It shows signs of use bordering on abuse: we find a ring-shaped stain and knife marks that suggest it has been used as a coaster and as a cutting board, and its final pages are pocked and scarred, burned by what appears to have been a mislaid firebrand.

The Nowell Codex, also known as the *Beowulf* Manuscript, contains the poems *Beowulf* and *Judith* as well as some prose pieces. It is also fire damaged, the edges of its pages scorched in 1731 by a terrible library fire that damaged or destroyed about a quarter of the medieval manuscript collection of Sir Robert Cotton.

The Vercelli Book is well traveled, having found its way at some point after the eleventh century to the Italian cathedral whose name it bears, where it was rediscovered in 1822. Containing over twenty prose homilies and five religious poems (including *The Dream of the Rood*) it was perhaps carried to Italy by a pilgrim headed for Rome.

The Junius Manuscript was once called the Cædmon Manuscript, as early scholars proposed that its four biblical retellings were authored by the legendary Anglo-Saxon poet Cædmon. This manuscript is known for the fine line drawings illustrating its texts.

ANGLO-SAXON LITERATURE AND CULTURE

Often, newcomers to Anglo-Saxon poetry expect to find either swashbuckling stories of derring-do with romantic knights, alabaster-skinned ladies, and fearsome dragons, or else Tolkienesque tales of dwarves and elves, shape-shifting werewolves, trickster gods, and magic swords. But the former were the product of the great twelfth-century French romances of Arthur and his knights, and the latter are more readily found in Scandinavian eddas and sagas or in Celtic tales. Instead, most Old English poetry is decidedly meditative, grounded in clear-eyed pragmatism and concerned largely with religious, ethical, and sociological themes.

The more well-known short poems are sober—perhaps even downright doleful—evocations of exile, alienation, and loss. The narrators of two such poems, *The Wanderer* and *The Seafarer*, are castoffs, adrift and lonely on a harsh and unforgiving sea. With their isolation comes stoicism, an ethic of suffering-as-strength that finds a victory in accepting the inevitable. The wanderer tells us that "fate dictates," while the displaced court poet Deor finds a balm for his own misfortunes in repeating "That passed over, this can too" (as rendered by Seamus Heaney). Nevertheless, the narrators of *The Wanderer* and *The Seafarer* are not passive in their acceptance of fate; they must actively resist the turbulent distress of sorrow, shoring up their inner reserves, not baring their souls but binding them, suffering in silence. The wanderer reminds us, as Greg Delanty translates:

> I know
> it's the noble custom for an earl
> to bind fast what's in his breast,
> hoard inmost thoughts, think what he will.

The seafarer more vividly describes the force of such dangerous inner turmoil, in Mary Jo Salter's words, as "A hunger from within" that "tore at [his] mind." This unrest must be turned and directed to good: "A man must steer his passions, / be strong in staying steady" so that he may avoid losing control.

Turmoil of the inner self can be caused by many things, not only the sorrow of exile. The moralizing poet of *Vainglory,* here in Alan Jenkins's translation, warns of drinking's dangers:

> A lordly feaster   far gone in wine
> craftily his words   creep out, creatures
> pushing proudly   puffed with self-yeast
> vainglory gluts him   he glows with envy
> and treacherous hatred.

To allow prideful speech to escape the breast's confines puts both body and soul in peril. The mental fortitude required to control one's inner self is a hallmark of the Anglo-Saxon ethos, in all walks of life. The pivotal moment of *The Battle of Maldon,* a historical fiction based on a battle between the English home guard and a band of rampaging Vikings in the year 991, turns on such an act of mental containment. The English military commander Byrhtnoth must decide whether to allow the Vikings, who have landed on a small island in an estuary, free access to the mainland so that they may fight a full-scale battle:

        The earl, overconfident,
granted them passage,   too much land
to those hateful people,   and Byrhthelm's son, Byrhtnoth,
called across the chill water   as his host harkened:
"The pathway is open.   Come to us quickly,
war-men meeting war-men.   God alone knows
who will win control   of this killing field."

The Old English word *ofermod,* rendered here as "overconfident" by translator David Slavitt, suggests that Byrhtnoth's decision, if not necessarily foolish, was rooted in an abundance or even an excess of *mod*—the stuff that fills the hearts of heroes and drunkards alike. Thus we name the warming slug of whiskey "courage." But to be useful, *mod* must be constrained and directed, as a seasoned veteran reminds the troop after Byrhtnoth has been killed:

        "Your minds put in order,
and settle your hearts.   Our courage must grow
as the strength we have ebbs."

Mod sceal þe mare writes the Anglo-Saxon poet, "*mod* must be the greater," but at the same time "settled," under control.

Attempts to control one's fate through mental fortitude or physical action pervade Old English poetry: the poets often ask whether people can direct the course of their lives, or whether their fates are in the hands of a higher power (or of random chance, another kind of higher power). At the same time, many poems acknowledge a tendency toward decay in the world and the steady progress toward death. So notes the poet of *The Ruin,* here translated by Yusef Komunyakaa, about the great swordsmen of the past:

> Their fortress became a tomb; the city rotted away:
> those who should have braced it up, the multitudes,
> were bones on the ground.

In some poems, fate is simply the passage of time—an unstoppable force, as Solomon says in his dialogue with Saturn: "On earth, age overpowers everything / with press-gang prison-irons." Because of this,

> . . . a mother has no power over the child's destiny
> when she conceives, but from birth
> one thing follows another, as is the way of the world.

This "way of the world" (as Fiona Sampson translates *eald gesceaft,* "the ancient decree") cannot be changed, but what we do within its constraints is up to us.

The heroic ethos requires the warrior to trust in himself, in fate, and in God (not necessarily in that order). Either he will live on or, if he does everything he can to survive and fails, his heroic memory will outlive him. We can easily recognize a similar courage needed to bear up in *The Wanderer, The Seafarer, The Battle of Maldon,* and other poems of men pulling themselves together to face their fate. But poems of a warrior's life, whether in camaraderie or exile, can overshadow other poems' dramatic themes. This collection includes, for instance, poignant poems about estranged couples, one member venting frustration or seeking reconciliation with the other. But these poems do not address absent lovers with one voice; the speaker in *Wulf and Eadwacer* paints a vivid picture of longing in her plaintive cry, as translated by Paul Muldoon: "Wulf—Wulf—it was my hunger for you / and your all-too-seldom visits / rather than any lack of food made me ill." *The Wife's Lament,* in contrast, given modern voice by Eavan Boland, finally scorns the man who left ("Let my weary friend beside the sea / suffer his cruel anxiety"), while Michael Schmidt's narrator in *The Husband's Message* offers a more hopeful scenario as he calls on his wife to join him across the sea. And the poem *Maxims I* (part B, by Brigit Kelly), which tells of a Frisian couple reunited after the seafaring husband returns, shows the wife take up such domestic tasks as washing his clothes.

The detail of washing clothes can seem odd in a poem written within a culture with a poetic preoccupation with the warrior class, but a concern with the practical—a down-to-earth matter of factness—characterizes this poetry as well. The *Maxims* referenced above offer a series of observations about the world, philosophical claims rooted in the observable everyday:

> A tree must shed leaves,   its branches be barren;
> the traveler must embark   on the start of travels;
> all mortals must   meet their fate;

Sententiousness becomes poetry in the observance of small details, such as a description of how a falling man is "waving / His arms like wings but they are not wings" (*The Fortunes of Men,* translated by Kelly Cherry), or how "The thief must walk in dirty weather" (*Maxims II,* by Rachel Hadas). Everyday truths emerge in these texts, what we might call Anglo-Saxon conventional wisdom, as we find in *The Rune Poem:*

> Riding seems like a pleasant thing
> to warriors indoors
> but tests a man who's galloping
> upon a sturdy horse.

To express the abstract through the physical is to create meta-
phor, but in Old English the stress always seems to circle back to
the physical. For instance, in *Soul and Body,* here translated by
Maurice Riordan as *The Damned Soul Addresses the Body,* a bitter
and resentful damned soul returns to berate the buried body it
blames for its infernal punishment. Though about the eternal
wages of sin, the poem seeks to frighten us not with extended
scenes of hellish torment, but instead by describing creatures feast-
ing on a dead body:

> Its head is broken in, its hands disjointed,
> The jaws lie gaping, the gums fester,
> The fingers have already fallen off.
> Wriggling worms are raiding the rib cage,
> Their tongues active in ten directions
> Struggling to satisfy the hungry horde.

Similarly, from A. E. Stallings's version of *The Riming Poem*:

> | | Wassailing worms |
> | --- | --- |
> | Feast afresh | where limbs lie slain |
> | Devouring flesh: | only bones remain. |
> | Body bereft, | the frame rotted, |
> | Naught is left | but what fate's allotted |

The shock and horror of imagining one's own body deteriorate
was not a cheap thrill for the Anglo-Saxons; it was central to a Chris-
tian theology that stressed crime and punishment, confession and pen-
ance, and intense glorification of God. *The Seafarer,* for instance, is a
confessional poem; the narrator reveals his inner self to disassociate
himself from those aspects of earthly life that impede his progress
toward heaven. Ezra Pound, however, in his boldly unfaithful and
brilliant 1912 rendition of *The Seafarer,* famously amputated its final

twenty-five lines (which make up twenty percent of the poem). By opting to excise all overtly Christian sentiments in the original, Pound performed what literary critic Harold Bloom would call a "strong misreading." This idea that stripping Anglo-Saxon poetry of its Christian clothing might reveal an originary, pagan Germanic past has held great appeal for many eager to discover an ancient Germanic religion. But Anglo-Saxon poetry is far from being a record of a pagan culture co-opted and rewritten by Christian monks. Christianity is the sea Anglo-Saxon poetry swims in.

While some number of the Britons under the Roman Empire had been Christians, the pagan Anglo-Saxons were pressed in a kind of missionary pincer movement. Saint Columba (also known as Colum Cille) had arrived from Ireland to establish his monastery on the northern Scottish island of Iona in 563. Missionaries from Iona later founded a monastery at Lindesfarne, in Northumbria, in 633 to aid in missionary work in the northern kingdoms of England. Meanwhile, Pope Gregory sent Augustine to convert Æthelberht of Kent, a powerful English king. In 597 Augustine landed at Thanet, and with remarkable efficiency achieved his mission. But such successes were intermittent: King Edwin of Northumbria was converted by another missionary, Paulinus, in 627, but was killed by the pagan king Penda of Mercia five years later.

The waves of missionaries and the ongoing struggles between Christians and the followers of Germanic beliefs (or the followers of purely secular interests) left their impressions. We can see the warrior ethic and Christian theology meet in much Old English writing. Sweeping, epic poems retell parts of the first two books of the Bible as well as the later stories of Daniel and Judith. In other poems Christ appears as a warrior-king as he harrows hell or presides over the Last Judgment, and many saints are the subjects of elaborately told saints' lives (including *Andreas,* excerpted in this collection), in which men and women fight the enemies of Christianity using elaborately interwoven powers of physical endurance, rhetorical skill, and divine favor. The most famous poem to weave heroic ideals within Christian salvation theology and ethics is *The Vision of the Cross* (also known as *The Dream of the Rood*), a dream-vision in which the Cross retells the crucifixion from its point of view as a loyal retainer to the warrior Christ. Paradoxically, this perfectly recognizable Anglo-Saxon warrior seeks not to kill his enemies, but to be killed by them, and the Cross-retainer must be the instrument of his death rather than his defender or avenger:

> This man of mettle—God Almighty—then stripped off
> for battle; stern and strong, he climbed the gallows,
> brave before the throng, that he might free mankind.
> I trembled when the warrior embraced me,
> but dared not bow to earth. I had to stand fast.

We see the poet (here in Ciaran Carson's words) use the ideal of the Anglo-Saxon warrior-lord and his loyal retainer to create his characters of Christ and Cross, his poetic imagery forging a unity out of the paradox of the hero who seeks not victory but death and of the loyal retainer who refuses to come to his lord's aid.

Less grandiose examples of a similar merging of traditions appear in the many remedies the Anglo-Saxons had for everything from aches and pains to trouble in childbirth, from lost cattle to attacks from invisible supernatural assailants. Such remedies appear in both prose and verse; those that contain verse are translated in this book. These remedies usually involve some combination of spoken incantation, herbal concoction, and physical action. As religious folk charms, they reference Woden as readily as Christ, and appeal to the four cardinal directions as easily as to communion wafers.

Such mergers appear not to have been as puzzling to the Anglo-Saxons as they now appear to us. Still, the juxtaposition of unlike ideas is a hallmark of Old English poetry. *The Fortunes of Men, Precepts,* and other "catalogue poems" offer insight through contrast rather than direct statement, juxtaposing surprising image-pairs to move ideas forward. The *Maxims* poems do much the same, though they demand their readers take on more of the work of making connections among their images. But the true mergers come in the playful shape-shifters of the Old English riddles. The riddle tradition is old and wide spread, so the Anglo-Saxon interest in riddles might trace to a Germanic interest echoed in Scandinavian literature, or to the Latin tradition of Symphosius, or most likely to both. Regardless of provenance, the simple presence of the bulk of riddles collected in the Exeter Book tells us they were to be taken seriously as an artistic enterprise.

This book includes nearly all the undamaged riddles from the Exeter Book, as well as some of the damaged ones. The range of subjects disguised in riddles is staggering: wild and domestic animals (a vixen, a magpie, a bullock, a fish); household tools (a rake, a bellows, a loom, a plow); weapons of war (swords, a helmet, a coat of mail, a shield); astronomical bodies and natural phenomena (sun, moon, stars, wind, water, and creation itself) all make their way into the Exeter collection. Some riddles are philosophical, some devotional, and others offer double entendres and outright dirty jokes. But they all share a poet's fascination with a word's ability to point in many directions at once while maintaining a palpable aptness. To cut precisely while opening up an unending vista of meaning is the riddler's challenge. In this collection, we have opted to distribute small gatherings of riddles throughout the book rather than group them all in one place. They are more likely to surprise this way, and to reveal themselves as poems.

Old English writings encompass a world of experience and points of view, from prayers to bawdy riddles, from heroic saints to drunken louts, from farmers hoping to improve their fields to sermonizers looking to save your soul. This range might surprise us somewhat considering the texts were preserved only by monks copying them into manuscripts that were very expensive to produce—indeed, that required slaughtering animals for their skins to make pages (we hear from one of these animals in Jane Hirshfield's translation of *Riddle 26*, beginning "Some Enemy Took My Life"). The poetry in these pages is about life and death, war and peace, sickness and health, pleasure and pain—a world so like and unlike our own.

—Michael Matto

GUIDE TO READING ALOUD

OLD ENGLISH POETRY WAS COMPOSED FOR ORAL PERFORMANCE. For those who would like to read the facing page Old English texts aloud, a few rules will lead to passable if not perfect pronunciation. For a fuller explanation of OE pronunciation and meter, please consult one of the handbooks in *For Further Reading on Old English*.

PRONUNCIATION

Vowels sound in Old English like they do in modern Romance languages: *a* = "ah"; *e* = "eh"; *i* = "ee"; *o* = "oh"; and *u* = "oo." The letter *y* is pronounced "ee," but with lips rounded as if saying "oo." Another vowel, *æ,* has the vowel sound of "ash," which is also the letter's name.

Consonants are pronounced as in modern English with a few exceptions: *c* usually sounds like modern "k," but sometimes "ch" (generally before *e* or *i*), but never "s"; *g* can sound like modern "g" of "good" or like modern "y" (again, before *e* or *i*). In the middle of a word, *g* can be pronounced as a "w." The modern "sh" sound is spelled *sc* in Old English; the final sound of "edge" is spelled *cg*. Two commonly found letters, *þ* (thorn) and *ð* (eth), are interchangeable, both representing the modern voiced and voiceless sounds of "th," as heard in "thy" and "thigh."

In Old English, there are no silent letters—every letter is pronounced. For instance, an "e" on the end of a word is to be said aloud, so *wine* ("friend") is pronounced "wee-neh," not as modern "wine."

METER

In its manuscripts, Old English poetry is written like prose, from margin to margin. The meter would be heard, however, when the verses were spoken aloud. The editorial convention (followed in this book) of printing each line as two separated half-lines—an "on-verse" and an "off-verse"—offers a visual representation of the prosody perceived in oral performance. Old English meter is based on an earlier Germanic alliterative oral tradition echoed in other Scandinavian and Northern Germanic literatures. It features alliteration (head rhyme) probably because the Germanic languages tended to accent the first syllable of words.

In general, each line of Old English poetry will have four dominant stresses, two in each half-line. The third overall stress anchors the alliterative pattern for the line—either the first stress, the second, or both must alliterate with it. The fourth stress normally does not alliterate. (Consonants alliterate with themselves, while vowels alliterate with any other vowel.)

Usually nouns, adjectives, and often verbs receive stress; rarely do pronouns or other parts of speech. Prefixes on verbs are generally not stressed, nor is the prefix *ge-* on any word, so the alliterating sound will at times appear after the first syllable of a word. Occasionally an on-verse will be "light," having only one stress, as in the first line below. In this example, stressed syllables are *italicized,* alliteration is also **bolded**.

> Mæg ic be me *sy***l**fum   *so***ð**gied *w***re**can,
> *si***þ**as *se***c**gan,   hu ic ge*sw***i**nc-*da***g**um
> *ear*fo**ð**h*wí*le   *o***ft** **þ**rowade,
> **bi**tre **b**reostceare ge**b**iden *hæ***b**be. . . .
> (*The Seafarer,* lines 1–4)

Some syllables that are stressed do not receive alliteration, and not all words that begin with the alliterating sound are necessarily stressed.

Still, one wishing to read Old English poetry aloud will do pretty well simply to stress the alliterating syllables in a line while maintaining the pronunciation rules above.

The acceptable patterns of stressed and unstressed syllables in a line were fairly constrained. For more information about these patterns, and about Old English prosody and pronunciation in general, consult any of the standard introductory textbooks in *For Further Reading on Old English*. And to hear some of the poems in this book read aloud in both Old and Modern English, visit the Poems Out Loud Web site at http://poemsoutloud.net.

ABOUT THE OLD ENGLISH TEXT

THE FACING-PAGE TEXT IN OLD ENGLISH IS BASED ON THE WORK of many scholars over many decades (as detailed in the acknowledgments) who poured over manuscripts that are sometimes damaged or otherwise unreliable. Many poems (such as *Waldere, The Battle of Finnsburh,* and many riddles) survive only as fragments, and appear as such in this book. Bold-faced type in the Old English indicates words emended or reconstructed by previous editors. Ellipses indicate damage to the manuscripts: a three-dot ellipsis marks a relatively small gap in the text; six dots mean a longer stretch of damage. For further details on specific emendations or other textual notes, one should consult the *Anglo-Saxon Poetic Records,* or individual editions of the poems, some of which are listed in the bibliography.

On occasion, a translator has opted for a manuscript reading or emendation at variance with the source we have used for the Old English. Among the riddles, what some editors have read as one riddle we on occasion have treated as two, or vice versa, often following Craig Williamson's readings in his edition, *Old English Riddles of the Exeter Book.* Similarly, the three parts of *Maxims I* have been treated as three individual poems.

Poems of Exile
and Longing

The Seafarer

Mæg ic be me sylfum   soðgied wrecan,
siþas secgan,   hu ic geswincdagum
earfoðhwile   oft þrowade,
bitre breostceare   gebiden hæbbe,
5 gecunnad in ceole   cearselda fela,
atol yþa gewealc,   þær mec oft bigeat
nearo nihtwaco   æt nacan stefnan,
þonne he be clifum cnossað.   Calde geþrungen
wæron mine fet,   forste gebunden,
10 caldum clommum,   þær þa ceare seofedun
hat ymb heortan;   hungor innan slat
merewerges mod.   þæt se mon ne wat
þe him on foldan   fægrost limpeð,
hu ic earmcearig   iscealdne sæ
15 winter wunade   wræccan lastum,
winemægum bidroren,
bihongen hrimgicelum;   hægl scurum fleag.
þær ic ne gehyrde   butan hlimman sæ,
iscaldne wæg.   Hwilum ylfete song
20 dyde ic me to gomene,   ganetes hleoþor

The Seafarer

Mary Jo Salter

I can sing my own true story
of journeys through this world,
how often I was tried
by troubles. Bitterly scared,
I would be sick with sorrow
on my night watch as I saw
so many times from the prow
terrible, tall waves
pitching close to cliffs.
My feet were frozen stiff,
seized and locked by frost,
although my heart was hot
from a host of worries.
A hunger from within
tore at my mind, sea-weary.

But men on solid ground
know nothing of how a wretch
like me, in so much pain,
could live a winter alone,
exiled, on the ice-cold sea
where hail came down in sheets,
and icicles hung from me
while friendly hall-companions
feasted far away.
The crashing sea was all
I heard, the ice-cold wave.
I made the wild swan's song

ond huilpan sweg   fore hleahtor wera,

mæw singende   fore medodrince.

Stormas þær stanclifu beotan,   þær him stearn oncwæð

isigfeþera;   ful oft þæt earn bigeal,

25 urigfeþra;   **ne** ænig hleomæga

feasceaftig ferð   **frefran** meahte.

Forþon him gelyfeð lyt,   se þe ah lifes wyn

gebiden in burgum,   bealosiþa hwon,

wlonc ond wingal,   hu ic werig oft

30 in brimlade   bidan sceolde.

Nap nihtscua,   norþan sniwde,

hrim hrusan bond,   hægl feol on eorþan,

corna caldast.   Forþon cnyssað nu

heortan geþohtas,   þæt ic hean streamas,

35 sealtyþa gelac   sylf cunnige;

monað modes lust   mæla gehwylce

ferð to feran,   þæt ic feor heonan

elþeodigra   eard gesece.

Forþon nis þæs modwlonc   mon ofer eorþan,

40 ne his gifena þæs god,   ne in geoguþe to þæs hwæt,

my game; sometimes the gannet
and curlew would cry out
though elsewhere men were laughing;
and the sea-mew would sing
though elsewhere men drank mead.
Storms beat against the stone
cliffs, and the ice-feathered
tern called back, and often
the sea-sprayed eagle too.
No kinsman can console
or protect a sorry soul.

In fact, a city-dweller
who revels and swills wine
far from travel's perils,
barely could believe
how often, wearily,
I weathered the sea paths.
The shadows of night deepened,
snow fell from the north,
and on the frost-bound earth
hail fell like cold grain.
For all that, my heart's thoughts
pound now with the salt
wave's surging; on high seas
my spirit urges me
forward, to seek far
from here a foreign land.

The truth is that no man—
however generous
in gifts, however bold
in youth, however brave,

ne in his dædum to þæs deor,   ne him his dryhten to þæs hold,

þæt he a his sæfore   sorge næbbe,

to hwon hine dryhten   gedon wille.

Ne biþ him to hearpan hyge   ne to hringþege,

45 ne to wife wyn   ne to worulde hyht,

ne ymbe owiht elles,   nefne ymb yða gewealc,

ac a hafað longunge   se þe on lagu fundað.

Bearwas blostmum nimað,   byrig fægriað,

wongas **wlitigað**,   woruld onetteð;

50 ealle þa gemoniað   modes fusne

sefan to siþe,   þam þe swa þenceð

on flodwegas   feor **gewitan**.

Swylce geac monað   geomran reorde,

singeð sumeres weard,   sorge beodeð

55 bitter in breosthord.   þæt se beorn ne wat,

esteadig secg,   hwæt þa sume dreogað

þe þa wræclastas   widost lecgað.

however loyally
his own lord may attend him—
is ever wholly free
in his seafaring from worry
at what is the Lord's will.

No, it is not for him,
the harp's song, nor the rings
exchanged, nor pleasure in women,
nor any worldly glory,
nothing but welling waves;
a seagoing man's longing
is what he always has.
Groves break into blossom,
the towns and fields grow fair
and the world once more is new:
all of this spurs on
the man whose mind and spirit
are eager for the journey,
who yearns to steer his course
far across the sea.

Mournfully the cuckoo's
voice cries out in warning,
the harbinger of summer
bitterly foretells
in song the soul's distress.
To the wealthy warrior
blessed with worldly fortune,
this is all unknown—
what we face who follow
the vast and alien way.

Forþon nu min hyge hweorfeð   ofer hreþerlocan,
min modsefa   mid mereflode
60 ofer hwæles eþel   hweorfeð wide,
eorþan sceatas,   cymeð eft to me
gifre ond grædig,   gielleð anfloga,
hweteð on **hwælweg**   hreþer unwearnum
ofer holma gelagu.   Forþon me hatran sind
65 dryhtnes dreamas   þonne þis deade lif,
læne on londe.   Ic gelyfe no
þæt him eorðwelan   ece **stondað**.
Simle þreora sum   þinga gehwylce,
ær his tid **aga**,   to tweon weorþeð;
70 adl oþþe yldo   oþþe ecghete
fægum fromweardum   feorh oðþringeð.
Forþon þæt **bið** eorla gehwam   æftercweþendra
lof lifgendra   lastworda betst,
þæt he gewyrce,   ær he on weg scyle,
75 **fremum** on foldan   wið feonda niþ,
deorum dædum   deofle togeanes,
þæt hine ælda bearn   æfter hergen,
ond his lof siþþan   lifge mid englum
awa to ealdre,   ecan lifes **blæd**,

And now my thought roams far
beyond my heart; my mind
flows out to the water,
soars above the whale's path
to the wide world's corners
and returns with keen desire;
the lone bird, flying, shrieks
and leads the willing soul
to the whale-road, and over
the tumbling of the waves.

The joys of the Lord can kindle
more in me than dead
and fleeting life on land.
I do not believe the riches
of this world will last forever.
Always, without fail,
of three things one will turn
uncertain for a man
before his fatal hour:
sickness, age, or the sword
will rip the life right out
of the doomed and done for.
So it is for every man:
the best praise will come after,
from people who outlive him;
today, then, he must toil
against enemies and the Devil;
undaunted he must dare
so that sons of men extol him,
that in time to come his fame
endures amid the angels,
and his glory goes on, ceaseless,

80 dream mid dugeþum.   Dagas sind gewitene,
    ealle onmedlan   eorþan rices;
    næron nu cyningas   ne caseras
    ne goldgiefan   swylce iu wæron,
    þonne hi mæst mid him   mærþa gefremedon
85 ond on dryhtlicestum   dome lifdon.
    Gedroren is þeos duguð eal,   dreamas sind gewitene,
    wuniað þa wacran   ond þas woruld healdaþ,
    brucað þurh bisgo.   Blæd is gehnæged,
    eorþan indryhto   ealdað ond searað,
90 swa nu monna gehwylc   geond middangeard.
    Yldo him on fareð,   onsyn blacað,
    gomelfeax gnornað,   wat his iuwine,
    æþelinga bearn,   eorþan forgiefene.
    Ne mæg him þonne se flæschoma,   þonne him þæt feorg losað,
95 ne swete forswelgan   ne sar gefelan,
    ne hond onhreran   ne mid hyge þencan.
    þeah þe græf wille   golde stregan
    broþor his geborenum,   byrgan be deadum,
    maþmum mislicum   þæt hine mid wille,

among the celestial hosts.

The days are dwindling now
of the kingdoms of this earth;
there are no kings or Caesars
as before, and no gold-givers
as once, when men of valor
performed great deeds and lived
majestically among
themselves in high renown.
Their delights too are dead.
The weakest hold the world
in their hands, and wear it out
with labor, while all splendor,
like the earth, grows older;
its noble aspect withers
as man does everywhere.

Age creeps up on him,
his face grows pale; his head,
gray-haired, bewails old friends,
sons of princes, already
given to the earth.
As his body fails,
life leaks away, he tastes
sweetness in things no more,
nor feels pain, nor can move
his hand, nor use his mind.
When a kinsman dies, he wants
to strew the grave with gold,
or bury with the dead
treasures he amassed.
But no, it cannot be;

100 ne mæg þære sawle   þe biþ synna ful
    gold to geoce   for godes egsan,
    þonne he hit ær hydeð   þenden he her leofað.
    Micel biþ se meotudes egsa,   forþon hi seo molde oncyrreð;
    se gestaþelade   stiþe grundas,
105 eorþan sceatas   ond uprodor.
    Dol biþ se þe him his dryhten ne ondrædeþ;   cymeð him se dead
        unþinged.
    Eadig bið se þe eaþmod leofaþ;   cymeð him seo ar of heofonum,
    meotod him þæt mod gestaþelað,   forþon he in his meahte gelyfeð.
    Stieran **mon** sceal strongum mode,   ond þæt on staþelum healdan,
110 ond gewis werum,   wisum clæne,
    scyle monna gehwylc   mid gemete healdan
    wiþ leofne ond wið laþne   bealo,
    þeah þe he hine wille fyres   fulne
    oþþe on bæle   forbærnedne
115 his geworhtne wine.   Wyrd biþ **swiþre**,
    meotud meahtigra   þonne ænges monnes gehygd.
    Uton we hycgan   hwær **we** ham agen,
    ond þonne geþencan   hu we þider cumen,
    ond we þonne eac tilien,   þæt we to moten

gold once hid and hoarded
in life is no good now
for the soul full of sin
before the force of God.

Terrible and great
is the Lord, and the very world
turns from Him in awe.
He made the firm foundations,
the earth's face and the heavens.
Foolish is he who does not fear
his Lord; death comes to him
though he is unprepared.
Blessed is he who lives in all
humility; what comes to him
in Heaven is forgiveness.
God gave to him that spirit
to bow to all His power.
A man must steer his passions,
be strong in staying steady;
keep promises, be pure.
He must be wise and fair
with foes as much as friends,
well-tempered in himself.
He dreads to see a dear one
engulfed in flames, yet patience
tells him to trust the sway
of Fate, and that God's might
is greater than we know.

Let us ponder where our true
home is, and how to reach it.
Let us labor to gain entry

120 in þa ecan   eadignesse,
    þær is lif gelong   in lufan dryhtnes,
    hyht in heofonum.   þæs sy þam halgan þonc,
    þæt he usic geweorþade,   wuldres ealdor,
    ece dryhten,   in ealle tid.
125 Amen.

into the eternal,
to find the blessedness
of belonging to the Lord
joyfully on high.
Thanks be to God who loved us,
the endless Father, the Prince
of Glory forever. Amen.

The Wife's Lament

Ic þis giedd wrece   bi me ful geomorre,
minre sylfre sið.   Ic þæt secgan mæg,
hwæt ic yrmþa gebad,   siþþan ic up weox,
niwes oþþe ealdes,   no ma þonne nu.
5 A ic wite wonn   minra wræcsiþa.
ærest min hlaford gewat   heonan of leodum
ofer yþa gelac;   hæfde ic uhtceare
hwær min leodfruma   londes wære.
ða ic me feran gewat   folgað secan,
10 wineleas wræcca,   for minre weaþearfe.
Ongunnon þæt þæs monnes   magas hycgan
þurh dyrne geþoht,   þæt hy todælden unc,
þæt wit gewidost   in woruldrice
lifdon laðlicost,   ond mec longade.
15 Het mec hlaford min   herheard niman,
ahte ic leofra lyt   on þissum londstede,
holdra freonda.   Forþon is min hyge geomor,
ða ic me ful gemæcne   monnan funde,

The Wife's Lament

Eavan Boland

I sing this poem full of grief.
        Full of sorrow about my life.
Ready to say the cruel state
        I have endured, early and late,
And never more I will tell
        Than now—now that exile
Has fallen to me with all its pain.
        My lord had gone, had fled away
Over the sea. The break of day
        Found me grieving for a prince
Who had left his people. Then at once
        I set out on my journey,
Little more than a refugee,
        Lacking a retinue and friends,
With needy means and needy ends.
        They plotted together, his kith and kin.
They met in secret, they made a plan
        To keep us as far apart, away
From each other, night and day
        As ever they could while making sure
I would feel anguish and desire.
        My lord and master made his will
Plain to me: He said, be still:
        Stay right here, in this place.
And here I am—penniless, friendless,
        Lacking him, my heart's companion
And sad indeed because our union
        Suited me so well, so well

heardsæligne, hygegeomorne,
20 mod miþendne, morþor **hycgendne**.
Bliþe gebæro ful oft wit beotedan
þæt unc ne gedælde nemne deað ana
owiht elles; eft is þæt onhworfen,
is nu swa hit no wære
25 freondscipe uncer. **Sceal** ic feor ge neah
mines felaleofan fæhðu dreogan.
Heht mec mon wunian on wuda bearwe,
under actreo in þam eorðscræfe.
Eald is þes eorðsele, eal ic eom oflongad,
30 sindon dena dimme, duna uphea,
bitre burgtunas, brerum beweaxne,
wic wynna leas. Ful oft mec her wraþe begeat
fromsiþ frean. Frynd sind on eorþan,
leofe lifgende, leger weardiað,
35 þonne ic on uhtan ana gonge
under actreo geond þas eorðscrafu.
þær ic **sittan** mot sumorlangne dæg,
þær ic wepan mæg mine wræcsiþas,
earfoþa fela; forþon ic æfre ne mæg
40 þære modceare minre gerestan,
ne ealles þæs longaþes þe mec on þissum life begeat.
A scyle geong mon wesan geomormod,
heard heortan geþoht, swylce habban sceal
bliþe gebæro, eac þon breostceare,
45 sinsorgna gedreag, sy æt him sylfum gelong

And for so long. And yet the real
                    State of his heart, the actual weakness
Of his mind, the true darkness
                    Of murderous sin was hidden away.
And yet I well remember the day,
                    Our singular joy on this earth
When we two vowed that only death
                    Could separate us. Now I see
Love itself has deserted me:
                    Love that was so true, so trusted
Is now as if it never existed.
                    Wherever I go, far or near,
Enmity springs from what is dear.
                    I was commanded to this grove
Under an oak tree, to this cave—
                    An ancient cave—and I am filled
With longing here where hedges, wild
                    With briars, valleys, rolling,
Steep hills make a joyless dwelling.
                    Often here, the fact of his leaving
Seizes my heart. There are lovers living
                    On this earth who keep their beds
While I am walking in the woods
                    Through these caves alone at dawn.
Here I sit. Here I mourn,
                    Through the summer hours, all my woes,
My exiled state. I can't compose
                    My careworn heart nor ease the strife
Of that desire which is my life.
                    Let a young man be sober, tough
And sunny withal however weighed
                    Down his soul, however sad.
And if it happens joy is his choice

eal his worulde wyn,   sy ful wide fah
feorres folclondes,   þæt min freond siteð
under stanhliþe   storme behrimed,
wine werigmod,   wætre beflowen
50 on dreorsele.   Dreogeð se min wine
micle modceare;   he gemon to oft
wynlicran wic.   Wa bið þam þe sceal
of langoþe   leofes abidan.

May his self be its only source.
My lost lord, my lover-felon—
　　　Let him be cast from his land alone
By an icy cliff in a cold storm.
　　　Let his own mind bedevil him
With weariness as the water flows
　　　Far below his makeshift house.
Let my weary friend beside the sea
　　　Suffer his cruel anxiety.
Let him be reminded in this place
　　　Of another dwelling: all its grace,
And all the affliction, all the cost
　　　Of longing for a love that's lost.

Deor

Welund him be wurman   wræces cunnade,
anhydig eorl   earfoþa dreag,
hæfde him to gesiþþe   sorge ond longaþ,
wintercealde wræce;   wean oft onfond,
5   siþþan hine Niðhad on   nede legde,
swoncre seonobende   on syllan monn.
þæs ofereode,   þisses swa mæg!
Beadohilde ne wæs   hyre broþra deaþ
on sefan swa sar   swa hyre sylfre þing,
10   þæt heo gearolice   ongieten hæfde
þæt heo eacen wæs;   æfre ne meahte
þriste geþencan,   hu ymb þæt sceolde.
þæs ofereode,   þisses swa mæg!
We þæt Mæðhilde   monge gefrugnon
15   wurdon grundlease   Geates frige,
þæt hi seo sorglufu   slæp ealle binom.
þæs ofereode,   þisses swa mæg!
ðeodric ahte   þritig wintra
Mæringa burg;   þæt wæs monegum cuþ.
20   þæs ofereode,   þisses swa mæg!
We geascodan   Eormanrices
wylfenne geþoht;   ahte wide folc
Gotena rices.   þæt wæs grim cyning.
Sæt secg monig   sorgum gebunden,

Deor

Seamus Heaney

Weland the blade-winder   suffered woe.
That steadfast man   knew misery.
Sorrow and longing   walked beside him,
wintered in him,   kept wearing him down
after Nithad   hampered and restrained him,
lithe sinew-bonds   on the better man.
    That passed over,   this can too.

For Beadohilde   her brother's death
weighed less heavily   than her own heartsoreness
once it was clearly   understood
she was bearing a child.   Her ability
to think and decide   deserted her then.
    That passed over,   this can too.

We have heard tell   of Mathilde's laments,
the grief that afflicted   Geat's wife.
Her love was her bane,   it banished sleep.
    That passed over,   this can too.

For thirty winters—   it was common knowledge—
Theodric held   the Maerings' fort.
    That passed over,   this can too.

Earmonric   had the mind of a wolf,
by all accounts   a cruel king,
lord of the far flung   Gothic outlands.
Everywhere men sat   shackled in sorrow,

25 wean on wenan,   wyscte geneahhe
   þæt þæs cynerices   ofercumen wære.
   þæs ofereode,   þisses swa mæg!
   Siteð sorgcearig,   sælum bidæled,
   on sefan sweorceð,   sylfum þinceð
30 þæt sy endeleas   **earfoða** dæl.
   Mæg þonne geþencan,   þæt geond þas woruld
   witig dryhten   wendeþ geneahhe,
   eorle monegum   are gesceawað,
   wislicne blæd,   sumum weana dæl.
35 þæt ic bi me sylfum   secgan wille,
   þæt ic hwile wæs   Heodeninga scop,
   dryhtne dyre.   Me wæs Deor noma.
   Ahte ic fela wintra   folgað tilne,
   holdne hlaford,   oþþæt Heorrenda nu,
40 leoðcræftig monn   londryht geþah,
   þæt me eorla hleo   ær gesealde.
   þæs ofereode,   þisses swa mæg!

expecting the worst,   wishing often
he and his kingdom   would be conquered.
    That passed over,   this can too.

A man sits mournful,   his mind in darkness,
so daunted in spirit   he deems himself
ever after   fated to endure.
He may think then   how throughout this world
the Lord in his wisdom   often works change—
meting out honor,   ongoing fame
to many, to others   only their distress.
Of myself, this much   I have to say:
for a time I was poet   of the Heoden people,
dear to my lord.   Deor was my name.
For years I enjoyed   my duties as minstrel
and that lord's favor,   but now the freehold
and land titles   he bestowed upon me once
he has vested in Heorrenda,   master of verse-craft.
    That passed over,   this can too.

Wulf and Eadwacer

Leodum is minum   swylce him mon lac gife;
willað hy hine aþecgan,   gif he on þreat cymeð.
Ungelic is us.
Wulf is on iege,   ic on oþerre.
5 Fæst is þæt eglond,   fenne biworpen.
Sindon wælreowe   weras þær on ige;
willað hy hine aþecgan,   gif he on þreat cymeð.
Ungelice is us.
Wulfes ic mines widlastum   wenum dogode;
10 þonne hit wæs renig weder   ond ic reotugu sæt,
þonne mec se beaducafa   bogum bilegde,
wæs me wyn to þon,   wæs me hwæþre eac lað.
Wulf, min Wulf,   wena me þine
seoce gedydon,   þine seldcymas,
15 murnende mod,   nales meteliste.
Gehyrest þu, Eadwacer?   Uncerne earne hwelp
bireð wulf to wuda.
þæt mon eaþe tosliteð   þætte næfre gesomnad wæs,
uncer giedd geador.

Wulf and Eadwacer

Paul Muldoon

My tribe would welcome him with open arms
were he to show up with a war party or otherwise pose a threat.
How differently it goes for us . . .
Wulf on one island and myself on another,
an island made safe by the swamp thrown up about it,
an island full of hard men
who would welcome him with open arms . . .
How very differently it goes for us . . .
It was after my far-flung Wulf I was sighing
as the rain came down and my tears flowed
when a hard man took me under his wing
and I was filled with glee and gloom in equal measure . . .
Wulf—Wulf—it was my hunger for you
and your all-too-seldom visits
rather than any lack of food made me ill.
Be mindful, Eadwacer, be mindful of our cub
carried off by a Wulf into the woods,
of how soon may be cut short what's scarely been composed—
the song of us two together.

The Husband's Message

Nu ic onsundran þe   secgan wille
. . . . . . treocyn   ic tudre aweox;
in mec æld . . . sceal   ellor londes
settan . . . . . .   sealte streamas
5 . . . sse.   Ful oft ic on bates
. . . . . . gesohte
þær mec mondryhten   min . . . . . .
ofer heah hofu;   eom nu her cumen
on ceolþele,   ond nu cunnan scealt
10 hu þu ymb **modlufan**   mines frean
on hyge hycge.   Ic gehatan dear
þæt þu þær tirfæste   treowe findest.
Hwæt, þec þonne biddan het   se þisne beam agrof
þæt þu sinchroden   sylf gemunde
15 on gewitlocan   wordbeotunga,
þe git on ærdagum   oft gespræcon,
þenden git moston   on meoduburgum
eard weardigan,   an lond bugan,
freondscype fremman.   Hine fæhþo adraf
20 of sigeþeode;   heht nu sylfa þe
lustum **læran**,   þæt þu lagu drefde,
siþþan þu gehyrde   on hliþes oran
galan geomorne   geac on bearwe.
Ne læt þu þec siþþan   siþes getwæfan,
25 lade gelettan   lifgendne monn.

The Husband's Message

Michael Schmidt

To you far away   I carry this message
I remain true   to the tree I was hacked from
Wood I am, bearing   the marks of a man
Letters and runes   the words of his heart
I come from afar   borne on salt currents
Hiss . . .   in a hull I sought and I sought you
Where would I find you   my lord despatched me
Over fathomless seas   I've come, here I am
Do you think of him still   my lord in your dear heart
Do you recall him   or is your mind bare
He remains true to you   true and with fixed desire
You try his faith   you'll find it stands firm

But hear me now, read   what is scratched on my surface

You, cherished treasure, dear   you in your youthful
Your hidden heart, dear   remember your vows
Your heart and his heart   when together you haunted
The lovely hamlets   the mead hall, the promise
To perform your love
                              Well, all of that ended
In feud and in flight   he was forced from that place
Now he has sent me   to ask you come to me
Cross the seas, come to me   come here with joy
When to your listening   on the steep hillside
First comes the cuckoo's voice   sad in the trees
Don't pause don't linger   come at that calling
Don't stay or delay   come at that call

Ongin mere secan,   mæwes eþel,
onsite sænacan,   þæt þu suð heonan
ofer merelade   monnan findest,
þær se þeoden is   þin on wenum.
30 Ne mæg him worulde   willa **gelimpan**
mara on gemyndum,   þæs þe he me sægde,
þonne inc geunne   alwaldend god
. . . . . . ætsomne   siþþan motan
secgum ond gesiþum   s . . .
35 næglede beagas;   he genoh hafað
fædan **goldes**
. . . d elþeode   eþel healde,
fægre foldan
. . . ra hæleþa,   þeah þe her min wine . . .
40 nyde gebæded,   nacan ut aþrong,
ond on yþa geong . . . . . . sceolde
faran on flotweg,   forðsiþes georn,
mengan merestreamas.   Nu se mon hafað
wean oferwunnen;   nis him wilna gad,
45 ne meara ne maðma   ne meododreama,
ænges ofer eorþan   eorlgestreona,
þeodnes dohtor,   gif he þin beneah
ofer eald gebeot   incer twega.
Gecyre ic ætsomne   ᚻ ᚱ geador
50 ᛏ ᚹ ond ᛗ   aþe benemnan,
þæt he þa wære   ond þa winetreowe
be him lifgendum   læstan wolde,
þe git on ærdagum   oft gespræconn.

Go down to the shore   set out to sea then
To the tern's chilly home   go south go south
Over the ragged sea   south find your lord
Come to him, there   he waits for you wedded
To your sure arrival   no other wish
But only the wish of you   You're in his mind
Almighty God's there   his power rebind you
One to the other   again as you were
Able to rule then   able to raise up
Your people, comrades   and endow you with jewels
Bracelets and carcanets   collars and combs
He has set aside for you   fair gold, bright gemstones
In a land far away   among foreign folk
A handsome mansion   hectares and cattle
Faithful retainers

                              though when he set out
Pursued and a pauper   he pointed his prow
Out to the sea   alone set out sailing
Lost in his exile   yet eager to go
Weaving the currents   time in his veins

Now truly that man   has passed beyond pain
He has all he wants   has horses, has treasure
The great hall's warm welcome   gifts the earth yields
Princess, Princess   you too are his portion
Remember the promises   each of you vowed
The sealing silences   he made and you made
A letter, a syllable   nothing is lost
What seem erasures   are kisses and praying
Are runes that keep counsel   a promise in touch
A promise in looking   how staunch he has stayed to you
Above him the heavens   the earth under foot
A man of his word he is   true to your contract
The twining of wills   in those days gone in time

The Wanderer

Oft him anhaga   are gebideð,
metudes miltse,   þeah þe he modcearig
geond lagulade   longe sceolde
hreran mid hondum   hrimcealde sæ,
5 wadan wræclastas.   Wyrd bið ful aræd!
Swa cwæð eardstapa,   earfeþa gemyndig,
wraþra wælsleahta,   winemæga hryre:
"Oft ic sceolde ana   uhtna gehwylce
mine ceare cwiþan.   Nis nu cwicra nan
10 þe ic him modsefan   minne durre
sweotule asecgan.   Ic to soþe wat
þæt biþ in eorle   indryhten þeaw,
þæt he his ferðlocan   fæste binde,
healde his hordcofan,   hycge swa he wille.
15 Ne mæg werig mod   wyrde wiðstondan,
ne se hreo hyge   helpe gefremman.
Forðon domgeorne   dreorigne oft
in hyra breostcofan   bindað fæste;
swa ic modsefan   minne sceolde,
20 oft earmcearig,   eðle bidæled,
freomægum feor   feterum sælan,
siþþan geara iu   goldwine **minne**
hrusan heolstre biwrah,   ond ic hean þonan
wod wintercearig   ofer **waþema** gebind,
25 sohte sele dreorig   sinces bryttan,
hwær ic feor oþþe neah   findan meahte
þone þe in meoduhealle   **min** mine wisse,
oþþe mec **freondleasne**   frefran wolde,

The Wanderer

Greg Delanty

The loner holds out for grace
—the Maker's mercy—though full of care
he steers a course, forced to row
the freezing, fierce sea with bare hands,
take the exile's way; fate dictates.
The earth-stepper spoke, heedful of hardship,
of brutal battle, the death of kith and kin:
    "Often at first lick of light
I lament my sole way—no one left
to open my self up to wholly,
heart and soul. Sure, I know
it's the noble custom for an earl
to bind fast what's in his breast,
hoard inmost thoughts, think what he will.
    The weary mind can't fight fate
nor will grim grit help.
Driven men often harbor
chill dread fast in their chests.
So I, at sea in my angst,
(wretched outcast from my land,
far from kind kindred) brace myself,
having buried my large-hearted lord
years back in black earth. Abject,
I wander winter-weary the icy waves,
longing for lost halls, a helping hand
far or near. Maybe I'll find
one who'd host me in the toasting hall,
who'd comfort me, friendless,

weman mid wynnum.   Wat se þe cunnað,
30 hu sliþen bið   sorg to geferan,
þam þe him lyt hafað   leofra geholena.
Warað hine wræclast,   nales wunden gold,
ferðloca freorig,   nalæs foldan blæd.
Gemon he selesecgas   ond sincþege,
35 hu hine on geoguðe   his goldwine
wenede to wiste.   Wyn eal gedreas!
Forþon wat se þe sceal   his winedryhtnes
leofes larcwidum   longe forþolian,
ðonne sorg ond slæp   somod ætgædre
40 earmne anhogan   oft gebindað.
þinceð him on mode   þæt he his mondryhten
clyppe ond cysse,   ond on cneo lecge
honda ond heafod,   swa he hwilum ær
in geardagum   giefstolas breac.
45 ðonne onwæcneð eft   wineleas guma,
gesihð him biforan   fealwe wegas,
baþian brimfuglas,   brædan feþra,
hreosan hrim ond snaw,   hagle gemenged.
þonne beoð þy hefigran   heortan benne,
50 sare æfter swæsne.   Sorg bið geniwad,
þonne maga gemynd   mod geondhweorfeð;
greteð gliwstafum,   georne geondsceawað
secga geseldan.   Swimmað **eft** on weg!
Fleotendra ferð   no þær fela bringeð
55 cuðra cwidegiedda.   Cearo bið geniwad
þam þe sendan sceal   swiþe geneahhe
ofer waþema gebind   werigne sefan.
Forþon ic geþencan ne mæg   geond þas woruld
for hwan **modsefa**   min ne gesweorce,
60 þonne ic eorla lif   eal geondþence,
hu hi færlice   flet ofgeafon,

gladly entertain me. Any who attempt it
know what cruel company sorrow can be
for a soul without a single mate;
exile's path holds him, not finished gold;
a frozen heart, not the world's wonders;
he recalls retainers, reaping treasure,
how in youth his lavish liege
feted and feasted him. All is history.

　　　He who lacks a loved lord's
counsel knows this story:
whenever sorrow and sleep combine
the wretched recluse often dreams
that he is with his loyal lord.
He clasps and kisses him, lays
his hands and head on those knees, loves
the liberal ruler as in whilom days.

　　　As soon as the sober man wakes
he sees nothing but fallow furrows;
seabirds paddle and preen feathers;
snow and frost combine forces.
Then his heart weighs heavier, sore
for the loved lord, sorrow renewed.
He recalls friends from the past,
gladly greets them, feasts his eyes.
His mates swim in waves of memory.
Those fellows float away in his mind,
barely utter a word. Down again
the man knows he must cast
his harrowed heart over frigid waves.

　　　It's not hard to guess why in the world
my spirit's in such a stark state
as I consider the lives of those lords,
how they abruptly quit the halls,

modge maguþegnas.   Swa þes middangeard
ealra dogra gehwam   dreoseð ond fealleþ,
forþon ne mæg **weorþan** wis   wer, ær he age
65   wintra dæl in woruldrice.   Wita sceal geþyldig,
ne sceal no to hatheort   ne to hrædwyrde,
ne to wac wiga   ne to wanhydig,
ne to forht ne to fægen,   ne to feohgifre
ne næfre gielpes to georn,   ær he geare cunne.
70   Beorn sceal gebidan,   þonne he beot spriceð,
oþþæt collenferð   cunne gearwe
hwider hreþra gehygd   hweorfan wille.
Ongietan sceal gleaw hæle   hu gæstlic bið,
þonne **ealre** þisse worulde wela   weste stondeð,
75   swa nu missenlice   geond þisne middangeard
winde biwaune   weallas stondaþ,
hrime bihrorene,   hryðge þa ederas.
Woriað þa winsalo,   waldend licgað
dreame bidrorene,   duguþ eal gecrong,
80   wlonc bi wealle.   Sume wig fornom,
ferede in forðwege,   sumne fugel oþbær
ofer heanne holm,   sumne se hara wulf
deaðe gedælde,   sumne dreorighleor
in eorðscræfe   eorl gehydde.
85   Yþde swa þisne eardgeard   ælda scyppend
oþþæt burgwara   breahtma lease
eald enta geweorc   idlu stodon.
Se þonne þisne wealsteal   wise geþohte
ond þis **deorce** lif   deope geondþenceð,
90   frod in ferðe,   feor oft gemon
wælsleahta worn,   ond þas word acwið:
"Hwær cwom mearg? Hwær cwom mago?   Hwær cwom maþþumgyfa?
Hwær cwom symbla gesetu?   Hwær sindon seledreamas?
Eala beorht bune!   Eala byrnwiga!

the bold youth. In this way the world,
day after day, fails and falls.
For sure, no man's wise without his share
of winters in this world. He must be patient,
not too keen, not hot tongued,
not easily led, not foolhardy,
not timid, not all gusto, not greedy
not too cocky till he knows life.
A man should take stock before a vow,
brace for action, be mindful
of the mind's twists and turns.

      The wise man knows how ghostly it will be
when all the world's wealth is wasted
as in many regions on Earth today,
the still-standing walls wind-wracked,
ice-bound; each edifice under snow.
The halls fall, the lords lie low,
no more revels, troops of gallant veterans
lie valiant by the wall. Some fell in battle,
borne away: one was borne by vultures
over the ocean; one the hoar wolf
wolfed down; another a noble laid in a cave
—his mien a death mask of grief.
So the Shaper laid the Earth waste,
until, bereft of human life,
the ancient works of giants stand empty.

      Anyone who dwells on these battlements,
ponders each stage of our dark life,
will wisely survey the distant past,
the myriad struggles, and exclaim:
Where is the horse gone? The young bucks? The kind king?
Where is the banquet assembly gone? The merrymaking?
O the glittering glass. O the uniformed man.

95 Eala þeodnes þrym!　　Hu seo þrag gewat,
　　　genap under nihthelm,　　swa heo no wære.
　　　Stondeð nu on laste　　leofre duguþe
　　　weal wundrum heah,　　wyrmlicum fah.
　　　Eorlas fornoman　　asca þryþe,
100　wæpen wælgifru,　　wyrd seo mære,
　　　ond þas stanhleoþu　　stormas cnyssað,
　　　hrið hreosende　　**hrusan** bindeð,
　　　wintres woma,　　þonne won cymeð,
　　　nipeð nihtscua,　　norþan onsendeð
105　hreo hæglfare　　hæleþum on andan.
　　　Eall is earfoðlic　　eorþan rice,
　　　onwendeð wyrda gesceaft　　weoruld under heofonum.
　　　Her bið feoh læne,　　her bið freond læne,
　　　her bið mon læne,　　her bið mæg læne,
110　eal þis eorþan gesteal　　idel weorþeð!"
　　　Swa cwæð snottor on mode,　　gesæt him sundor æt rune.
　　　Til biþ se þe his treowe gehealdeþ,　　ne sceal næfre his torn to rycene
　　　beorn of his breostum acyþan,　　nemþe he ær þa bote cunne,
　　　eorl mid elne gefremman.　　Wel bið þam þe him are seceð,
115　frofre to fæder on heofonum,　　þær us eal seo fæstnung stondeð.

O the general's glory. How that time has passed.
Night shrouds all as if nothing ever was.
Now all that is left of those veterans
is a tower wall ringed with serpent devils;
missiles slaughtered those who served,
weapons amassed for mass murder, an incredible end.
Hurricanes attack the rocky coast.
Snowstorms sheet the earth.
Winter's tumult (dark comes then,
nightshadows deepen) drives hailstorms
out of the north to try us sorely.
This earthly realm is fraught.
Fate changes everything under the sun.
Here wealth is brief, friendship brief,
man brief, kinship brief.
All human foundation falls to naught."

      So spoke the wise man from his heart, musing apart.
Blest is he who holds true. No man should openly bare
his heart's hardships unless he knows the cure,
that is his great feat. It's well to seek solace
from the Maker, our only security.

First
Riddle-Hoard

Riddles 1-3

1.

Hwylc is hæleþa þæs horsc ond þæs hygecræftig
þæt þæt mæge asecgan, hwa mec on sið wræce,
þonne ic astige strong, stundum reþe,
þrymful þunie, þragum wræce
5 fere geond foldan, folcsalo bærne,
ræced reafige? Recas stigað,
haswe ofer hrofum. Hlin bið on eorþan,
wælcwealm wera, þonne ic wudu hrere,
bearwas bledhwate, beamas fylle,
10 holme gehrefed, **heahum** meahtum
wrecen on waþe, wide sended;
hæbbe me on hrycge þæt ær hadas wreah
foldbuendra, flæsc ond gæstas,
somod on sunde. Saga hwa mec þecce,
15 oþþe hu ic hatte, þe þa hlæst bere.

2.

Hwilum ic gewite, swa ne wenaþ men,
under yþa geþræc eorþan secan,
garsecges grund. Gifen biþ gewreged,
fam gewealcen;
5 hwælmere hlimmeð, hlude grimmeð,
streamas staþu beatað, stundum weorpaþ
on stealc hleoþa stane ond sonde,
ware ond wæge, þonne ic winnende,
holmmægne biþeaht, hrusan styrge,
10 side sægrundas. Sundhelme ne mæg
losian ær mec læte se þe min latteow bið

Who Is So Smart, So Crafty-Spirited

Peter Campion

Who is so smart, so crafty-spirited
that he can tell who drives my outcast force
when I arise along fate's road in wrath
and, groaning so grandly, spume down that power
on earth, on village homes, cracking their rafters
as I plunder? Smoke and ash plume out
and cries of the dying. Then in the woodland
I splinter flowering branches and slash down
trees as I wander, water for my roof,
this path enclosed by . . . whose enclosing might?
The rains that sluice from me once wrapped the flesh
and souls of men. So say who shrouds my force.
Say who I am. Who makes me bear these pains?
Sometimes I plunge to ocean, and to shock him,
swivel some poor sea-spearman's wobbling stance.
The sawtooth waves fly back. The foam swipes round.
The whale-road roars and pummels shoreward
strewing the cliff-face with sand and seaweed
as I wrangle that wave-strength on my back
and writhe, inside the long expanse of blue.
I can't escape the water-cover till my ruler

on siþa gehwam.   Saga, þoncol mon,
hwa mec bregde   of brimes fæþmum,
þonne streamas eft   stille weorþað,
15 yþa geþwære,   þe mec ær wrugon.

3.

Hwilum mec min frea   fæste genearwað,
sendeð þonne   under **salwonges**
bearm **þone** bradan,   ond on bid wriceð,
þrafað on þystrum   þrymma sumne,
5 **hæste** on enge,   þær me heord siteð
hruse on hrycge.   Nah ic hwyrftweges
of þam **aglace**,   ac ic eþelstol
hæleþa **hrere**;   hornsalu wagiað,
wera wicstede,   weallas beofiað,
10 steape ofer stiwitum.   Stille þynceð
lyft ofer londe   ond lagu swige,
oþþæt ic of enge   up aþringe,
efne swa mec wisaþ   se mec wræde on
æt frumsceafte   furþum legde,
15 bende ond clomme,   þæt ic onbugan ne mot
of þæs gewealde   þe me wegas tæcneð.
Hwilum ic sceal ufan   yþa wregan,
streamas styrgan   ond to staþe **þywan**
flintgrægne flod.   Famig winneð
20 wæg wið wealle,   wonn ariseð
dun ofer dype;   hyre deorc on last,
eare geblonden,   oþer fereð,
þæt hy gemittað   mearclonde neah
hea hlincas.   þær bið hlud wudu,
25 brimgiesta breahtm,   bidað stille
stealc stanhleoþu   streamgewinnes,

lets me escape. So tell me, thoughtful man,
who plucks me upward when my struggle's through?
Sometimes this leader sends his follower
under wide fields, and pens my power there,
cramped in the dark with earth to saddle me.
I can't twist free from tortures yet I shake
men's sanctuaries. Horn-hung walls and earthworks
towering above householders I make tremble.
The air goes tranquil, spreading over land
until I spiral out once more: the Lord
who chained me at creation hurls me.
Soon I'm at sea again to rouse the breakers.
I lace bright foam along their crests and smash
their faces into the cliff-face, the hill
on hill of ocean blotting out the coast.
A keel creaks and the spattered sailors scream
while rocks stand waiting, while the ocean broil

hopgehnastes,   þonne heah geþring
on cleofu crydeþ.   þær bið ceole wen
sliþre sæcce,   gif hine sæ byreð
30 on þa grimman tid,   gæsta fulne,
þæt he scyle rice   birofen weorþan,
feore bifohten   fæmig ridan
yþa hrycgum.   þær bið egsa sum
ældum geywed,   þara þe ic hyran sceal
35 strong on stiðweg.   Hwa gestilleð þæt?
Hwilum ic þurhræse,   þæt me on bæce rideð
won wægfatu,   wide toþringe
lagustreama full,   hwilum læte eft
slupan tosomne.   Se bið swega mæst,
40 breahtma ofer burgum,   ond gebreca hludast,
þonne scearp cymeð   sceo wiþ oþrum,
ecg wið ecge;   earpan gesceafte
fus ofer folcum   fyre swætað,
blacan lige,   ond gebrecu ferað
45 deorc ofer **dryhtum**   gedyne micle,
farað feohtende,   feallan lætað
sweart sumsendu   seaw of bosme,
wætan of wombe.   Winnende fareð
atol eoredþreat,   egsa astigeð,
50 micel modþrea   monna cynne,
brogan on burgum,   þonne blace scotiað
scriþende scin   scearpum wæpnum.
Dol him ne ondrædeð   ða deaðsperu,
swylteð hwæþre,   gif him soð meotud
55 on geryhtu   þurh regn ufan
of gestune læteð   stræle fleogan,
farende flan.   Fea þæt gedygað,
þara þe geræceð   rynegiestes wæpen.
Ic þæs orleges   or anstelle,

batters and thrashes landward. Then the crew
crazily scurries as their sail and rudder
fail in the swell: they scurry to survive.
The terror of this passage . . . who will still it?
Sometimes I ride the clouds that ride my back
and spill their water all across the earth.
And sometimes I collide them. Sword on sword's
no louder when they lash against each other
shedding their angled flames. Bare terror fills
the townships as the battle gleams and bellows.
Only a dullard never fears the arrow.
He dies regardless when my leader flies
down through the rain to loose his fire-shower.
Few live to tell about its simmering touch.
I drive that charge, lash on the cloud stampede

60 þonne gewite   wolcengehnaste
   þurh geþræc þringan   þrimme micle
   ofer byrnan bosm.   Biersteð hlude
   heah hloðgecrod;   þonne hnige eft
   under lyfte helm   londe near,
65 ond me **on** hrycg hlade   þæt ic habban sceal,
   meahtum **gemagnad**   mines frean.
   Swa ic þrymful þeow   þragum winne,
   hwilum under eorþan,   hwilum yþa sceal
   hean underhnigan,   hwilum holm ufan
70 streamas styrge,   hwilum stige up,
   wolcnfare wrege,   wide fere
   swift ond swiþfeorm.   Saga hwæt ic hatte,
   oþþe hwa mec rære,   þonne ic restan ne mot,
   oþþe hwa mec stæðþe,   þonne ic stille beom.

over the sky-borne rivers. Then I bend

close to the ground at my master's command.

Sometimes I rush through channels under land.
Sometimes I whip the ocean from below
and sometimes from above. Sometimes I climb
cloud-tumult to incite the crash and roil.
You, strong and quick, say who I am, and say
who wakens and who calms my frenzied power.

Riddle 4

Ic sceal þragbysig   þegne minum,
hringum hæfted,   hyran georne,
min bed brecan,   breahtme cyþan
þæt me halswriþan   hlaford sealde.
5 Oft mec slæpwerigne   secg oðþe meowle
gretan eode;   ic him gromheortum
winterceald oncweþe.   Wearm lim
gebundenne bæg   hwilum bersteð;
se þeah biþ on þonce   þegne minum,
10 medwisum men,   me þæt sylfe,
þær wiht wite,   ond wordum min
on sped mæge   spel gesecgan.

Busy from Time to Time, in Rings

Phillis Levin

Busy from time to time, in rings
bound, I shall obey my servant eagerly,
break my bed and suddenly call out
that my lord has given me a neck-collar.
Often a man or a maid will greet me,
sleepweary; grim-hearted, I give
a winter-cold answer. A warm limb
sometimes bursts the bound ring,
which is pleasing to my servant,
a feeble-minded man; to me, as well,
if you'd like to know, and if my words
ring true my story may be told.

Riddle 5

Ic eom anhaga   iserne wund,
bille gebennad,   beadoweorca sæd,
ecgum werig.   Oft ic wig seo,
frecne feohtan.   Frofre ne wene,
5   þæt **me** geoc cyme   guðgewinnes,
ær ic mid ældum   eal **forwurðe**,
ac mec hnossiað   homera lafe,
heardecg heoroscearp,   **hondweorc** smiþa,
bitað in burgum;   ic abidan sceal
10   laþran gemotes.   Næfre læcecynn
on folcstede   findan meahte,
þara þe mid wyrtum   wunde gehælde,
ac me ecga dolg   eacen weorðað
þurh deaðslege   dagum ond nihtum.

Riddle 7

Hrægl min swigað,   þonne ic hrusan trede,
oþþe þa wic buge,   oþþe wado drefe.
Hwilum mec ahebbað   ofer hæleþa byht
hyrste mine,   ond þeos hea lyft,
5   ond mec þonne wide   wolcna strengu
ofer folc byreð.   Frætwe mine
swogað hlude   ond swinsiað,
torhte singað,   þonne ic getenge ne beom
flode ond foldan,   ferende gæst.

I Am a Monad Gashed by Iron

David Curzon

I am a monad   gashed by iron,
savaged by the sword,   worn by battles,
drained by blades.   I often watch war,
fierce fighting.   I trust in no comfort,
no solace to come   from the trouble of conflict,
until my murder   among men,
but on me beat   hard hammers,
smiths' handwork,   deep bites
in my battlements.   I wait for further
hateful conclaves.   In no abode
can I discover   the clan of doctors
who might heal   my hurts with herbs,
but sword wounds   widen in me
through deadly blows   day and night.

All That Adorns Me Keeps Me

Lawrence Raab

All that adorns me keeps me
silent as I step among the grasses
or trouble the water. Sometimes
I'm lifted by the high winds far above
your houses, and when the sweep
of clouds carries me away you may think
you can hear my song—how clear
and strange it is—the voice of a being
traveling alone and far from sleep—
a spirit, a ghost, no one like yourself.

Riddle 8

Ic þurh muþ sprece   mongum reordum,
wrencum singe,   wrixle geneahhe
heafodwoþe,   hlude cirme,
healde mine wisan,   hleoþre ne miþe,
5 eald æfensceop,   eorlum bringe
blisse in burgum,   þonne ic bugendre
stefne styrme;   stille on wicum
sittað nigende.   Saga hwæt ic hatte,
þe swa scirenige   sceawendwisan
10 hlude onhyrge,   hæleþum bodige
wilcumena fela   woþe minre.

I Can Chortle Away in Any Voice

Patricia McCarthy

I can chortle away in any voice,
an impresario of impersonations.
I broadcast my deathless lyrics,
never backward in coming forward.
Ancient soloist of eventides, I perform
for those unwinding at home.
They sit quietly in their houses,
downcast. Guess who I am?
I parody as loudly as I can the japes
of comedians. I top the charts,
karaoke the most popular songs.

Riddle 9

Mec on þissum dagum   deadne **ofgeafun**
fæder ond modor;   ne wæs me feorh þa gen,
ealdor in innan.   þa mec **an** ongon,
welhold mege,   wedum **þeccan,**
5   heold ond freoþode,   hleosceorpe wrah
swa arlice   swa hire agen bearn,
oþþæt ic under sceate,   swa min gesceapu wæron,
ungesibbum wearð   eacen gæste.
Mec seo friþe mæg   fedde siþþan,
10   oþþæt ic aweox,   widdor meahte
siþas asettan.   Heo hæfde swæsra þy læs
suna ond dohtra,   þy heo swa dyde.

Days before Birth I Was Left Here for Dead

James McGonigal

Days before birth
by both parents
of life there at all.

my mother's cousin
in her finest cloth
as her own dear boy
and to my destiny
strong at heart
And she fed me then
until stout enough
on my far travels.

So few children left
and dear daughters

I was left here for dead
not a prick or a pulse

Then lovely and gracious
came by and covered me
gathered me close
to her breast
so that daily I grew
among strangers.
my beautiful friend
I could set out at last

Tough luck on her.
to cherish now—all her sons
undone by that one kind deed.

Riddle 11

Hrægl is min hasofag,   hyrste beorhte,
reade ond scire   on reafe **minum**.
Ic dysge dwelle   ond dole hwette
unrædsiþas,   oþrum styre
5 nyttre fore.   Ic þæs nowiht wat
þæt heo swa gemædde,   mode bestolene,
dæde gedwolene,   deoraþ mine
won wisan gehwam.   Wa him þæs þeawes,
siþþan heah **bringað**   horda deorast,
10 gif hi unrædes   ær ne geswicaþ.

My Jacket Is Polished Gray

Billy Collins

My jacket is polished gray
Emblazoned with roses and fire.
I drive some men crazy; others are
merely foolish or they grow quiet.
Who knows why the weak
And the loony hold me up?
But sharp pain comes to those who lift me
Higher than man's treasure most dear.
Accustomed to their sad pleasure,
They won't get used to their bitter woe.

Riddle 12

Fotum ic fere,   foldan slite,
grene wongas,   þenden ic gæst bere.
Gif me feorh losað,   fæste binde
swearte Wealas,   hwilum sellan men.
5 Hwilum ic deorum   drincan selle
beorne of bosme,   hwilum mec bryd triedeð
felawlonc fotum,   hwilum feorran broht
wonfeax Wale   wegeð ond þyð,
dol druncmennen   deorcum nihtum,
10 wæteð in wætre,   wyrmeð hwilum
fægre to fyre;   me on fæðme sticaþ
hygegalan hond,   hwyrfeð geneahhe,
swifeð me geond sweartne.   Saga hwæt ic hatte,
þe ic lifgende   lond reafige
15 ond æfter deaþe   dryhtum þeowige.

I Crush and Compress, Ruin and Ravage the Raw

Elizabeth Powell

I crush and compress, ruin and ravage the raw,
Muddy land forever thick with clash and brawl.
Victor or not, slave or master,
Both I bind in my death. They are
Warrior-fortified, drink a soldier's brew
Made from my belly-sac. Sometimes
A young bride weaves and walks on me;
Care has not yet trampled her. Her feet
Won't touch the earth. The laborer is worthy
Of his reward, if there is one. The drunken slave-
Girl is dark haired in the velvet closing
Of night and lifts me to the hell-hot fire,
So that I may lull and invite—
Her hot hands are full of kneading,
Pressing, shoving, pulling. Say what
I am whom they kill so that they can
Remember who they are
And that in slaying me they may not die.

Riddle 13

Ic seah turf tredan,   X wæron ealra,
VI gebroþor   ond hyra sweostor mid;
hæfdon feorg cwico.   Fell hongedon
sweotol ond gesyne   on seles wæge
5   anra gehwylces.   Ne wæs hyra ængum þy wyrs,
ne **siðe** þy **sarre**,   þeah hy swa sceoldon
reafe birofene,   rodra weardes
meahtum aweahte,   muþum slitan
haswe blede.   Hrægl bið geniwad
10   þam þe ær forðcymene   frætwe leton
licgan on laste,   gewitan lond tredan.

I Saw Ten of Them Ramble across the Land

Enda Wyley

I saw ten of them ramble across the land—
six brothers and their sisters strutting about
all in high spirits. A fine robe of skin—
it was quite clear to see—hung on the wall
of each of their houses. And not one of them
was hard done by, nor did it pain them
to move about, robbed of their delicate skin,
gnawing the withering shoots, roused
by the power of the guardian of heaven.
New clothes are there for the taking
by those who before roamed out naked;
they strutted over the ground.

Riddle 14

Ic wæs wæpenwiga.　　Nu mec wlonc þeceð
geong hagostealdmon　　golde ond sylfore,
woum wirbogum.　　Hwilum weras cyssað,
hwilum ic to hilde　　hleoþre bonne
5　wilgehleþan,　　hwilum wycg byreþ
mec ofer mearce,　　hwilum merehengest
fereð ofer flodas　　frætwum beorhtne,
hwilum mægða sum　　minne gefylleð
bosm beaghroden;　　hwilum ic bordum sceal,
10　heard, heafodleas,　　behlyþed licgan,
hwilum hongige　　hyrstum frætwed,
wlitig on wage,　　þær weras drincað,
freolic fyrdsceorp.　　Hwilum folcwigan
on wicge wegað,　　þonne ic winde sceal
15　sincfag swelgan　　of sumes bosme;
hwilum ic gereordum　　rincas laðige
wlonce to wine;　　hwilum **wraþum** sceal
stefne minre　　forstolen hreddan,
flyman feondsceaþan.　　Frige hwæt ic hatte.

Armed and Deadly Those Were My Early Days

James McGonigal

Armed and deadly those were my early days.
Now a young captain coats me with silver and gold
twisting and turning the wires tightly round me.
Men often kiss me yet I can move the whole crowd
with my war songs. Sometimes a horse will carry me
into the borderlands or a buoyant stallion bears me
sparkling over salty surging seas. Sometimes those
fine jeweled fingers of a young girl can fill me
right to the brim. Other times I'm abandoned
empty and hard headless on the table. Sometimes
you'll find me set up here in my finery
high on the wall with drunk men below me.
Riding to fight I'm the finest equipment
a soldier can get. Gleaming and glittering
I suck out the breath from the broadest man's chest.
My voice is a clarion call: "More wine for the captains!"—
the very same voice sends you deep into battle
to ride to the rescue and rout out a brutalized foe.
What is my name? Do you not know?

Poems about Historical
Battles, People,
and Places

The Battle of Maldon

brocen wurde.
Het þa hyssa hwæne   hors forlætan,
feor afysan,   and forð gangan,
hicgan to handum   and **to** hige godum.
5 þa þæt Offan mæg   ærest onfunde,
þæt se eorl nolde   yrhðo geþolian,
he let him þa of handon   leofne fleogan
hafoc wið þæs holtes,   and to þære hilde stop;
be þam man mihte oncnawan   þæt se cniht nolde
10 wacian æt þam **wige**,   þa he to wæpnum feng.
Eac him wolde Eadric   his ealdre gelæstan,
frean to gefeohte,   ongan þa forð beran
gar to guþe.   He hæfde god geþanc
þa hwile þe he mid handum   healdan mihte
15 bord and bradswurd;   beot he gelæste
þa he ætforan his frean   feohtan sceolde.
ða þær Byrhtnoð ongan   beornas trymian,
rad and rædde,   rincum tæhte
hu hi sceoldon standan   and þone stede healdan,
20 and bæd þæt hyra **randas**   rihte heoldon
fæste mid folman,   and ne forhtedon na.
þa he hæfde þæt folc   fægere getrymmed,
he lihte þa mid leodon   þær him leofost wæs,
þær he his heorðwerod   holdost wiste.
25 þa stod on stæðe,   stiðlice clypode
wicinga ar,   wordum mælde,
se on beot abead   brimliþendra
ærænde to þam eorle,   þær he on ofre stod:

The Battle of Maldon

David R. Slavitt

         . . . was broken.
He had each man abandon his horse
driving it far so he could march
forward unfettered his mind on his hands
and the blade of his sword with its edge of honor.
Great Offa's kinsman when he first understood
the earl would not now tolerate cowards
set free from his hand his favorite hawk
to fly high on the wind away to the forest.
Forging them forward shoreward, warward,
that lusty lad would not shrink from the moment
as any man might see for himself
when it was time to hold his weapon.
Eadric likewise, eager to serve
his lord in the combat, carried his spear,
daring, determined with sword hand and shield hand
to vindicate vows given the master.
Byrhtnoth then began to arrange in order
his muster of men in the best dispositions,
how they should hold homestead ground
their round-shields aligned together in good grip
and with broadswords ready and not be frightened.
When they were rightly arrayed as he wanted
he dismounted at last to stand on the turf
hard by his hearth's men closest and most loyal.

The Viking herald, strident, shouting
from shore declared the Vikings' clear purpose.

"Me sendon to þe   sæmen snelle,
30 heton ðe secgan   þæt þu most sendan raðe
beagas wið gebeorge;   and eow betere is
þæt ge þisne garræs   mid gafole forgyldon,
þon we swa hearde   **hilde** dælon.
Ne þurfe we us spillan,   gif ge spedaþ to þam;
35 we willað wið þam golde   grið fæstnian.
Gyf þu þat gerædest,   þe her ricost eart,
þæt þu þine leoda   lysan wille,
syllan sæmannum   on hyra sylfra dom
feoh wið freode,   and niman frið æt us,
40 we willaþ mid þam sceattum   us to scype gangan,
on flot feran,   and eow friþes healdan."
Byrhtnoð maþelode,   bord hafenode,
wand wacne æsc,   wordum mælde,
yrre and anræd   ageaf him andsware:
45 "Gehyrst þu, sælida,   hwæt þis folc segeð?
Hi willað eow to gafole   garas syllan,
ættrynne ord   and ealde swurd,
þa heregeatu   þe eow æt hilde ne deah.
Brimmanna boda,   abeod eft ongean,
50 sege þinum leodum   miccle laþre spell,
þæt her stynt unforcuð   eorl mid his werode,
þe wile gealgean   eþel þysne,
æþelredes eard,   ealdres mines,
folc and foldan.   Feallan sceolon
55 hæþene æt hilde.   To heanlic me þinceð
þæt ge mid urum sceattum   to scype gangon
unbefohtene,   nu ge þus feor hider
on urne eard   in becomon.
Ne sceole ge swa softe   sinc gegangan;
60 us sceal ord and ecg   ær geseman,
grim guðplega,   ær **we** gofol syllon."

His errand: to tell   the earl the terms
of the seafarers' message   from the ships on the bank:
"Send in all speed   to the valiant seamen
treasure to take.   Buy your safety,
paying them tribute   to avoid battle.
We see no need   for wanton destruction
for you are wealthy   and we can deal—
for gold to give   the advantage of truce.
If you and your council   consider our offer
you will send us seafarers   away from Essex
and redeem your people   with the peace all men want.
We will go willingly,   your gold in our coffers,
traveling elsewhere   and leave you alone."
Byrhtnoth spoke   hefting his shield
and ashen spear,   to answer for all:
"Hear them, seaman?   Hark at my host.
What they will pay   is spears they will send
with poisoned points   and their family swords,
those heriot weapons   not for your profit.
Go then, envoy,   say to your seamen
our terse terms: that the English earl
stands fast with his troops,   defends his homeland,
and defies your demands   upon Æthelred's realm,
his land and his people.   In hard battle
heathens will fall,   for it would be shameful
that you should depart   in your plundering ships
without the fight   that we must give you.
Thus far have you come   into our country,
but fare no farther   or think to extort
what is ours from us.   Point and sharp edge
must carve the conclusion,   who gives and who takes,
and settle the terms   before we pay tribute.

Het þa bord beran, beornas gangan,
þæt hi on þam easteðe ealle stodon.
Ne mihte þær for wætere werod to þam oðrum;
65 þær com flowende flod æfter ebban,
lucon lagustreamas. To lang hit him þuhte,
hwænne hi togædere garas beron.
Hi þær Pantan stream mid prasse bestodon,
Eastseaxena ord and se æschere.
70 Ne mihte hyra ænig oþrum derian,
buton hwa þurh flanes flyht fyl gename.
Se flod ut gewat; þa flotan stodon gearowe,
wicinga fela, wiges georne.
Het þa hæleða hleo healdan þa bricge
75 wigan wigheardne, se wæs haten Wulfstan,
cafne mid his cynne, þæt wæs Ceolan sunu,
þe ðone forman man mid his francan ofsceat
þe þær baldlicost on þa bricge stop.
þær stodon mid Wulfstane wigan unforhte,
80 ælfere and Maccus, modige twegen,
þa noldon æt þam forda fleam gewyrcan,
ac hi fæstlice wið ða fynd weredon,
þa hwile þe hi wæpna wealdan moston.
þa hi þæt ongeaton and georne gesawon
85 þæt hi þær bricgweardas bitere fundon,
ongunnon lytegian þa laðe gystas,
bædon þæt hi **upgang** agan moston,
ofer þone ford faran, feþan lædan.
ða se eorl ongan for his ofermode
90 alyfan landes to fela laþere ðeode.
Ongan ceallian þa ofer cald wæter
Byrhtelmes bearn (beornas gehlyston):
"Nu eow is gerymed, gað ricene to us,
guman to guþe; god ana wat

He bade them then   to heft their shields
and all advance   to the bank of the river
where water would ward   one troop from the other
while the flood tide took   its own time turning.
They waited for water,   the Pante's current,
where waterstreams locked   to ebb and allow
the spearmen to move   and, patient, watched
the ship-army   of Viking invaders.
Both sides were harmless   except for arrows'
feathered flight   till the tide moved out,
and the many Vikings in ranks   eager for war
stood in massed menace.   Byrhtnoth then ordered
Wulfstan, Ceola's son,   his hero to guard the bridge
the bravest of brethren.   When the first of the Danes
approached the bridge,   with sharp spear-shot
he cut him down.   Alongside Wulfstan,
stood Ælfhere and Maccus,   a fine pair of steadfast men
who would not deign   to flee from that ford
but defied the foe   with the weapons they wielded.
When the Vikings discovered   these gallant bridge-guards
they fell back, dissembling,   and craved, as if craven,
permission to put ashore   to lead their men safely
into battle and blood-risk.   The earl, overconfident,
granted them passage,   too much land
to those hateful people,   and Byrhthelm's son, Byrhtnoth,
called across the chill water   as his host harkened:
"The pathway is open.   Come to us quickly,
war-men meeting war-men.   God alone knows

95 hwa þære wælstowe   wealdan mote."
   Wodon þa wælwulfas   (for wætere ne murnon),
   wicinga werod,   **west** ofer Pantan,
   ofer scir wæter   scyldas wegon,
   lidmen to lande   linde bæron.
100 þær ongean gramum   gearowe stodon
    Byrhtnoð mid beornum;   he mid bordum het
    wyrcan þone wihagan,   and þæt werod healdan
    fæste wið feondum.   þa wæs **feohte** neh,
    tir æt getohte.   Wæs seo tid cumen
105 þæt þær fæge men   feallan sceoldon.
    þær wearð hream ahafen,   hremmas wundon,
    earn æses georn;   wæs on eorþan cyrm.
    Hi leton þa of folman   feolhearde speru,
    gegrundene   garas fleogan;
110 bogan wæron bysige,   bord ord onfeng.
    Biter wæs se beaduræs,   beornas feollon
    on gehwæðere hand,   hyssas lagon.
    Wund **wearð** Wulfmær,   wælræste geceas,
    Byrhtnoðes mæg;   he mid billum wearð,
115 his swuster sunu,   swiðe forheawen.
    þær **wearð** wicingum   wiþerlean agyfen.
    Gehyrde ic þæt Eadweard   anne sloge
    swiðe mid his swurde,   swenges ne wyrnde,
    þæt him æt fotum   feoll fæge cempa;
120 þæs him his ðeoden   þanc gesæde,
    þam burþene,   þa he byre hæfde.
    Swa stemnetton   stiðhicgende
    hysas æt hilde,   hogodon georne
    hwa þær mid orde   ærost mihte
125 on fægean men   feorh gewinnan,
    wigan mid wæpnum;   wæl feol on eorðan.
    Stodon stædefæste;   stihte hi Byrhtnoð,

who will win control   of this killing field."

Advancing then, the Viking army,   careless of water,
crossed the Pante westward,   lifting high
their linden shields.   Opposed, the fierce
forces of Byrhtnoth   then formed a war-wall,
shield next to shield,   to hold off the attack,
for the crisis had come,   the time of trial
where the men who are fated   will fall as they must.
Overhead ravens   and carrion-hungry
screeching eagles   made leisurely circles,
while below the massed men   sent their roar skyward,
followed by sharp-filed   spears they flung.
Bows, too, were busy,   and Viking shields
bristled with arrows.   The war-charge then
was fierce, and men fell   leaving the ground
a clutter of corpses,   and Wulfmar wounded
and sliding to death-rest   he could not refuse.
Byrhtnoth's kinsman,   his sister's son,
was hard-hacked   by many swords.
But the wound was redressed   as Edward offered
payment in kind,   and a doomed fighter,
as I have heard,   fell at his feet.
For this his lord thanked him   at the earliest moment,
telling his chamberlain.   Thus, they stood,
firm and strong-minded,   men in hard battle,
keen in competing   whose pointed weapons might
find their way   to fated men
and garner the lives   of those men of war.
Dying men fell   but the steadfast and resolute
still stood as Byrhtnoth gave   his heartening words,

bæd þæt hyssa gehwylc   hogode to wige
þe on Denon wolde   dom gefeohtan.
130 Wod þa wiges heard,   wæpen up ahof,
bord to gebeorge,   and wið þæs beornes stop.
Eode swa anræd   eorl to þam ceorle,
ægþer hyra oðrum   yfeles hogode.
Sende ða se særinc   suþerne gar,
135 þæt gewundod wearð   wigena hlaford;
he sceaf þa mid ðam scylde,   þæt se sceaft tobærst,
and þæt spere sprengde,   þæt hit sprang ongean.
Gegremod wearð se guðrinc;   he mid gare stang
wlancne wicing,   þe him þa wunde forgeaf.
140 Frod wæs se fyrdrinc;   he let his francan wadan
þurh ðæs hysses hals,   hand wisode
þæt he on þam færsceaðan   feorh geræhte.
ða he oþerne   ofstlice sceat,
þæt seo byrne tobærst;   he wæs on breostum wund
145 þurh ða hringlocan,   him æt heortan stod
ætterne ord.   Se eorl wæs þe bliþra,
hloh þa, modi man,   sæde metode þanc
ðæs dægweorces   þe him drihten forgeaf.
Forlet þa drenga sum   daroð of handa,
150 fleogan of folman,   þæt se to forð gewat
þurh ðone æþelan   æþelredes þegen.
Him be healfe stod   hyse unweaxen,
cniht on gecampe,   se full caflice
bræd of þam beorne   blodigne gar,
155 Wulfstanes bearn,   Wulfmær se geonga,
forlet forheardne   faran eft ongean;
ord in gewod,   þæt se on eorþan læg
þe his þeoden ær   þearle geræhte.
Eode þa gesyrwed   secg to þam eorle;
160 he wolde þæs beornes   beagas gefecgan,

that whoever strove now   to achieve great glory
should look to the Danes   to drag it from them.

The bold one, Byrhtnoth,   raised up his weapon
and set his shield   to stride toward a soldier,
the earl to the churl   and each meaning evil.
That seaman marauder   hurled his southern spear
and wounded was   the warriors' lord.
Byrhtnoth banged the shaft,   shaking it free
and stabbed with the spear-point   its Viking owner,
giving him back   the bite of its wound.
Skillful was Byrhtnoth   and he struck with his lance,
hitting the Viking   and piercing his neck
and in that quick thrust   reaching his life.
He turned to another   and hurled at this Viking
that lance that landed   and pierced through his chain mail
the hard point   hitting his heart.
Elated, the earl,   the valiant victor,
laughed aloud   and gave thanks to his God.
for the work of the day,   the deity's grant.
But one Viking then   loosed from his hand
a javelin striking   Æthelred's noble thane,
Byrhtnoth, and biting   into his body.
Hard by his side   a fledgling fighter,
Wulfstane's son   the young Wulfmaer
drew from his lord   the bloodied spear
and flung it forward   back at that Viking
to get him for getting   the lad's lord.
This strike was successful   and the Viking lay down dying.
Came then another   Viking marauder
up to the earl   to harvest rich pickings,

reaf and hringas   and gerenod swurd.
þa Byrhtnoð bræd   bill of sceðe,
brad and bruneccg,   and on þa byrnan sloh.
To raþe hine gelette   lidmanna sum,
165 þa he þæs eorles   earm amyrde.
Feoll þa to foldan   fealohilte swurd;
ne mihte he gehealdan   heardne mece,
wæpnes wealdan.   þa gyt þæt word gecwæð
har hilderinc,   hyssas bylde,
170 bæd gangan forð   gode geferan;
ne mihte þa on fotum leng   fæste **gestandan.**
He to heofenum wlat:
"Geþancie þe,   ðeoda waldend,
ealra þæra wynna   þe ic on worulde gebad.
175 Nu ic ah, milde metod,   mæste þearfe
þæt þu minum gaste   godes geunne,
þæt min sawul to ðe   siðian mote
on þin geweald,   þeoden engla,
mid friþe ferian.   Ic eom frymdi to þe
180 þæt hi helsceaðan   hynan ne moton."
ða hine heowon   hæðene scealcas
and begen þa beornas   þe him big stodon,
ælfnoð and Wulmær   begen lagon,
ða onemn hyra frean   feorh gesealdon.
185 Hi bugon þa fram beaduwe   þe þær beon noldon.
þær **wearð** Oddan bearn   ærest on fleame,
Godric fram guþe,   and þone godan forlet
þe him mænigne oft   mear gesealde;
he gehleop þone eoh   þe ahte his hlaford,
190 on þam gerædum   þe hit riht ne wæs,
and his broðru mid him   begen **ærndon,**
Godwine and Godwig,   guþe ne gymdon,
ac wendon fram þam wige   and þone wudu sohton,

rings and armor   and patterned sword.
But Byrhtnoth could draw   his blade from its scabbard
to strike at that sailor   and would have, but one
of the cutthroat's comrades   hit the earl's arm
and rendered it useless.   His biting blade then
fell to the earth,   for Byrhtnoth could no more
hold the weapon's weight.   Still, he could speak,
that white-haired war man,   to encourage his people
and urge them onward.   His legs were unsteady
and footing uncertain,   as the hero to heaven
spoke his last words: "I give you my thanks,
O King of Kings,   for all my achievements
in this life I have lived.   Now, my king Maker,
I ask a last favor,   that you may admit me
into your high domain.   Lord of the Angels,
grant peaceful passage   and hear my petition
that the demons of hell   not snare my spirit."
Then heathen men hacked him   and his two companions,
Ælfnoth and Wulfmaer   who had stood beside him
and, along with their lord,   they too gave their lives.

They then fled the battle   whose spirit for the fighting
began now to quaver: Odda's son, Godric,
was the first man who fled,   abandoning Byrhtnoth
who had given him many mares   and their trappings and tack.
He leapt on his lord's   own charger
who had not ever earned   the right to ride and use,
and he and his brothers,   Godwine and Godwig,
flew from the battle   they could not bear,
away from the fighting   to hide in the forest.

flugon on þæt fæsten   and hyra feore burgon,
195 and manna ma   þonne hit ænig mæð wære,
gyf hi þa geearnunga   ealle gemundon
þe he him to duguþe   gedon hæfde.
Swa him Offa on dæg   ær asæde
on þam meþelstede,   þa he gemot hæfde,
200 þæt þær **modiglice**   manega spræcon
þe eft æt **þearfe**   þolian noldon.
þa wearð afeallen   þæs folces ealdor,
æþelredes eorl;   ealle gesawon
heorðgeneatas   þæt hyra heorra læg.
205 þa ðær wendon forð   wlance þegenas,
unearge men   efston georne;
hi woldon þa ealle   oðer twega,
lif **forlætan**   oððe leofne gewrecan.
Swa hi bylde forð   bearn ælfrices,
210 wiga wintrum geong,   wordum mælde,
ælfwine þa cwæð,   he on ellen spræc:
"**Gemunan** þa mæla   þe we oft æt meodo spræcon,
þonne we on bence   beot ahofon,
hæleð on healle,   ymbe heard gewinn;
215 nu mæg cunnian   hwa cene sy.
Ic wylle mine æþelo   eallum gecyþan,
þæt ic wæs on Myrcon   miccles cynnes;
wæs min ealda fæder   Ealhelm haten,
wis ealdorman,   woruldgesælig.
220 Ne sceolon me on þære þeode   þegenas ætwitan
þæt ic of ðisse fyrde   feran wille,
eard gesecan,   nu min ealdor ligeð
forheawen æt hilde.   Me is þæt hearma mæst;
he wæs **ægðer** min mæg   and min hlaford."
225 þa he forð eode,   fæhðe gemunde,
þæt he mid orde   anne geræhte

to find there some refuge and save their hides,
they and many more   spiritless men
who each had received   Byrhtnoth's favors.
Offa had warned him   early that day
at the morning meeting   in the counsel-place
that many who spoke   the speeches of warriors
might not at need   be worth their fine words.

Æthelred's earl,   their leader, lay dead,
and all who saw   Byrhtnoth's body,
the proud thanes   and the household troops,
brave men now   hastened keenly,
seeing but two   choices of honor:
either to die there   along with their lord,
or else to avenge him,   and kill many Danes.
Ælfwin, Ælfric's young son,   urged them all onward
making his valorous speech: "Remember those times
after much mead   there in the great hall
we were such heroes   making proud vows
of our bearing in battle,   the times of tough fighting.
Now we discover   which ones are brave.
I pray that my progeny   declare with some pride
among Mercian men   of noble line
that I was here.   My grandfather, Ealhelm,
an earl of much wisdom,   did well in the world.
Let no one now taunt me   that I wanted to go
away from this army   home and to safety
when my leader lay   cut down in the fighting,
my kinsman, my lord,   the greatest of griefs."
Then he moved forward   hot with his hatred
and with his weapon-point   found one of the Vikings

flotan on þam folce,   þæt se on foldan læg
forwegen mid his wæpne.   Ongan þa winas manian,
frynd and geferan,   þæt hi forð eodon.
230 Offa gemælde,   æscholt asceoc:
"Hwæt þu, ælfwine, hafast   ealle gemanode
þegenas to þearfe,   nu ure þeoden lið,
eorl on eorðan.   Us is eallum þearf
þæt ure æghwylc   oþerne bylde
235 wigan to wige,   þa hwile þe he wæpen mæge
habban and healdan,   heardne mece,
gar and godswurd.   Us Godric hæfð,
earh Oddan bearn,   ealle beswicene.
Wende þæs formoni man,   þa he on meare rad,
240 on wlancan þam wicge,   þæt wære hit ure hlaford;
forþan wearð her on felda   folc totwæmed,
scyldburh tobrocen.   Abreoðe his angin,
þæt he her swa manigne   man aflymde!"
Leofsunu gemælde   and his linde ahof,
245 bord to gebeorge;   he þam beorne oncwæð:
"Ic þæt gehate,   þæt ic heonon nelle
fleon fotes trym,   ac wille furðor gan,
wrecan on gewinne   minne winedrihten.
Ne þurfon me embe Sturmere   stedefæste hælæð
250 wordum ætwitan,   nu min wine gecranc,
þæt ic hlafordleas   ham siðie,
wende fram wige,   ac me sceal wæpen niman,
ord and iren."   He ful yrre wod,
feaht fæstlice,   fleam he forhogode.
255 Dunnere þa cwæð,   daroð acwehte,
unorne ceorl,   ofer eall clypode,
bæd þæt beorna gehwylc   Byrhtnoð wræce:
"Ne mæg na wandian   se þe wrecan þenceð
frean on folce,   ne for feore murnan."

impaling the pirate   to leave him lying
dead on the ground.   With this he could rally
as much as his words did   his friends and his comrades
to advance toward the enemy.   Offa spoke up
shaking his ash-spear: "Yea, Ælfwin has said it
to urge you all on,   the good thanes at need-time.
Byrhtnoth lies dead,   our earl on the earth,
and this is our moment   to rally each other
forward to war,   holding our hard blades
of spear and sharp sword.   The coward, Godric,
Odda's get, has betrayed us,   fleeing the field
on Byrhtnoth's own mount,   thus dispersing the army
and breaking the shield-wall.   Damn him for what he did,
spreading his foul fear   among the formation!"
Leofsun then spoke,   raising his linden shield:
"I offer my oath.   Not one step backward!
I fare only forward   to avenge in hard battle
my good lord's death.   The brave men of my village,
the people of Sturmer,   will not have the need
to reproach my behavior.   My friend has fallen
and I am lordless.   I will not go home
or turn away from the fight,   but a weapon must take me,
point or sharp blade edge."   He advanced in his anger
and steadfast he fought,   scorning the flight.
Dunner spoke up   as he brandished his weapon.
An honest peasant,   he called out to all,
bidding each soldier   to avenge great Byrhtnoth:
"Let no one hesitate   who intends to wreak vengeance
on the Viking horde,   nor fear for his life!"

260 þa hi forð eodon,   feores hi ne rohton;
    ongunnon þa hiredmen   heardlice feohtan,
    grame garberend,   and god bædon
    þæt hi moston gewrecan   hyra winedrihten
    and on hyra feondum   fyl gewyrcan.
265 Him se gysel ongan   geornlice fylstan;
    he wæs on Norðhymbron   heardes cynnes,
    Ecglafes bearn,   him wæs æscferð nama.
    He ne wandode na   æt þam wigplegan,
    ac he fysde forð   flan genehe;
270 hwilon he on bord sceat,   hwilon beorn tæsde,
    æfre embe stunde   he sealde sume wunde,
    þa hwile ðe he wæpna   wealdan moste.
    þa gyt on orde stod   Eadweard se langa,
    gearo and geornful,   gylpwordum spræc
275 þæt he nolde fleogan   fotmæl landes,
    ofer bæc bugan,   þa his betera leg.
    He bræc þone bordweall   and wið þa beornas feaht,
    oðþæt he his sincgyfan   on þam sæmannum
    wurðlice wrec,   ær he on wæle læge.
280 Swa dyde æþeric,   æþele gefera,
    fus and forðgeorn,   feaht eornoste.
    Sibyrhtes broðor   and swiðe mænig oþer
    clufon cellod bord,   cene hi weredon;
    bærst bordes lærig,   and seo byrne sang
285 gryreleoða sum.   þa æt guðe sloh
    Offa þone sælidan,   þæt he on eorðan feoll,
    and ðær Gaddes mæg   grund gesohte.
    Raðe wearð æt hilde   Offa forheawen;
    he hæfde ðeah geforþod   þæt he his frean gehet,
290 swa he beotode ær   wið his beahgifan
    þæt hi sceoldon begen   on burh ridan,
    hale to hame,   oððe on here **crincgan**,

And then they moved forward,   indifferent to death.

Into the fight, then,   the brave spear-bearers
advanced to avenge   their stricken good lord,
and prayed to the Lord   that they might destroy Danes.
Their hostage helped them,   a Northumbrian captive,
Edglaf's son, Ashfroth,   of hardy kin.
He joined in the struggle,   firing arrows.
Some stuck in shields   but some pierced Vikings,
and on and on he fought,   wielding his weapon
as long as he could.   The tall Edward,
fierce in the front line,   shouted defiance
and said he would never   yield one foot of land
when his lord lay dead.   He broke through their shield-wall
and with fellow fighters   collecting from Vikings
blood for Byrhtnoth's blood.   Æthric, also,
a noble warrior,   pressing forward
wreaked worthy vengeance.   He, Sibricht's brother,
and many more with him   split the Danes' targes
and defended themselves   as chain mail sang
its shrill terror-songs.   Offa in battle
struck one of the seamen   who fell to the turf:
Gad's kinsman fell,   cut down in the fighting.
Still, he had fulfilled   his oath to his lord,
the ring-giver Byrhtnoth,   that they return together
into the town   or else die together

on wælstowe   wundum sweltan;
he læg ðegenlice   ðeodne gehende.
295 ða wearð borda gebræc.   Brimmen wodon,
guðe gegremode;   gar oft þurhwod
fæges feorhhus.   Forð þa eode Wistan,
þurstanes **sunu**,   wið þas secgas feaht;
he wæs on **geþrange**   hyra þreora bana,
300 ær him Wigelines bearn   on þam wæle læge.
þær wæs stið gemot;   stodon fæste
wigan on gewinne,   wigend cruncon,
wundum werige.   Wæl feol on eorþan.
Oswold and Eadwold   ealle hwile,
305 begen þa gebroþru,   beornas trymedon,
hyra winemagas   wordon bædon
þæt hi þær æt ðearfe   þolian sceoldon,
unwaclice   wæpna neotan.
Byrhtwold maþelode   bord hafenode
310 (se wæs eald geneat),   æsc acwehte;
he ful baldlice   beornas lærde:
"Hige sceal þe heardra,   heorte þe cenre,
mod sceal þe mare,   þe ure mægen lytlað.
Her lið ure ealdor   eall forheawen,
315 god on greote.   A mæg gnornian
se ðe nu fram þis wigplegan   wendan þenceð.
Ic eom frod feores;   fram ic ne wille,
ac ic me be healfe   minum hlaforde,
be swa leofan men,   licgan þence."
320 Swa hi æþelgares bearn   ealle bylde,
Godric to guþe.   Oft he gar forlet,
wælspere windan   on þa wicingas,
swa he on þam folce   fyrmest eode,
heow and hynde,   oðþæt he on hilde gecranc.
325 Næs þæt na se Godric   þe ða **guðe** forbeah

from wounds on the slaughter-field.   Noble, he lay there
close to his lord.   Then were shields crashing
as the Vikings, enraged,   fought their way forward,
their sharp spears   piercing life-boxes.
Wystan advanced,   Thurstan's son,
and hot in the hurly-burly   felled three of their fighters
before he himself   lay dead on the ground.
There was hard fighting   with warriors standing firm
in the hard struggle.   Worn down by wounds
fighters fell.   All the while,
Oswold and Eadwold,   two brawny brothers,
exhorted the men,   their cousins and kinsmen,
to stand firm   and to use their good weapons.
Then Byrhtwold spoke up,   raising his shield,
an older fighter,   shaking his ash-spear
and exhorting the men: "Your minds put in order,
and settle your hearts.   Our courage must grow
as the strength we have ebbs.   Here lies our leader,
a good man in the dirt.   Any who leave now
will ever be sorry   for quitting this war work
to survive then in shame.   I have lived long
and I know much of life,   but I shall not leave here.
My firm intention   is here to be killed
to lie by the side   of the lord I have loved."
Godric, too,   Ethelgar's son,
called them to battle,   and hurling his javelin,
a death-spear flying   into the Vikings.
And he with his friends   advanced on the Danes,
hacking at them   and cutting them down
until he, himself,   was killed in the combat—
a far different Godric   than he who had run. . . .

The Battle of Brunanburh

This poem is found in the *Anglo-Saxon Chronicle* entry for 937.

Her æþelstan cyning,   eorla dryhten,
beorna beahgifa,   and his broþor eac,
Eadmund æþeling,   ealdorlangne tir
geslogon æt sæcce   sweorda ecgum
5 ymbe Brunanburh.   Bordweal clufan,
heowan heaþolinde   hamora lafan,
afaran Eadweardes,   swa him geæþele wæs
from cneomægum,   þæt hi æt campe oft
wiþ laþra gehwæne   land ealgodon,
10 hord and hamas.   Hettend crungun,
Sceotta leoda   and scipflotan
fæge feollan,   feld dænnede
secga **swate**,   siðþan sunne up
on morgentid,   mære tungol,
15 glad ofer grundas,   godes condel beorht,
eces drihtnes,   oð sio æþele gesceaft
sah to setle.   þær læg secg mænig
garum ageted,   guma norþerna
ofer scild scoten,   swilce Scittisc eac,
20 werig, wiges sæd.   Wesseaxe forð
ondlongne dæg   eorodcistum
on last legdun   laþum þeodum,
heowan herefleman   hindan þearle
mecum mylenscearpan.   Myrce ne wyrndon
25 **heardes** hondplegan   hæleþa nanum
þæra þe mid Anlafe   ofer æra gebland
on lides bosme   land gesohtun,

The Battle at Brunanburh

Robert Hass

In that year Æthelstan, thane of thanes,
King, ring-giver, won great glory
In a battle at Brunanburh with the blade of his sword.
Also the atheling, his younger brother, Edmund.
They broke the shield wall, hewed linden-boards
With sword edge, hacked them with hammered metal.
They were the sons of Eadward, Alfred's grandsons.
It suited their Saxon birth to spill the blood
of a loathed foe, defending their lands,
their homesteads and hoard-goods.

                                   The enemy was stove through,
The Scotsmen and ship-raiders
fell as if fated. The fields soaked up blood
from dawn light, when the Lord's star,
the eternal Lord's bright candle, rose
to glide over earth, till it had gone to its rest,
glorious Being, and left behind bodies
that spears had destroyed, bodies of Norsemen
sprawled on their scutcheons, and the Scotsmen as well,
exhausted and war-gorged.

                              The men of Wessex
harried them hard while the light lasted,
herded in troops the fugitives fleeing before them
and slashed at them sorely with swords ground sharp.
Nor did the Mercians refuse hard hand-play
to any of the foe who turned to face them
from among the warriors who had followed Anlaf
over the sea surge, crouched in the ship's breast,

fæge to gefeohte.   Fife lægun
on þam campstede   **cyningas** giunge,
sweordum aswefede,   swilce seofene eac
eorlas Anlafes,   unrim heriges,
flotan and Sceotta.   þær geflemed wearð
Norðmanna bregu,   nede gebeded,
to lides stefne   litle weorode;
cread cnear **on** flot,   cyning ut gewat
on fealene flod,   feorh generede.
Swilce þær eac se froda   mid fleame com
on his cyþþe norð,   Costontinus,
har **hilderinc**,   hreman ne þorfte
mæca gemanan;   he wæs his mæga sceard,
freonda gefylled   on folcstede,
beslagen æt sæcce,   and his sunu forlet
on wælstowe   wundun **forgrunden**,
giungne æt guðe.   Gelpan ne þorfte
beorn blandenfeax   bilgeslehtes,
eald inwidda,   ne Anlaf þy ma;
mid heora herelafum   hlehhan ne þorftun
þæt heo beaduweorca   beteran wurdun
on campstede   **cumbolgehnastes**,
garmittinge,   gumena gemotes,
wæpengewrixles,   þæs hi on wælfelda
wiþ Eadweardes   afaran plegodan.
Gewitan him þa Norþmen   nægledcnearrum,
dreorig daraða laf,   on Dinges mere
ofer deop wæter   Difelin secan,
eft Iraland,   æwiscmode.
Swilce þa gebroþer   begen ætsamne,
cyning and æþeling,   cyþþe sohton,
Wesseaxena land,   wiges hremige.

to seek out the land they were fated to die in.
Five lay dead on the field of battle, young kings
the sword put to sleep, and another seven
of Anlaf's earls, and an untold number
of shipmen and Scots. And they sent fleeing
the Norsemen's chief. Need drove him
to the ship's prow with what remained of his people
they pushed out on the tide, took the king out
on the fallow flood-tide, and that saved his life.
Constantinus, in the same way, fled the fighting,
that crafty man homed to his north country,
the hoary old soldier had nothing to sing of,
the clash of weapons had robbed him of kinsmen,
of friends who fell at the field of battle,
slain in the strife. He had left his own son
young to the sword, on that slaughtering ground,
wounded and maimed. Not much for the graybeard
to sing praise of in that sword-work,
the old fraud, nor for Anlaf either.
With his army lost no reason to laugh
that they were the better in deeds of war,
in collision of banners on the battlefield,
in the spear thrusts, the meeting of men
and trading of blows, when in that blood-test
they played with the offspring of Eadward.

So the Northmen departed in their nailed ships.
Sad leavings of spears, and shamed in their spirits,
They sailed from Dinges Mere over deep waters,
seeking Dublin Bay again and Ireland.
In the same way the brothers, both together,
The king and the prince, sought out their kin
In the West Saxon lands, wild with their winning.

60   Letan him behindan   hræw bryttian
       saluwigpadan,   þone sweartan hræfn,
       hyrnednebban,   and þane hasewanpadan,
       earn æftan hwit,   æses brucan,
       grædigne guðhafoc   and þæt græge deor,
65   wulf on wealde.   Ne wearð wæl mare
       on þis eiglande   **æfre** gieta
       folces gefylled   beforan þissum
       sweordes ecgum,   þæs þe us secgað bec,
       ealde uðwitan,   siþþan eastan hider
70   Engle and Seaxe   up becoman,
       ofer brad brimu   Brytene sohtan,
       wlance wigsmiþas,   **Wealas** ofercoman,
       eorlas arhwate   eard begeatan.

They left behind a scattering of corpses,
For the dark ones, for the black raven
With its horned beak, and for the dusky eagle
With its white back, for that greedy war hawk,
A carrion feast, and for the wild gray beast,
The wolf in the woods.

There was never more killing
On this island, never before so many cut down
By the sword's edge. Never so many bodies,
The old books say, the wise old rememberers,
Not since Angles and Saxons came from the east
Over the brimming sea, looking for Britain,
And, bold men, war-smiths, eager for glory,
smashed the Welshmen, and battened on this earth.

The Death of Alfred

This poem is found in the *Anglo-Saxon Chronicle* entry for 1036.

Her com Ælfred, se unsceððiga æþeling, Æþelrædes
sunu cinges, hider inn and wolde to his meder, þe on Win-
cestre sæt, ac hit him ne geþafode Godwine eorl, ne ec oþre
men þe mycel mihton wealdan, forðan hit hleoðrode þa
5 swiðe toward Haraldes, þeh hit unriht wære.
  Ac Godwine hine þa gelette   and hine on hæft sette,
and his geferan he todraf,   and sume mislice ofsloh;
sume hi man wið feo sealde,   sume hreowlice acwealde,
sume hi man bende,   sume hi man blende,
10 sume hamelode,   sume hættode.
  Ne wearð dreorlicre dæd   gedon on þison earde,
syþþan Dene comon   and her frið namon.
  Nu is to gelyfenne   to ðan leofan gode,
þæt hi blission   bliðe mid Criste
15 þe wæron butan scylde   swa earmlice acwealde.
  Se æþeling lyfode þa gyt;   ælc yfel man him gehet,
oðþæt man gerædde   þæt man hine lædde
to Eligbyrig   swa gebundenne.
  Sona swa he lende,   on scype man hine blende,
20 and hine swa blindne   brohte to ðam munecon,
and he þar wunode   ða hwile þe he lyfode.
  Syððan hine man byrigde,   swa him wel gebyrede,
ful wurðlice,   swa he wyrðe wæs,
æt þam westende,   þam styple ful gehende,
25 on þam suðportice;   seo saul is mid Criste.

The Death of Alfred

Robert Hass

1036. In this year Alfred, innocent prince, son of King Æthelred, came
into the country and wished to go to his mother who was living at
Winchester, but Godwin did not permit him to do this, nor the other
barons, because—wrong as it was—sentiment had swung to Harald.

So Godwin seized the young prince and put him in prison.
The retinue he destroyed; he found various ways to kill them:
Some were sold for cash, some cut down cruelly,
Some put in fetters, some were blinded,
Some hamstrung, and some of them scalped.
No bloodier deed was ever done in this land,
Not since the Danes came and made peace here.
Now it's to be believed that the hands of God
Have put them in bliss with Jesus Christ,
For they were guiltless and wretchedly slain.
The prince was kept alive, set about by every evil,
Until, under advisement, they led him
As they had bound him to Ely-in-the-Fens.
As soon as he landed, he was blinded,
Right there on shipboard, and, blinded,
He was brought to the good monks
And he dwelled there as long as he lived
And afterward he was buried, as befitted him,
Very worthily, for he was a worthy man,
At the west end of the chapel, very near the steeple,
Under the church porch. His soul is with Christ.

The Death of Edgar

Her geendode   eorðan dreamas
Eadgar, Engla cyning,   ceas him oðer leoht,
wlitig and wynsum,   and þis wace forlet,
lif þis læne.   Nemnað leoda bearn,
5   men on moldan,   þæne monað gehwær
in ðisse eðeltyrf,   þa þe ær wæran
on rimcræfte   rihte getogene,
Iulius monoð,   þær se geonga gewat
on þone eahteðan dæg   Eadgar of life,
10   beorna beahgyfa.   Feng his bearn syððan
to cynerice,   cild unweaxen,
eorla ealdor,   þam wæs Eadweard nama.
And him tirfæst hæleð   tyn nihtum ær
of Brytene gewat,   bisceop se goda,
15   þurh gecyndne cræft,   ðam wæs Cyneweard nama.
ða wæs on Myrceon,   mine gefræge,
wide and welhwær   waldendes lof
afylled on foldan.   Fela wearð todræfed
gleawra godes ðeowa;   þæt wæs gnornung micel
20   þam þe on breostum wæg   byrnende lufan
metodes on mode.   þa wæs mærða fruma
to swiðe forsewen,   sigora waldend,
rodera rædend,   þa man his riht tobræc.
And þa wearð eac adræfed   deormod hæleð,
25   Oslac, of earde   ofer yða gewealc,

The Death of Edgar

Paul McLoughlin

Here ended Edgar's earthly joy,
the English chieftain choosing that other
light, serene and lovely, relinquishing
this lean and transitory life on earth.

So is it known to people near and far
of all lands, those who have learned
the calendar because correctly
taught, that on the eighth day of July

young Edgar from his years of peace
was borne away, to be succeeded
as England's chieftain by his child,
Edward, named to emulate his forbear

but a fledgling still. Ten nights before,
Cyneward the Good, God's much-loved
mild-mannered bishop of Milton, left.
And many were expelled from Mercia,

willing servants, embodiments of wisdom,
leaving behind bewildered grief
for those whose bosoms burned with love
of home, whose hurried banishment

brought in its wake willful contempt
for the glorious word of God in heaven.
And the fair-haired, faithful Oslac,

ofer ganotes bæð,   gamolfeax hæleð,
wis and wordsnotor,   ofer wætera geðring,
ofer hwæles eðel,   hama bereafod.
And þa wearð ætywed   uppe on roderum
30 steorra on staðole,   þone stiðferhþe,
hæleð higegleawe,   hata ð wide
cometa be naman,   cræftgleawe men,
wise **woðboran.**   Wæs geond werðeode
waldendes wracu   wide gefrege,
35 hungor ofer hrusan;   þæt eft heofona weard
gebette, brego engla,   geaf eft blisse gehwæm
egbuendra   þurh eorðan westm.

wise and eloquent, was exiled, driven

from his country over crashing waves,
over the gannet-bath, beyond the whale's
home, his own dwelling-house destroyed.
There was moreover at this time observed

a star fixed high up in the heavens
the learnèd through the lettered world
and skillful orators call Comet. Then
vain men felt the vengeance of the Lord

over England's length and breadth
and a fearful famine afflicted the isle.
Until God revealed in all its glory
his abundance, allowed once more

the bliss that is his blessèd fruit.

Durham

Is ðeos burch breome   geond Breotenrice,
steppa gestaðolad,   stanas ymbutan
wundrum gewæxen.   Weor ymbeornad,
ea yðum stronge,   and ðer inne wunað
5   **feola** fisca kyn   on floda gemonge.
And ðær gewexen is   wudafæstern micel;
wuniad in ðem wycum   wilda deor monige,
in deope dalum   deora ungerim.
Is in ðere byri eac   bearnum gecyðed
10   ðe arfesta   eadig Cudberch
and ðes clene   **cyninges** heafud,
Osuualdes, Engle leo,   and Aidan biscop,
Eadberch and Eadfrið,   æðele geferes.
Is ðer inne midd heom   **Æðelwold** biscop
15   and breoma bocera Beda,   and Boisil abbot,
ðe clene Cudberte   on gecheðe
lerde lustum,   and he **his** lara wel genom.
Eardiæð æt ðem eadige   in in ðem minstre
unarimeda   reliquia,
20   **ðær** monia wundrum gewurðað,   ðes ðe writ seggeð,
midd ðene drihnes wer   domes bideð.

Durham

Derek Mahon

Known throughout Britain this noble city.
Its steep slopes and stone buildings
are thought a wonder; weirs contain
its fast river; fish of all kinds
thrive here in the thrusting waters.
A great forest has grown up here,
thickets throng with wild creatures;
deer drowse in the deep dales.
Everyone knows this renowned town
holds the body of blessèd Cuthbert,
also the holy head of Oswald,
lion of England, Eadberch and Eadfrith,
brothers in battle, the bishop Aidan
and here besides the bishop Athelwold,
learnèd Bede and the abbot Basil,
inspiring tutor to Cuthbert in youth
who gladly took his grave instruction.
Together with these tombs in the minster
numerous recognized relics remain
that work wonders, as records say,
where worthy men await Judgment Day.

The Battle of Finnsburh

. . . "nas byrnað?"

Hnæf hleoþrode ða,   **heaþogeong** cyning:

"Ne ðis ne dagað **eastan**,   ne her draca ne fleogeð,

ne her ðisse healle   hornas ne byrnað.

5 Ac her forþ berað;   fugelas singað,

gylleð græghama,   guðwudu hlynneð,

scyld scefte oncwyð.   Nu scyneð þes mona

waðol under wolcnum.   Nu arisað weadæda

ðe ðisne folces nið   fremman willað.

10 Ac onwacnigeað nu,   wigend mine,

habbað eowre **linda**,   **hicgeaþ** on ellen,

winnað on orde,   wesað onmode!"

ða aras mænig goldhladen ðegn,   gyrde hine his swurde.

ða to dura eodon   drihtlice cempan,

15 Sigeferð and Eaha,   hyra sword getugon,

and æt oþrum durum   Ordlaf and Guþlaf,

and Hengest sylf   hwearf him on laste.

ða gyt Garulf   Guðere **styrde**

ðæt he swa freolic feorh   forman siþe

20 to ðære healle durum   hyrsta ne **bære**,

nu hyt niþa heard   anyman wolde,

ac he frægn ofer eal   undearninga,

deormod hæleþ,   hwa ða duru heolde.

"Sigeferþ is min nama," cweþ he,   "ic eom Secgena leod,

25 **wreccea** wide cuð;   fæla ic **weana** gebad,

heardra hilda.   ðe is gyt her witod

swæþer ðu sylf to me   secean wylle."

ða wæs on healle   wælslihta gehlyn;

The Battle of Finnsburh: a fragment

X. J. Kennedy

. . . "Are this hall's gables burning?"
Then King Hnaef answered,   though callow in battle,
"That glow is not dawn,   nor a dragon in flight,
nor are this hall's horns,   its high gables, burning.
It's our foes in bright armor   preparing attack
Birds shall scream, gray wolf howl,   and war's wooden spears rattle,
shield shall stand up to shaft.   Now behold: the moon shines
as it wanders through clouds.   Deadly deeds are to follow
from this host who hate us.   Hard struggle impends.
Awake! Take up linden-wood shields,   my good soldiers!
Now muster your bravery,   gird up your minds
to be dauntless today   at the forefront of battle."
Then up rose those thanes clad in gold,   strapped on sword-belts.
great Eaha and Sigeferth   strode to the door
with drawn swords, to the other door   Ordlaf and Guthlaf
did spring, and with Hengest   himself close behind.

At the sight of their foes   Guthere pled with Garulf,
"Do not rush to the fore   in the very first onslaught
on the doors of the hall   at the cost of your life,
from which powerful Sigeferth   means to undo you."
Yet Garulf the gallant   to the hall-holders boldly
called out his demand,   "What man holds the door?"
"I am Sigeferth," said he,   "a prince of the Secgan,
a wandering warrior   known the world wide
for my many fierce combats.   Your fate now awaits you,
my hand shall deliver   whatever you want."
Then in the hall burst   clash and clatter of battle,

sceolde **cellod bord** **cenum** on handa,
30 banhelm berstan (buruhðelu dynede),
oð æt ðære guðe Garulf gecrang,
ealra ærest eorðbuendra,
Guðlafes sunu, ymbe hyne godra fæla,
hwearflicra hræw. Hræfen wandrode,
35 sweart and sealobrun. Swurdleoma stod,
swylce eal Finnsburuh fyrenu wære.
Ne gefrægn ic næfre wurþlicor æt wera hilde
sixtig sigebeorna sel **gebæran**,
ne nefre **swetne** medo sel forgyldan
40 ðonne Hnæfe guldan his hægstealdas.
Hig fuhton fif dagas, swa hyra nan ne feol
drihtgesiða, ac hig ða duru heoldon.
ða gewat him wund hæleð on wæg gangan,
sæde þæt his byrne abrocen wære,
45 heresceorp **unhror**, and eac wæs his helm **ðyrel**.
ða hine sona frægn folces hyrde,
hu ða wigend hyra wunda genæson,
oððe hwæþer ðæra hyssa

with shields shaped like ships   that a warrior wields.
The sound of swords clanging   shook planks in the floor.
Then at the door Garulf   was first man to fall,
Garulf, son of Guthlaf,   the foremost of Frisians
died surrounded by good men   while dark overhead
the black ravens circled.   Men's blades blazed so brightly
you would think from their flash   Finnsburh were all aflame.
I have never heard tell   of warriors more worthy
than that band sixty strong   who so bravely bore
war's brunt, nor of any   who so well repaid
those cups of sweet mead   Hnaef gave to his guards.
For five days they fought,   not a man of them toppled
but fearless, united,   held fast at the doors.
Then one warrior, wounded,   withdrew to the sidelines,
his armor in tatters,   breastplate split apart,
his helmet impaled.   And the folk's stout defender
asked that weary warrior   how the wounded fared
and which of the young men . . .

Waldere A & B

PART A

          hyrde hyne georne:

"Huru Welande . . .   worc ne geswiceð

monna ænigum   ðara ðe Mimming can

heardne gehealdan.   Oft æt hilde gedreas

5   swatfag and sweordwund   **secg** æfter oðrum.

ætlan ordwyga,   ne læt ðin ellen nu gy . . .

gedreosan to dæge,   dryhtscipe

    is se dæg cumen

þæt ðu scealt aninga   oðer twega,

10 lif forleosan   oððe l . . . gne dom

agan mid eldum,   ælfheres sunu.

Nalles ic ðe, wine min,   wordum cide,

ðy ic ðe gesawe   æt ðam **sweordplegan**

ðurh edwitscype   æniges monnes

15 wig forbugan   oððe on weal fleon,

lice beorgan,   ðeah þe laðra fela

ðinne byrnhomon   billum heowun,

ac ðu symle furðor   feohtan sohtest,

mæl ofer mearce;   ðy ic ðe metod ondred,

20 þæt ðu to fyrenlice   feohtan sohtest

æt ðam ætstealle   oðres monnes,

wigrædenne.   Weorða ðe selfne

godum dædum,   ðenden ðin god recce.

Ne murn ðu for ði mece;   ðe wearð maðma cyst

25 **gifeðe** to **geoce**,   mid ðy ðu Guðhere scealt

Waldere: two fragments

Matthew Hollis

FRAGMENT A

    —She heartened him:
"No work of Weyland shall fail
a master of Mimming, or any man
whose grip is true—one after another,
good men have fallen at its blade, bloodied and sword-swung.

Attila's champion, dig deep;
keep about you your courage and your heart,
now that the day is come
when you must make a choice:
let go on life or find a lasting glory—
Waldere, remembered among men.

Never shall I say that in battle
I saw you turn in shame
from any man's taunt
or flee to the rampart to save your skin,
though the foes were many
at your sword-hewn armor.
No, always you went further, carrying the fight
so far into the field that I feared your life;
and still you went on, onto marked land.
Honor your name then, true to yourself,
stay in God's keeping.

And fear not for your sword, for this it was made.
With it you shall humble Guthere's boast,

beot forbigan,   ðæs ðe he ðas beaduwe ongan
. . . d unryhte   ærest secan.
Forsoc he ðam swurde   and ðam syncfatum,
beaga mænigo,   nu sceal bega leas
30 hworfan **from** ðisse hilde,   hlafurd secan
ealdne ᚷ   oððe her ær swefan,
gif he ða"

PART B

". . . ce bæteran
buton ðam anum   ðe ic eac hafa
on stanfate   stille gehided.
Ic wat þæt **hit** ðohte   ðeodric Widian
5   selfum onsendon,   and eac sinc micel
maðma mid ði mece,   monig oðres mid him
golde gegirwan   (iulean genam),
þæs ðe hine of nearwum   Niðhades mæg,
Welandes bearn,   Widia ut forlet;
10 ðurh fifela gewe . . . ld   forð onette."
Waldere **maðelode**,   wiga ellenrof,
hæfde him on handa   **hildefrofre**,
guðbilla gripe,   gyddode wordum:
"Hwæt! ðu huru wendest,   wine Burgenda,
15 þæt me Hagenan hand   hilde gefremede
and getwæmde . . . ðewigges.   Feta, gyf ðu dyrre,
æt ðus heaðuwerigan   hare byrnan.
Standeð me her on eaxelum   ælfheres laf,
god and geapneb,   golde geweorðod,
20 ealles unscende   æðelinges reaf
to habbanne,   þonne **hand** wereð
feorhhord feondum.   **Ne** bið fah wið me,
þonne . . . . . . unmægas   eft ongynnað,

since it was he who undertook this quarrel
without right on his side,
he who forsook the blade and the treasures,
the ring hoard. Send him from this field,
empty armed, a lord long seeking home;
unless he lie here. . . ."

FRAGMENT B

". . . no better blade,
save one, in my own keeping,
sleeping in its sheath,
that Theodric himself
thought to pass to Widia,
and much treasure besides:
an army in a skin of gold;
such gifts bestowed because once,
in the narrow, Widia had delivered him from durance
and given him safe passage, through a land of Giants."

Then Waldere spoke,
sword in hand, his guide in battle,
the keener blade; these were his words:
"So, King of Burgundians, did you think
Hagen stood here for you? Was it he
who was to end Waldere's days?
I grow tired from the fight:
come, take my casings if you can:
it is my father's coat that lies across
my shoulders, worth every bit its weight
to the man who must face down foes
and guard his own. It will not fail
when men again assail me and turn

mecum gemetað,   swa ge me dydon.
25 ðeah mæg sige syllan   se ðe symle byð
recon and rædfest   ryh . . . a gehwilces.
Se ðe him to ðam halgan   helpe gelifeð,
to gode gioce,   he þær gearo findeð
gif ða earnunga   ær geðenceð.
30 þonne **moten** wlance   welan britnian,
æhtum wealdan,   þæt is"

their swords on mine, as you yourself have done.

Know this. Only He, swift and resolute in judgment,
can truly bestow victory. Whoever seeks the Holy One,
and looks to God's guidance, will find it,
if he has first given himself truly.
Only then will men rule over riches,
men of mettle, that is. . . ."

Widsith

Widsið maðolade,   wordhord onleac,
se þe **monna** mæst   **mægþa** ofer eorþan,
folca geondferde;   oft he **on** flette geþah
mynelicne maþþum.   **Him** from Myrgingum
5 æþele onwocon.   He mid Ealhhilde,
fælre freoþuwebban,   forman siþe
Hreðcyninges   ham gesohte
eastan of Ongle,   Eormanrices,
wraþes wærlogan.   Ongon þa worn sprecan:
10 "Fela ic monna gefrægn   mægþum wealdan!
Sceal **þeodna** gehwylc   þeawum lifgan,
eorl æfter oþrum   eðle rædan,
se þe his þeodenstol   geþeon wile.
þara wæs **Hwala**   hwile selast,
15 ond Alexandreas   ealra ricost
monna cynnes,   ond he mæst geþah
þara þe ic ofer foldan   gefrægen hæbbe.
ætla weold Hunum,   Eormanric Gotum,
Becca Baningum,   Burgendum Gifica.
20 Casere weold Creacum   ond Cælic Finnum,
Hagena **Holmrygum**   ond **Heoden** Glommum.
Witta weold Swæfum,   Wada Hælsingum,
Meaca Myrgingum,   Mearchealf Hundingum.
þeodric weold Froncum,   þyle Rondingum,
25 Breoca Brondingum,   Billing Wernum.
Oswine weold Eowum   ond Ytum Gefwulf,

Widsith

Bernard O'Donoghue

Widsith spoke
and unlocked his heart: of all men he had visited
the most places and peoples on earth,
and been best rewarded where riches were given.
His own descent was from the Myrgings;
with Ealhhild, gracious peace-weaver,
he first came from the land of the East-Angles
to seek out the home of that savage,
the treacherous Eormanric.

His speech ranged widely:
"I have heard of many rulers of peoples.
All princes must rule with virtue,
following each other in rightful order,
if their reign is to be successful.
For a while Wala was dominant,
as Alexander was the greatest of all
the race of men. He prospered the most
of those I have known of across the world.
Attila ruled the Huns and Eormanric the Goths;
Becca ruled the Banings and Gifica the Burgundians.
Caesar ruled the Greeks and Caelic the Finns;
Hagen the Island-Rugians and Heoden the Glommas.
Witta ruled the Swabians and Wade the Hælsings;
Macca the Myrgings and Marchalf the Hundings.
Theodoric ruled the Franks and Thula the Rondings;
Breca the Brondings and Billing the Wernas.
Oswin ruled the Eowas and Gefwulf the Jutes.

Fin Folcwalding   Fresna cynne.

Sigehere lengest   Sædenum weold,

Hnæf Hocingum,   Helm Wulfingum,

30 Wald Woingum,   Wod þyringum,

Sæferð Sycgum,   Sweom Ongendþeow,

Sceafthere Ymbrum,   Sceafa Longbeardum,

Hun Hætwerum   ond Holen Wrosnum.

Hringweald wæs haten   Herefarena cyning.

35 Offa weold Ongle,   Alewih Denum;

se wæs þara manna   modgast ealra,

no hwæþre he ofer Offan   eorlscype fremede,

ac Offa geslog   ærest monna,

cnihtwesende,   cynerica mæst.

40 Nænig efeneald him   eorlscipe maran

on orette.   Ane sweorde

merce gemærde   wið Myrgingum

bi Fifeldore;   heoldon forð siþþan

Engle ond Swæfe,   swa hit Offa geslog.

45 Hroþwulf ond Hroðgar   heoldon lengest

sibbe ætsomne   suhtorfædran,

siþþan hy forwræcon   wicinga cynn

ond Ingeldes   ord forbigdan,

forheowan æt Heorote   Heaðobeardna þrym.

50 Swa ic geondferde fela   fremdra londa

geond ginne grund.   Godes ond yfles

þær ic cunnade   cnosle bidæled,

freomægum feor   folgade wide.

Forþon ic mæg singan   ond secgan spell,

55 mænan fore mengo   in meoduhealle

hu me cynegode   cystum dohten.

Ic wæs mid Hunum   ond mid Hreðgotum,

mid Sweom ond mid Geatum   ond mid Suþdenum.

Fin Folcwalding ruled over the Frisians.
Sighere ruled longest over the SeaDanes,
Hnaef ruled the Hocings and Helm the Wulfings.
Wald ruled the Woings and Wod the Thuringians;
Sigeferth the Secgan and Ongentheow the Swedes,
Shafthere the Ymbras and Sheaf the Langobards,
Hun the Hetware and Holen the Wrosnas.
Ringwald was called the King of the Seafarers;
Offa ruled the Angles and Alewih the Danes.

"Whoever was the bravest of all the men named
couldn't supersede Offa in prowess.
Offa in his youth slew the most men
of the most numerous kingdoms.
No one so young had more strength in battle.
With a single sword he secured the border
against the Myrgings along the Eider.
Later the Angles and Swabians kept it
as Offa had won it. For a long time
Hrothulf and Hrothgar, uncle and nephew,
kept peace together, after defeating
the race of the Vikings. They overcame
the battle line of Ingeld, and cut down
in Heorot the Heathobards' power.

"So I traveled through many far lands
over the wide world. I explored good and evil,
journeyed far, away from my people.
That's why I can compose and tell the story,
report to the company in the great hall
how well I was treated by all these great nations.
I was with the Huns and the Glory-Goths,
With the Swedes and the Geats and the Southern Danes.

Mid Wenlum ic wæs ond mid Wærnum   ond mid wicingum.

60   Mid Gefþum ic wæs ond mid Winedum   ond mid Gefflegum.

Mid Englum ic wæs ond mid Swæfum   ond mid ænenum.

Mid Seaxum ic wæs ond Sycgum   ond mid Sweordwerum.

Mid Hronum ic wæs ond mid Deanum   ond mid Heaþoreamum.

Mid þyringum ic wæs   ond mid þrowendum,

65   ond mid Burgendum,   þær ic beag geþah;

me þær Guðhere forgeaf   glædlicne maþþum

songes to leane.   Næs þæt sæne cyning!

Mid Froncum ic wæs ond mid Frysum   ond mid Frumtingum.

Mid Rugum ic wæs ond mid Glommum   ond mid Rumwalum.

70   Swylce ic wæs on Eatule   mid ælfwine,

se hæfde moncynnes,   mine gefræge,

leohteste hond   lofes to wyrcenne,

heortan unhneawaste   hringa gedales,

beorhtra beaga,   bearn Eadwines.

75   Mid Sercingum ic wæs   ond mid Seringum;

mid Creacum ic wæs ond mid Finnum   ond mid Casere,

se þe winburga   geweald ahte,

wiolena ond wilna,   ond Wala rices.

Mid Scottum ic wæs ond mid Peohtum   ond mid Scridefinnum;

80   mid Lidwicingum ic wæs ond mid Leonum   ond mid Longbeardum,

mid hæðnum ond mid hæleþum   ond mid Hundingum.

Mid Israhelum ic wæs   ond mid Exsyringum,

mid Ebreum ond mid Indeum   ond mid Egyptum.

Mid Moidum ic wæs ond mid Persum   ond mid Myrgingum,

85   ond Mofdingum   ond ongend Myrgingum,

ond mid Amothingum.   Mid Eastþyringum ic wæs

ond mid Eolum ond mid Istum   ond Idumingum.

Ond ic wæs mid Eormanrice   ealle þrage,

þær me Gotena cyning   gode dohte;

90   se me beag forgeaf,   burgwarena fruma,

I was with the Wendels and the Warnas, as well as the Vikings:
with the Gefthas and the Wends, and with the Gefflegas.
I was with the Angles and the Swabians, and with the Enenas:
with the Saxons and the Secgan, and the Suardones.
I was with the Hronas and the Danes, and with the Hathoremes:
with the Thuringians and with the Throwendas.
I was with the Burgundians and received an armlet:
there Gunther gave me a rich jewel
as payment for song: no small-minded king!
I was with the Franks and the Frisians, and with the Frumtings:
with the Rugas and the Glommas, and with the Romans.
Likewise I was in Italy with Alboin
who had, I've been told, of all mankind
the hand most ready to confer praise
and the heart most light in the giving of rings
and bright treasures, great son of Audoin!
I've been amongst Saracens and among the Serings:
with Greeks and with Finns and with Caesar himself
who wielded power over feasting cities,
over wealth and riches, and the kingdom of Wales.
I was with the Scots and the Irish, and with the Ski-Finns;
with the Bretons and the Leonas, and with the Langobards;
among heathens and heroes, and with the Hundings.
I was with Israelites, Assyrians,
with Jews and Indians, and with Egyptians.
I was with the Medes and the Persians, and with the Myrgings;
with the Ongendmyrgings and the Amothings;
with the Eastherings and with the Ofdings,
with the Eols and the Iste, and with the Idumings.

"And I was with Eormanric all the time,
and the king of the Goths treated me well.
That prince of citizens gave me a ring

on þam siex hund wæs   smætes goldes,
gescyred sceatta   scillingrime;
þone ic Eadgilse   on æht sealde,
minum hleodryhtne,   þa ic to ham bicwom,
95 leofum to leane,   þæs þe he me lond forgeaf,
mines fæder eþel,   frea Myrginga.
Ond me þa Ealhhild   oþerne forgeaf,
dryhtcwen duguþe,   dohtor Eadwines.
Hyre lof lengde   geond londa fela,
100 þonne ic be songe   secgan sceolde
hwær ic under **swegle**   selast wisse
goldhrodene cwen   giefe bryttian.
ðonne wit Scilling   sciran reorde
for uncrum sigedryhtne   song ahofan,
105 hlude bi hearpan   hleoþor swinsade,
þonne monige men,   modum wlonce,
wordum sprecan,   þa þe wel cuþan,
þæt hi næfre song   sellan ne hyrdon.
ðonan ic ealne geondhwearf   eþel Gotena,
110 sohte ic a **gesiþa**   þa selestan;
þæt wæs innweorud   Earmanrices.
Heðcan sohte ic ond Beadecan   ond Herelingas,
Emercan sohte ic ond Fridlan   ond Eastgotan,
frodne ond godne   fæder Unwenes.
115 Seccan sohte ic ond Beccan,   Seafolan ond þeodric,
Heaþoric ond Sifecan,   Hliþe ond Incgenþeow.
Eadwine sohte ic ond Elsan,   ægelmund ond Hungar,
ond þa wloncan gedryht   Wiþmyrginga.
Wulfhere sohte ic ond Wyrmhere;   ful oft þær wig ne alæg,
120 þonne Hræda here   heardum sweordum
ymb Wistlawudu   wergan sceoldon
ealdne eþelstol   ætlan leodum.

of six hundred pieces of beaten gold,
counted in shillings. I gave it into
the power of Adgils, my lord-protector
when I came home, for safekeeping,
because he, the prince of the Myrgings,
gave me land in my father's nation.
And then Ealhild, the powerful queen
and daughter of Edwin, gave me more.
Praise of her ran through many places,
wherever I was called on to sing a song
about who under heaven I knew was the best
of gold-adorned queens dispensing gifts.
When Shilling and I with clear voices
sang out a song for a triumphing prince
and loud to the harp the music rang out,
many men said, well-versed in that art
and speaking aloud with pride in their hearts,
that they'd never heard a song that was better.

"From there I traveled all the land of the Goths,
always seeking the best of companions
to be found in Eormanric's realm.
I sought Hethca and Badeca and the Harlungs;
I sought Emerca and Fridla and Eastgota too,
the wise and good father of Unwen.
I sought Secca and Becca, Seafola and Theodric,
Heathoric and Sifela, Hlithe and Ingentheow.
I sought Edwin and Elsa, Agelmund and Hungar,
and the proud company of the Withmyrgings.
I sought Wulfhere and Wyrmhere—often war lasted
when the army of the Goths with their hard swords
against Attila's troops had to defend
their ancient domains by the Vistula's wood-banks.

Rædhere sohte ic ond Rondhere,   Rumstan ond Gislhere,
Wiþergield ond Freoþeric,   Wudgan ond Haman;
125 ne wæran þæt gesiþa   þa sæmestan,
þeah þe ic hy anihst   nemnan sceolde.
Ful oft of þam heape   hwinende fleag
giellende gar   on grome þeode;
wræccan þær weoldan   wundnan golde
130 werum ond wifum,   Wudga ond Hama.
Swa ic þæt symle onfond   on þære feringe,
þæt se biþ leofast   londbuendum
se þe him god syleð   gumena rice
to gehealdenne,   þenden he her leofað."
135 Swa scriþende   gesceapum hweorfað
gleomen gumena   geond grunda fela,
þearfe secgað,   þoncword sprecaþ,
simle suð oþþe norð   sumne gemetað
gydda gleawne,   geofum unhneawne,
140 se þe fore duguþe wile   dom aræran,
eorlscipe æfnan,   oþþæt eal scæceð,
leoht ond lif somod;   lof se gewyrceð,
hafað under heofonum   heahfæstne dom.

I sought Radhere and Rondhere, Rumstan and Giselhere,
Withergild and Frederick, Wudga and Hama:
not the least formidable companions,
even if I come to name them last.
The yelling spear flew often, whining,
from that band against a hostile people.
The two outcasts, Wudga and Hama,
ruled man and woman there by twisted gold.
So I always found it in my travels,
that the man to whom God gives power to hold
is always most popular with dwellers on earth
for as long as he lives here below."

So the minstrels of men go wandering
by the dictates of fate through many lands.
They express what is needed and compose thanks.
Always, south or north, they find someone
with wise taste for poems, generous with gifts
who wants his name raised before the people,
to achieve valor, before everything fails,
light and life together. He earns their praise:
so under heaven gains exalted glory.

Second
Riddle-Hoard

Riddle 15

Hals is min hwit   ond heafod fealo,
sidan swa some.   Swift ic eom on feþe,
beadowæpen bere.   Me on bæce standað
her swylce swe on **hleorum**.   Hlifiað tu
5   earan ofer eagum.   Ordum ic steppe
in **grene** græs.   Me bið gyrn witod,
gif mec onhæle   an onfindeð
wælgrim wiga,   þær ic wic buge,
bold mid bearnum,   ond ic bide þær
10   mid geoguðcnosle,   hwonne gæst cume
to durum minum,   him biþ dead witod.
Forþon ic sceal of eðle   eaforan mine
forhtmod fergan,   fleame nergan,
gif he me æfterweard   ealles weorþeð;
15   hine berað breost.   Ic his **bidan** ne dear,
reþes on geruman,   (nele þæt ræd teale),
ac ic sceal fromlice   feþemundum
þurh steapne beorg   stræte wyrcan.
Eaþe ic mæg freora   feorh genergan,
20   gif ic mægburge mot   mine gelædan
on degolne weg   þurh **dune** þyrel
swæse ond gesibbe;   ic me siþþan ne þearf
wælhwelpes wig   wiht onsittan.
Gif **se** niðsceaþa   nearwe stige
25   me on swaþe seceþ,   ne tosæleþ him
on þam gegnpaþe   guþgemotes,
siþþan ic þurh hylles   hrof geræce,
ond þurh hest hrino   hildepilum
laðgewinnum,   þam þe ic longe fleah.

My Throat's a Torch, the Rest of Me Rust

David Barber

My throat's a torch, the rest of me rust
From head to haunch. I hotfoot it off,
Ready to rumble. That's my ruddy pelt
Bristling in streaks. Those spikes and sparks
Are my ears and eyes. I steal on my toes
Across the green downs. Dark will be the day
If the hellhound comes harrying here
Where I've gone to ground with my little ones.
The hot breath of the brute at our door
Will doom my brood to a bloody end
Unless I call on all my canny wiles
And seize on a scheme to save our skins.
If he bulls into our hidden burrow
On his belly, baying for our bones,
It would be folly to fight him there,
So with furious paws I'll forge a path
Headlong through our steep hillside.
Here's how a mother must make haste
To hustle her children out of harm:
Spirit them through a secret route
In the pitch-black peat, like a thing possessed.
Then I can face my foe with no fear
If the punk still wants a piece of me.
Bring it on: I'll double back
With fire in my belly, bolder than ever,
And terrible will be the turf-battle
On the hill-crest under the earth-candle
When I turn this time with tooth and nail
On the fiend I'll flee no longer.

Riddle 16

Oft ic sceal wiþ wæge winnan   ond wiþ winde feohtan,
somod wið þam sæcce,   þonne ic secan gewite
eorþan yþum þeaht;   me biþ se eþel fremde.
Ic beom strong þæs gewinnes,   gif ic stille weorþe;
5 gif me þæs tosæleð,   hi beoð swiþran þonne ic,
ond mec slitende   sona flymað,
willað oþfergan   þæt ic friþian sceal.
Ic him þæt forstonde,   gif min steort þolað
ond mec stiþne wiþ   stanas moton
10 fæste gehabban.   Frige hwæt ic hatte.

All My Life's a Struggle with Water and Wind

Lawrence Raab

All my life's a struggle with water and wind.
Two against one must be my story—
as I make my way into the earth
under the waves. There's no country
I can call my own. But I've learned
to grow strong by being still. I know
if I fail I'll be broken, and all
that's part of me will be torn from me.
Let me find my place
among the stones, and be held.

Riddle 20

Ic eom wunderlicu wiht,   on gewin sceapen,
frean minum leof,   fægre gegyrwed.
Byrne is min bleofag,   swylce beorht **seomað**
wir ymb þone wælgim   þe me waldend geaf,
5   se me widgalum   wisað hwilum
sylfum to sace.   þonne ic sinc wege
þurh hlutterne dæg,   hondweorc smiþa,
gold ofer geardas.   Oft ic gæstberend
cwelle compwæpnum.   Cyning mec gyrweð
10 since ond seolfre   ond mec on sele weorþað;
ne wyrneð wordlofes,   wisan mæneð
mine for mengo,   þær hy meodu drincað,
healdeð mec on heaþore,   hwilum læteð eft
radwerigne   on gerum sceacan,
15 orlegfromne.   Oft ic oþrum scod

Some Wonder Am I

Dennis O'Driscoll

Some wonder am I,
      made for mayhem,
eye-catchingly adorned,
      to my owner dear.
Variegated my mail,
      weaving its web
round the death-gem
      gifted by the lord
who leads me firmly forward
      toward the battle fray.
Arrayed in richest raiment
      a smith could style,
I glow like gold
      in the morning light.
Warring with my weapons,
      wounds I gouge
in body and in soul.
      Treasured by the king,
heaped with honors
      in his hall, I am object
of his silver-tongued tributes
      where wassailing
warriors splash out mead.
      Tightly confined I am,
tired of travel, but bold when
      freed for battle clash.
I deal a savage death
      blow to a man before

frecne æt his freonde;   fah eom ic wide,
wæpnum awyrged.   Ic me wenan ne þearf
þæt me bearn wræce   on bonan feore,
gif me gromra hwylc   guþe genægeð;
20 ne weorþeð sio mægburg   gemicledu
eaforan minum   þe ic æfter woc,
nymþe ic hlafordleas   hweorfan mote
from þam healdende   þe me hringas geaf.
Me bið forð witod,   gif ic frean hyre,
25 guþe fremme,   swa ic gien dyde
minum þeodne on þonc,   þæt ic þolian sceal
bearngestreona.   Ic wiþ bryde ne mot
hæmed habban,   ac me þæs hyhtplegan
geno wyrneð,   se mec **geara** on
30 bende legde;   forþon ic brucan sceal
on hagostealde   hæleþa gestreona.
Oft ic wirum dol   wife abelge,
wonie hyre willan;   heo me wom spreceð,
floceð hyre folmum,   firenaþ mec wordum,
35 ungod gæleð.   Ic ne gyme þæs compes

his friend can fend
        me off; cursed my
customs are by many.
        No progeny of mine
can I presume on
        to avenge a fatal
mutilation meted out
        to me; descendants
are denied me
        unless I cease
to serve the master who
        rewarded me with rings.
My fate it is
        to follow my lord
in combat as he wills,
        deprived of pleasurable prospect
of bride and brood.
        Chaste must I live
as my bond commands,
        bearing a bachelor's lot,
reaping manly recompense.
        Brightly filigreed,
I infuriate a woman,
        rob her of joy,
diminish her desire.
        Loud her accusations grow,
raucously she rails,
        her hands spell
out my shame.
        That battle is the one I shun. . . .

Riddle 21

Neb is min niþerweard;   neol ic fere
ond be grunde græfe,   geonge swa me wisað
har holtes feond,   ond hlaford min
woh færeð   weard æt steorte,
5 wrigaþ on wonge,   wegeð mec ond þyð,
saweþ on swæð min.   Ic snyþige forð,
brungen of **bearwe**,   bunden cræfte,
wegen on wægne,   hæbbe wundra fela;
me biþ gongendre   grene on healfe
10 ond min swæð sweotol   sweart on oþre.
Me þurh hrycg wrecen   hongaþ under
an orþoncpil,   oþer on heafde,
fæst ond forðweard.   Fealleþ on sidan
þæt ic toþum tere,   gif me teala þenaþ
15 hindeweardre,   þæt biþ hlaford min.

My Tooth Is Long, My Work Even Longer

Gary Soto

My tooth is long, my work even longer.
I snuffle, I grub that you may grub,
And I bite the earth without anger.
I come from the forest, was once the meat of forests.
Now I'm hounded by my earthly lord,
Who lowers me into the field and rams me down,
Who pushes and sows seed as I pass.
I spit wet clods, I a wooden tool shaved to a point.
The genius of man has brought me to life
And now rolls me on a wheel.
Think of my strange mechanics: as I plod
One flank of my trail gathers green,
The other shiny black. Consider me my lord's recruit,
His sword, his dagger, his bloodless claw.
What earth I slash falls in a curve
Of slaughter to one side.
If angled right, if pushed to my limits
I fill barrels, barns, and bellies.

Riddle 22

ætsomne cwom   LX monna
to wægstæþe   wicgum ridan;
hæfdon XI   eoredmæcgas
fridhengestas,   IIII sceamas.
5 Ne meahton magorincas   ofer mere feolan,
swa hi fundedon,   ac wæs flod to deop,
atol yþa geþræc,   ofras hea,
streamas stronge.   Ongunnon stigan þa
on wægn weras   ond hyra wicg somod
10 hlodan under hrunge;   þa þa hors oðbær
eh ond eorlas,   æscum dealle,
ofer wætres byht   wægn to lande,
swa hine oxa ne teah   ne esna mægen
ne fæthengest,   ne on flode swom,
15 ne be grunde wod   gestum under,
ne lagu drefde,   ne **on** lyfte fleag,
ne **under** bæc cyrde;   brohte hwæþre
beornas ofer burnan   ond hyra bloncan mid
from stæðe heaum,   þæt hy stopan up
20 on oþerne,   ellenrofe,
weras of wæge,   ond hyra wicg gesund.

Five Dozen Reached the Brink

Paul Farley

Five dozen reached the brink and pulled
their horses up (eleven spectrals,
four luminous whites). They'd trained for weeks
and were green to go, but the channel was tricky:
the swell a bastard, waves lit with foam,
the current strong. So the whole outfit
got scooped into a wagon, and under
the cosmic axle grease they rode,
both tooled-up man and horse, over
the waste to solid ground. No ox,
dray horse or slave sweat drew this wagon.
This was no sea or land haulage.
No feet got wet, all stayed airborne,
and there was no winding back, but by
degrees the wagon bore its load
from pickup point to mount the shore
on the other side: so this brave squad crossed
the deeps and landed safely home.

Riddle 23

Agof is min noma   eft onhwyrfed;
ic eom wrætlic wiht   on gewin sceapen.
þonne ic onbuge,   ond me of bosme fareð
ætren onga,   ic beom eallgearo
5   þæt ic me þæt feorhbealo   feor aswape.
Siþþan me se waldend,   se me þæt wite gescop,
leoþo forlæteð,   ic beo lengre þonne ær,
oþþæt ic spæte,   spilde geblonden,
ealfelo attor   þæt ic ær geap.
10   Ne togongeð þæs   gumena hwylcum,
ænigum eaþe   þæt ic þær ymb sprice,
gif hine hrineð   þæt me of hrife fleogeð,
þæt þone mandrinc   mægne geceapaþ,
fullwered fæste   feore sine.
15   Nelle ic unbunden   ænigum hyran
nymþe searosæled.   Saga hwæt ic hatte.

Wob Is My Name Approximately

James McGonigal

Wob is my name   approximately.   I had a difficult birth.
Now whenever I bend   some poison shoots   out of my chest
and I'm desperate   to get rid of the stuff   as far away from here
as I possibly can.   Someone is torturing me.   When he releases me
I'm taller than before   but then he gives me   more poison to swallow
and spit out again.   I'm a danger to society.   Will you just listen:
This stuff sticks.   If it touches anybody   it's a poison chalice
a final penance   life and strength totally   utterly gone.

Unless you restrain me   I'm out of control.   Tie me up.
And please tell me what is my name.

Riddle 24

Ic eom wunderlicu wiht,   wræsne mine stefne,
hwilum beorce swa hund,   hwilum blæte swa gat,
hwilum græde swa gos,   hwilum gielle swa hafoc,
hwilum ic onhyrge   þone haswan earn,
5 guðfugles hleoþor,   hwilum glidan reorde
muþe gemæne,   hwilum mæwes song,
þær ic glado sitte.   ᚷ mec nemnað,
swylce ᚠ ond ᚱ   ᚠ fullesteð,
ᚻ ond ᛁ   Nu ic haten eom
10 swa þa siex stafas   sweotule becnaþ.

Riddle 25

Ic eom wunderlicu wiht,   wifum on hyhte,
neahbuendum nyt;   nængum sceþþe
burgsittendra,   nymþe bonan anum.
Staþol min is steapheah,   stonde ic on bedde,
5 neoþan ruh nathwær.   Neþeð hwilum
ful cyrtenu   ceorles dohtor,
modwlonc meowle,   þæt heo on mec gripeð,
ræseð mec on reodne,   reafað min heafod,
fegeð mec on fæsten.   Feleþ sona
10 mines gemotes,   **seo** þe mec nearwað,
wif wundenlocc.   Wæt bið þæt eage.

I'm a Creature to Conjure With

David Barber

I'm a creature to conjure with, a chorus by myself.
I can bay like a bloodhound, bleat like a billygoat.
I can do the goose-honk and the hawk-shriek.
Here's how I keen in the key of the kite,
Here's an earful of the eagle's war-cry.
Now I'm a gyrfalcon, now I'm a gull—
A mime in my prime, making my name.
I've got a G, I've got an I,
An A and an E, an M and a P.
See what it spells and say who I am.

Call Me Fabulous

Gerry Murphy

Call me fabulous,
that rare thing,
a woman's delight.
Ever ready in the kitchen,
harming none but those
who would harm me.
Standing tall in my own bed,
my stalk rigid on its hairy root.
That haughty girl,
the churl's beautiful daughter,
deigns to take me in hand,
fribbles me to distraction,
stashes me in her sanctum,
weeps at our union.
Not a dry eye in the house.

Riddle 26

Mec feonda sum   feore besnyþede,
woruldstrenga binom,   wætte siþþan,
dyfde on wætre,   dyde eft þonan,
sette on sunnan,   þær ic swiþe beleas
5 herum þam þe ic hæfde.   Heard mec siþþan
snað seaxses **ecg**,   sindrum begrunden;
fingras feoldan,   ond mec fugles wyn
geond speddropum   spyrede geneahhe,
ofer brunne brerd,   beamtelge swealg,
10 streames dæle,   stop eft on mec,
siþade sweartlast.   Mec siþþan wrah
hæleð hleobordum,   **hyde** beþenede,
gierede mec mid golde;   forþon me gliwedon
wrætlic weorc smiþa,   wire bifongen.
15 Nu þa gereno   ond se reada telg
ond þa wuldorgesteald   wide mære
dryhtfolca helm,   nales dol wite.
Gif min bearn wera   brucan willað,
hy beoð þy gesundran   ond þy sigefæstran,
20 heortum þy hwætran   ond þy hygebliþran,
ferþe þy frodran,   habbaþ freonda þy ma,
swæsra ond gesibbra,   soþra ond godra,
tilra ond getreowra,   þa hyra tyr ond ead
estum ycað   ond hy arstafum

Some Enemy Took My Life

Jane Hirshfield

Some enemy took my life,
stripped me of my world strength,
doused me and drowned me in water,
then lifted me dry, set me in sun,
where I swiftly lost what hair I had left.
A knife-edge cut me then hard,
scraped from me every remnant of what I was.
Fingers reached to fold me
and what was once a bird's fine delight
rained over me a trail of encouraging droplets.
Crossing often over the brown-rimmed inkhorn,
it drank from there a stream the color of treebark,
then stepped back onto me
to mark once again its dark road. A hero came
next to cover me with guardian boards of oakwood,
stretched over them soft hide,
adorned me with gold until I came to shine
with the work of men who make things wondrous,
bound in rich threads of filigreed wire.
Now these bright trappings, my red dye
and gleaming jewels, proclaim in all directions
the savior of nations, no longer my old foolish sorrows.
If the children of men use me well
they will be safer, assured of more victories,
more courageous, freer of heart, wiser in spirit.
They will find more friends, dear and familiar,
good friends and true, faithful and helpful,
enlarging in honor and grace,

25 lissum bilecgað   ond hi lufan fæþmum
     fæste clyppað.   Frige hwæt ic hatte,
     niþum to nytte.   Nama min is mære,
     hæleþum gifre   ond halig sylf.

Riddle 27

     Ic eom weorð werum,   wide funden,
     brungen of bearwum   ond of burghleoþum,
     of denum ond of dunum.   Dæges mec wægun
     feþre on lifte,   feredon mid liste
5   under hrofes hleo.   Hæleð mec siþþan
     baþedan in bydene.   Nu ic eom bindere
     ond swingere,   sona **weorpe**
     esne to eorþan,   hwilum ealdne ceorl.
     Sona þæt onfindeð,   se þe mec fehð ongean,
10   ond wið mægenþisan   minre genæsteð,
     þæt he hrycge sceal   hrusan secan,
     gif he unrædes   ær ne geswiceð,
     strengo bistolen,   strong on spræce,
     mægene binumen;   nah his modes geweald,
15   fota ne folma.   Frige hwæt ic hatte,
     ðe on eorþan swa   esnas binde,
     dole æfter dyntum   be dæges leohte.

who will bring gifts and kindness, the firm clasp of love.
Ask who I am, useful to men, bringer of blessings.
My name is well-known, and itself is holy.

From Groves and Green Hills Girdling the City
Robert B. Shaw

From groves and green hills girdling the city,
from dales and downs, holding me dear,
foragers fan out far to fetch me.
Once wafted on wings through warm bright air,
I was put under thatch by practiced porters.
In time attendants gave me a tub-bath.
Now I bind men and belabor them brutally;
any young tough guy I'll toss on his tail
as quick as I can some old curmudgeon.
Any galoot going at me to grapple,
setting his strength against my strength,
soon realizes he's ripe for a rest,
finds himself flat on his foolish back
if he dares to endure what I dish out.
Gone all gimpy, gassing off big-time,
strength siphoned off, his sodden brain,
dazed feet and hands don't heed his edicts.
Tell what I'm called, daily taking captive
tyros whose trouncing ought to teach them,
but after each bout just beg for more.

Poems
about Living

Maxims I-A

Frige mec frodum wordum!   Ne læt þinne ferð onhælne,
degol þæt þu deopost cunne!   Nelle ic þe min dyrne gesecgan,
gif þu me þinne hygecræft hylest   ond þine heortan geþohtas.
Gleawe men sceolon gieddum wrixlan.   God sceal mon ærest hergan
5 fægre, fæder userne,   forþon þe he us æt frymþe geteode
lif ond lænne willan;   he usic wile þara leana gemonian.
Meotud sceal in wuldre,   mon sceal on eorþan
geong ealdian.   God us ece biþ,
ne wendað hine wyrda   ne hine wiht dreceþ,
10 adl ne yldo   ælmihtigne;
ne gomelað he in gæste,   ac he is gen swa he wæs,
þeoden geþyldig.   He us geþonc syleð,
missenlicu mod,   monge reorde.
Feorhcynna fela   fæþmeþ wide
15 eglond monig.   Eardas rume
meotud arærde   for moncynne,
ælmihtig god,   efenfela bega
þeoda ond þeawa.   þing sceal gehegan
frod wiþ frodne;   biþ hyra ferð gelic,
20 hi a sace semaþ,   sibbe gelærað,
þa ær wonsælge   awegen habbað.
Ræd sceal mid snyttro,   ryht mid wisum,
til sceal mid tilum.   Tu beoð gemæccan;
sceal wif ond wer   in woruld cennan
25 bearn mid gebyrdum.   Beam sceal on eorðan
leafum liþan,   leomu gnornian.
Fus sceal feran,   fæge sweltan
ond dogra gehwam   ymb gedal sacan

Maxims I–A

David Curzon

Scrutinize me with   shrewd words,
don't let your comprehension   be kept secret.
I won't speak my spirit   if you hide your heart.
Those who know   must traffic their maxims.

Let God, our Father,   be the first glorified
since from the beginning   his gifts were life, free will;
He wishes we ponder   on those loans.

The ordaining Lord   belongs in glory
as humans have the earth   and the young become elders.
Fate does not change Him,   or age or disease.
His patient spirit   is always as it was.
We've received reason,   temperaments, tongues,
many kinds of kindred   spread over islands,
the spacious places   for peoples and customs
the Almighty made   for homo sapiens.

The wise with the wise   must make common cause
since their minds are alike.   They must preach peace,
dissolve disputes   discontent induces.
The sage should counsel;   the just must deal justly;
the kind be kindly.   Such coupling must match
as man and woman   bring birth to the world.

A tree must shed leaves,   its branches be barren;
the traveler must embark   on the start of travels;
all mortals must   meet their fate;

middangeardes.   Meotud ana wat

30 hwær se cwealm cymeþ, þe heonan of cyþþe gewiteþ.

Umbor yceð, þa æradl nimeð;

þy weorþeð on foldan swa fela fira cynnes,

ne sy þæs magutimbres gemet ofer eorþan,

gif hi ne wanige se þas woruld teode.

35 Dol biþ se þe his dryhten nat, to þæs oft cymeð deað unþinged.

Snotre men sawlum beorgað, healdað hyra soð mid ryhte.

Eadig bið se þe in his eþle geþihð, earm se him his frynd geswicað.

Nefre sceal se him his nest aspringeð, **nyde** sceal þrage gebunden.

Bliþe sceal bealoleas heorte. Blind sceal his eagna þolian,

40 oftigen biþ him torhtre gesihþe. Ne magon **hi** tunglu bewitian,

swegltorht sunnan ne monan; þæt him biþ sar in his mode,

onge þonne he hit ana wat, ne weneð þæt him þæs edhwyrft cyme.

Waldend him þæt wite teode, se him mæg wyrpe syllan,

hælo of heofodgimme, gif he wat heortan clæne.

45 Lef mon læces behofað. Læran sceal mon geongne monnan,

trymman ond tyhtan þæt he teala cunne, oþþæt hine mon atemedne
    hæbbe,

sylle him wist ond wædo, oþþæt hine mon on gewitte alæde.

Ne sceal hine mon cildgeongne forcweþan, ær he hine acyþan mote;

þy sceal on þeode geþeon, þæt he wese þristhycgende.

50 Styran sceal mon strongum mode. Storm oft holm gebringeþ,

geofen in grimmum sælum; onginnað grome fundian

each day has a portion   of their steps toward it.
Only the Almighty   knows of death's departure.
Every baby must come   to the bane of ailment.
He who established   the family of man
conceived diminution   to limit increase.

Only the foolish   don't know their Lord;
to them death   arrives unexpected.
The wise shield their souls   with a righteous hold.
The fortunate flourish   in their own birthplace.
Hapless is he   whom friends betray.
When provisions diminish   prosperity palls
and men are bound   by knowledge of need.
Happy is the heart   immune from misery.

The blind have sight   deprived of vision,
they can't see stars,   tell constellations;
this is a misery   they know alone;
they can't envisage   a cure could come.
This torment was ordained   by He who can heal
the gems of the genuine   head and heart.

The sick know   they need a physician.

The young must be   persuaded to competence,
must be encouraged   until tamed,
given provisions until   conditioned by wisdom.
Don't accuse the childish   till they attain to adulthood.
The child must thrive   to come to courage.

The strong-willed   must steer straight.
Storms overcome oceans,   bring grim conditions.
Willful waves   sweep to shore

fealwe on feorran to londe,   hwæþer he fæste stonde.
Weallas him wiþre healdað,   him biþ wind gemæne.
Swa biþ sæ smilte,
55 þonne hy wind ne weceð;
swa beoþ þeoda geþwære,   þonne hy geþingad habbað,
gesittað him on gesundum þingum,   ond þonne mid gesiþum healdaþ
cene men gecynde rice.   Cyning biþ anwealdes georn;
lað se þe londes monað,   leof se þe mare beodeð.
60 þrym sceal mid wlenco,   þriste mid cenum,
sceolun bu recene   beadwe fremman.
Eorl sceal on eos boge,   **eorod** sceal getrume ridan,
fæste feþa stondan.   Fæmne æt hyre bordan geriseð;
widgongel wif word gespringeð,   oft hy mon wommum bilihð,
65 hæleð hy hospe mænað,   oft hyre hleor abreoþeð.
Sceomiande man sceal in sceade hweorfan,   scir in leohte geriseð.
Hond sceal heofod inwyrcan,   hord in streonum bidan,
gifstol gegierwed stondan,   hwonne hine guman gedælen.
70 Gifre biþ se þam golde onfehð,   guma þæs on heahsetle geneah;
lean sceal, gif we leogan nellað,   þam þe us þas lisse geteode.

to test whether   the land will stand steadfast.
The wind is weakened   against a cliff.
The sea is peaceful   when the wind is asleep
and peoples are peaceful   when agreement is reached.
They settle when   in safe circumstance,
when courageous comrades   rule law-filled nations.

A leader is one   who is eager to lead,
who hates him   who demands territory
and loves the one   who offers extra.
Power requires pride;   daring, a sharp spirit;
both are needed   to seek battle.
An earl is equestrian,   his charger is mounted;
a trooper must ride   among true company;
the infantry man   must stand his ground.

A woman is enjoined   to be with embroidery;
a wandering woman   engenders gossip;
she is often taunted   with sordid sayings,
slandered, insulted,   her complexion compromised.
A person nursing guilt   must move in darkness
but one unashamed   should not stay in shadow.

The head must hold the hand;   treasure must be hoarded.
The throne must be adorned   for when gifts are given.
He is always eager   who receives gold;
the one on high   has enough to divide.
We must repay   or we will deprive
the one who gave   such gold gifts to us.

Maxims I-B

Forst sceal freosan,   fyr wudu meltan,
eorþe growan,   is brycgian,
wæter helm wegan,   wundrum lucan
eorþan ciþas.   An sceal inbindan
75 forstes fetre   felameahtig god;
winter sceal geweorpan,   weder eft cuman,
sumor swegle hat,   sund unstille.
Deop deada wæg   dyrne bið lengest;
holen sceal inæled,   yrfe gedæled
80 deades monnes.   Dom biþ selast.
Cyning sceal mid ceape   cwene gebicgan,
bunum ond beagum;   bu sceolon ærest
geofum god wesan.   Guð sceal in eorle,
wig geweaxan,   ond wif geþeon
85 **leof** mid hyre leodum,   leohtmod wesan,
rune healdan,   rumheort beon
mearum ond maþmum,   meodorædenne

Maxims I–B

Brigit Pegeen Kelly

Frost must freeze, fire melt wood,
earth bear fruit, ice build bridges,
and, most wonderful, water put on a glass helmet
to protect the earth's sprouts.

Only one God, the God of all strength,
can unlock the shackles of ice, and cast out winter.
The water will melt, kind weather come again,
days hot with sun; the deep sea will seethe and sway—

but the way of the dead will long be hidden.

Holly must be burned,
and the goods of a dead man divided.
God's judgment will be just.

A royal man must buy his bride
with cups and with rings.
Both must first be generous with gifts.
A fighting spirit must grow in the man,
a brave battle spirit, and the woman
must find favor with her people—
gracious she must be, a keeper of secrets,
kind she must be, generous with horses and gifts.

for gesiðmægen   symle æghwær
eodor **æþelinga**   ærest gegretan,
90 forman fulle   to frean hond
ricene geræcan,   ond him ræd witan
boldagendum   bæm ætsomne.
Scip sceal genægled,   scyld gebunden,
leoht linden bord,   leof wilcuma
95 Frysan wife,   þonne flota stondeð;
biþ his ceol cumen   ond hyre ceorl to ham,
agen ætgeofa,   ond heo hine in laðaþ,
wæsceð his warig hrægl   ond him syleþ wæde niwe,
liþ him on londe   þæs his lufu bædeð.
100 Wif sceal wiþ wer wære gehealdan,   oft hi mon wommum **belihð**;
fela bið fæsthydigra,   fela bið **fyrwetgeornra**,
freoð hy fremde monnan,   þonne se oþer feor gewiteþ.
Lida biþ longe on siþe;   a mon sceal seþeah leofes wenan,

Always, in all festivities, she must greet
first her lord, among his companions,
and put the full cup in his hands.
She must be wise in the ways of her household,
giving her husband good counsel.

A ship must be nailed fast;
and the excellent shields,
the light linden-wood shields,
bound tight to the ship's sides.

When the sailor comes back,
when his ship is at rest,
the Frisian wife will embrace her welcome guest—
her freeman is home at last,
the one who protects her,
the one who provides.
She leads him in, washes his sea-stained clothes,
gives him new garments,
and yields to him on the land
the softness his love demands.

A woman must keep faith with her man.
Too often women defame their men.
Many are resolute, many restless—
taking up with strange men
when their husbands are away.

A sailor is on the sea for a long time.

gebidan þæs he gebædan ne mæg.   Hwonne him eft gebyre weorðe,
105 ham cymeð, gif he hal leofað,   nefne him holm gestyreð,
mere hafað mundum   mægðegsan wyn.
Ceapeadig mon   cyningwic þonne
leodon cypeþ,   þonne liþan cymeð;
wuda ond wætres nyttað,   þonne him biþ wic **alyfed**,
110 mete bygeþ, gif he maran þearf,   ærþon he to meþe weorþe.
Seoc se biþ þe to seldan ieteð;   þeah hine mon on sunnan læde,
ne mæg he be þy wedre wesan,   þeah hit sy wearm on sumera,
ofercumen biþ he, ær he acwele,   gif he nat hwa hine cwicne fede.
Mægen mon sceal mid mete fedan,   morþor under eorþan befeolan,
115 hinder under hrusan,   þe hit forhelan þenceð;
ne biþ þæt gedefe deaþ,   þonne hit gedyrned weorþeð.
Hean sceal gehnigan,   **hadl** gesigan,
ryht rogian.   Ræd biþ nyttost,
yfel unnyttost,   þæt unlæd nimeð.
120 God bið genge,   ond wiþ god lenge.

He, too, must hope for his return.
He, too, must be patient and endure hardship.
If the terrors of the sea do not take him,
or the wild raiders of the sea do not take him,
he will come back. And when he does,
the king will give him all he needs,
wood and water, food and a dwelling,
a place of respect among his people.

If a sick man does not eat, even if he is carried
into the warm weather, he will die—
the kindest weather will not save him.
If a sick man has no kinsman to care for him
and feed him, he will surely die.

If a man murders another man and hides
the crime under the ground,
he takes from that man both his life
and an honorable burial.

The poor are obliged to bend down,
the sick are obliged to fall,
but right will prevail.
Good counsel is the most useful thing,
evil the most useless.
Poor is the man who takes up evil.
God returns good for good, evil for evil.
God alone is useful.

Hyge sceal gehealden,   hond gewealden,

seo sceal in eagan,   snyttro in breostum,

þær bið þæs monnes   modgeþoncas.

Muþa gehwylc mete þearf,   mæl sceolon tidum gongan.

125 Gold geriseþ   on guman sweorde,

sellic sigesceorp,   sinc on cwene,

god scop gumum,   garniþ werum,

wig towiþre   wicfreoþa healdan.

Scyld sceal cempan,   sceaft reafere,

130 sceal bryde beag,   bec leornere,

husl halgum men,   hæþnum synne.

Woden worhte weos,   wuldor alwalda,

The mind must be trained,
as the hand must be trained.

Sight is found in the pupil of the eye,
and wisdom is found in the breast of man,
where his thoughts reside.

Every living thing needs food.
Time continues always.

Gold befits a warrior's sword.
Triumphant dress is a woman's treasure.

A poet sings to protect the people.
To protect the land a warrior fights.

A shield belongs to a warrior,
a blade to a robber,
a ring to a bride,
a book to a pupil,
the Eucharist to good men,
and to the sinner—his sins.

Woden made idols.

rume roderas;   þæt is rice god,

sylf soðcyning,   sawla nergend,

135 se us eal forgeaf   þæt we on lifgaþ,

ond eft æt þam ende   eallum wealdeð

monna cynne.   þæt is meotud sylfa.

The God of glory, the God of all strength,
made the wide firmament
and the kingdom of heaven.
He is the true King,
The Keeper of souls,
The One who forgives,
the One who bestows life here and hereafter—
the Ruler of mankind.
He is the One who is.

Maxims I-C

Ræd sceal mon secgan,   rune writan,
leoþ gesingan,   **lofes** gearnian,
140 dom areccan,   dæges onettan.
Til mon tiles   ond tomes meares,
cuþes ond gecostes   ond calcrondes;
nænig fira   to fela gestryneð.
Wel mon sceal wine healdan   on wega gehwylcum;
145 oft mon fereð feor bi tune,   þær him wat freond unwiotodne.
Wineleas, wonsælig mon   genimeð him wulfas to geferan,
felafæcne deor.   Ful oft hine se gefera sliteð;
gryre sceal for greggum,   græf deadum men;
hungre heofeð,   nales þæt heafe bewindeð,
150 ne huru wæl wepeð   wulf se græga,
morþorcwealm mæcga,   ac hit a mare wille.
Wræd sceal wunden,   wracu heardum men.
Boga sceal stræle,   sceal bam gelic
mon to gemæccan.   Maþþum oþres weorð,
155 gold mon sceal gifan.   Mæg god syllan
eadgum æhte   ond eft niman.
Sele sceal stondan,   sylf ealdian.
Licgende beam   læsest groweð.
Treo sceolon brædan   ond treow weaxan,
160 sio geond bilwitra   breost ariseð.
Wærleas mon ond wonhydig,
ætrenmod ond ungetreow,
þæs ne gymeð god.
Fela sceop meotud þæs þe fyrn gewearð,   het siþþan swa forð wesan.
165 Wæra gehwylcum wislicu   word gerisað,

Maxims I-C

Mark Halliday

To live well is to do what needs doing. If you have wise counsel,
speak it clearly; but when secrecy is wise, write silent words.
If you have a song, sing it. When you must judge, then judge.
The day for action is always today.

Be smart about what you have; if you find a good horse,
keep it and treat it well. Where is the man who owns enough?
Be true to your friends. The night will come when you'll wish
for a friend close by, when the road is dark and dusty

and something moves among the shadowy trees;
when the wolf finds you alone it will not consider
how important you were back in town. In this dark world
gray wolves are forever hungry and they show no mercy.

You must do the needful thing. When a wound bleeds
you must wrap it tightly; when too much harm is inflicted
you must exact revenge. Arrows are nothing without a bow;
bow and arrow are nothing without a strong arm.

When treasure is exchanged you must give fair weight,
but know that God allows strange outcomes. Guard your dwelling,
keep what can be kept, remember that when a tree has fallen
it can grow no more. In your dealings be true of heart

for God abandons the cheater. God watches, God knows,
there is a great and dark design. This is true for us all
even if each of us has favored ideas, favored songs.

gleomen gied   ond guman snyttro.

Swa monige beoþ men ofer eorþan,   swa beoþ modgeþoncas;

ælc him hafað sundorsefan.

Longað þonne þy læs   þe him con leoþa worn,

170 oþþe mid hondum con   hearpan gretan;

hafaþ him his gliwes giefe,   þe him god sealde.

Earm biþ se þe sceal ana lifgan,

wineleas wunian   hafaþ him wyrd geteod;

betre him wære þæt he broþor ahte,   begen hi anes monnes,

175 **eorles** eaforan wæran,   gif hi sceoldan eofor onginnan

oþþe begen beran;   biþ þæt sliþhende deor.

A scyle þa rincas   gerædan lædan

ond him ætsomne swefan;

næfre hy mon **tomælde**,

180 ær hy dead todæle.

Hy twegen sceolon tæfle ymbsittan,   þenden him hyra torn toglide,

forgietan þara geocran **gesceafta**,   habban him gomen on borde;

idle hond æmetlan geneah tæfles monnes,   þonne teoselum weorpeð.

Seldan in sidum ceole,   nefne he under segle yrne,

185 werig **scealc** wiþ winde roweþ;   ful oft mon wearnum tihð

eargne, þæt he elne forleose,   drugað his ar on borde.

Lot sceal mid lyswe,   list mid gedefum;

þy weorþeð se stan forstolen.

Oft hy wordum toweorpað,

190 ær hy bacum tobreden;

geara is hwær aræd.

Weard fæhþo fyra cynne,   siþþan furþum swealg

eorðe Abeles blode.   Næs þæt andæge nið,

of þam wrohtdropan   wide gesprungon,

200 micel mon ældum,   monegum þeodum

bealoblonden niþ.   Slog his **broðor** swæsne

Cain, þone cwealm nerede;   cuþ wæs wide siþþan,

þæt ece nið ældum scod,   swa aþolwarum

The wise man learns many songs and plays them on the harp

and feels less solitary while the songs are heard. Remember
how solitude becomes desperate; remember how danger comes
like a wild boar through the rustling forest! When it comes
you will need a kinsman standing bravely beside you

with a well-made spear. Never let false rumors and lies
divide you from your kinsman through all the years of life.
Be true and you will feel at ease playing chess with him
and forget grief, on winter nights when the wind outside is raw.

This world of hard days will make you weary, like a boatman
who strains to row against the wind; yet you must
keep on so that all will know you are a man of spirit.
Be true of heart, be steady, never cease to be ready!

Our world has no haven. Ever since the blood of Abel
soaked into the dirt of the first farmland where Cain struck him down
there has been hatred, envy, greed afoot in this world.
That is where you must live, among thieves and killers.

Drugon wæpna gewin   wide geond eorþan,
205 ahogodan ond ahyrdon   heoro sliþendne.
Gearo sceal guðbord,   gar on sceafte,
ecg on sweorde   ond ord spere,
hyge heardum men.   Helm sceal cenum,
ond a þæs heanan hyge   hord unginnost.

There is no other world. Every day they hone their long knives.
Therefore be ready: let your shield be hard, your spear be sharp,
your heart be bold. A coward's heart is no prize,
but the man of valor deserves his shining helmet.

Vainglory

Hwæt, me frod wita   on fyrndagum
sægde, snottor ar,   sundorwundra fela.
Wordhord **onwreah**   witgan larum
beorn boca gleaw,   bodan ærcwide,
5   þæt ic soðlice   siþþan meahte
ongitan bi þam gealdre   godes agen bearn,
wilgest on wicum,   ond þone wacran swa some,
scyldum bescyredne,   on gescead **witan**.
þæt mæg æghwylc mon   eaþe geþencan,
10   se þe hine **ne** læteð   on þas lænan tid
amyrran his gemyndum   modes gælsan
ond on his dægrime   **druncen** to rice,
þonne monige beoð   **mæþelhegendra**,
wlonce wigsmiþas   winburgum in,
15   sittaþ æt symble,   soðgied wrecað,
wordum wrixlað,   witan fundiaþ
hwylc æscstede   inne in ræcede
mid werum wunige,   þonne win hweteð
beornes breostsefan.   Breahtem stigeð,
20   cirm on corþre,   cwide scralletaþ
missenlice.   Swa beoþ modsefan
dalum gedæled,   sindon dryhtguman
ungelice.   Sum on oferhygdo
þrymme **þringeð**,   þrinteð him in innan
25   ungemedemad mod;   sindan to monige þæt!
Bið þæt æfþonca   eal gefylled
feondes fligepilum,   facensearwum;
breodað he ond bælceð,   boð his sylfes
swiþor micle   þonne se sella mon,

Vainglory

Alan Jenkins

Hwæt! Such wisdom   once was told me
a brave tale-bringer   broadcast wonders
unlocked the word-hoard   old head this herald
learned in teachings   long foretold us;
I heard sung the secret   the son of God
a welcome houseguest   and that weaker one
sundered by sin   I also saw—
all may grasp this   whose grip is not loosened
by lust for women,   wits overmastered
dragged down by drink   in life's short dream.
When men are gathered   for good times and men's talk
warlike helm-wearers   happy in wine-hall
ranged above others   reckon their song's truth
weave bold words   try boasts of battles
in hope one strikes home   to men's hearts;
wine heats the breast-hearth   of each hero
wine-fired, brazen   wielded wildly
words clash and clang.

                So path-cleaving
that person's price   and purpose part
from this other's,   they are not
alike in virtue.   Vainglory's victim
self-swelled, swanking—   no shortage of such.
The fiend fills him   full of envy,
stabs with sharp pricks   stokes his pride
bloated with self-wind   he boasts and belches
more than many   better men

30 þenceð þæt his wise   welhwam þince
    eal unforcuþ.   Biþ þæs oþer swice,
    þonne he þæs facnes   fintan sceawað.
    Wrenceþ he ond blenceþ,   worn geþenceþ
    hinderhoca,   hygegar leteð,
35 scurum sceoteþ.   He þa scylde ne wat
    fæhþe gefremede,   **feoþ** his betran
    eorl fore æfstum,   læteð inwitflan
    brecan þone burgweal,   þe him bebead meotud
    þæt he þæt wigsteal   wergan **sceolde**,
40 siteþ symbelwlonc,   searwum læteð
    wine gewæged   word ut faran,
    þræfte þringan   þrymme gebyrmed,
    æfæstum onæled,   oferhygda ful,
    niþum nearowrencum.   Nu þu cunnan meaht,
45 gif þu þyslicne   þegn gemittest
    wunian in wicum,   wite þe be þissum
    feawum forðspellum   þæt þæt biþ feondes bearn
    flæsce bifongen,   hafað fræte lif,
    grundfusne gæst   gode orfeormne,
50 wuldorcyninge.   þæt se witga song,
    gearowyrdig guma,   ond þæt gyd awræc:
    "Se þe hine sylfne   in þa sliþnan tid
    þurh oferhygda   up ahlæneð,
    ahefeð heahmodne,   se sceal hean wesan
55 æfter neosiþum   niþer gebiged,
    wunian witum fæst,   wyrmum beþrungen.
    þæt wæs geara iu   in godes rice

he fears no risk   of ill-repute
but will reap   rebuke in time.
He twists and turns   outwits truth-traps
shoots his arrow-showers   shafts of hatred
shame does not   shield him from harm
he sheds about him   hates his betters
virtue vexes him   envy's volleys
break down battlements   breach the bastion
God once bade him   guard with his life.
A lordly feaster   far gone in wine
craftily his words   creep out, creatures
pushing proudly   puffed with self-yeast
vainglory gluts him   he glows with envy
and treacherous hatred.   Know the truth
of this thane's might   if you should meet him
at home among men   in house and mead hall
these things bespeak him   the spawn of foulness
fear, suspect it   he is fiend's flesh
clings to uncleanness   hell will claim him
whose life is groundless   ghost goes graveward
unarmed and hungry   who goes without God
the king of glory.

            That prince's prophet
who sang his fore-praise   said: "The proud man
stunned at himself   and his high standing
who is haughty   in harsh times
he will have   a hard hereafter
will be brought low   at his life's end
dwell in torment   never-dwindling
will not escape   the serpent's coils."
Long ago   in the kingdom of God

þætte mid englum   oferhygd astag,
widmære gewin.   Wroht ahofan,
60 heardne heresiþ,   heofon **widledan**,
forsawan hyra sellan,   þa hi to swice þohton
ond þrymcyning   þeodenstoles
ricne beryfan,   swa hit ryht ne wæs,
ond þonne gesettan   on hyra sylfra dom
65 wuldres wynlond.   þæt him wige forstod
fæder frumsceafta;   wearð him seo feohte to grim.
ðonne bið þam oþrum   ungelice
se þe her on eorþan   eaðmod leofað,
ond wiþ gesibbra gehwone   simle healdeð
70 freode on folce   ond his **feond** lufað,
þeah þe he him abylgnesse   oft gefremede
willum in þisse worulde.   Se mot wuldres dream
in haligra hyht   heonan astigan
on engla eard.   Ne biþ þam oþrum swa,
75 se þe on ofermedum   eargum dædum
leofaþ in leahtrum,   ne beoð þa lean gelic
mid wuldorcyning."   Wite þe be þissum,
gif þu eaðmodne   eorl gemete,
þegn on þeode,   þam bið simle
80 gæst gegæderad   godes agen bearn
wilsum in worlde,   gif me se witega ne leag.
Forþon we sculon a hycgende   hælo rædes
gemunan in mode   mæla gehwylcum
þone selestan   sigora waldend.
85 Amen.

the revolt and high-vaunting   widely heard of
took hold on the angels   heaven was filled
with harsh raiding parties   who purposed wrongly
with blows and bloodlust   such their blame
to dethrone their greatest   good, their glorious king
their plan to set   themselves in his place
and lord it over   the land of joy;
the end of this was   our Father withstood them
become one who deals   in direst coin.
Nothing like this   known by him
who lives humbly   here on earth
who stands for peace   and steadfast friendship
loves his kinfolk   his foe likewise
though he did him   harm indeed
wanted, worked it   as is the world's way
he will journey hence   to wondrous joy
rise in hope   to heights of holiness
the angels' home.
                Not so who
believe themselves   already blessed
who parade their wickedness   with pride
these the great king   grants no riches—
they will lack him.   This their lesson
the humble man   who is high-born
serves a lord   everlasting
together in spirit   with God's own son
light of the world   —if the wise man did not lie.

Thus it is that we should think on   last things
and be mindful   at each moment
of the truest   triumphant Lord. Amen.

The Riming Poem

Me lifes onlah   se þis leoht onwrah,
ond þæt torhte geteoh,   tillice onwrah.
Glæd wæs ic gliwum,   glenged hiwum,
blissa bleoum,   blostma hiwum.
5 Secgas mec segon,   symbel ne alegon,
feohgiefe gefegon;   frætwed **wægon**
wicg ofer wongum   wennan gongum,
lisse mid longum   leoma **gehongum**.
þa wæs wæstmum aweaht,   world onspreht,
10 under roderum areaht,   rædmægne oferþeaht.
Giestas gengdon,   gerscype mengdon,
lisse lengdon,   lustum glengdon.
Scrifen scrad glad   þurh gescad in brad,
wæs on lagustreame lad,   þær me leoþu ne biglad.
15 Hæfde ic heanne had,   ne wæs me in healle gad,
þæt þær rof weord rad.   Oft þær rinc gebad,
þæt he in sele sæge   sincgewæge,
þegnum geþyhte.   þenden wæs **me** mægen,
horsce mec heredon,   hilde generedon,
20 fægre feredon,   feondon biweredon.
Swa mec hyhtgiefu heold,   hygedryht befeold,
staþolæhtum **steold**,   stepegongum weold
swylce eorþe ol,   ahte ic ealdorstol,
galdorwordum gol.   **Gomen** sibbe ne ofoll,
25 ac wæs gefest gear,   gellende sner,
wuniendo wær   wilbec bescær.
Scealcas wæron scearpe,   scyl wæs hearpe,

The Riming Poem

A. E. Stallings

The Lord lavished life on me   I had it all:
Blessings were rife for me,   honor in hall,
Clad in the gladsome   cloth of the looms
Dyed with the handsome   hues of the blooms,
Men then looked up to me,   friendship reigned
Filling the cup for me,   wine never waned.
Steeds in rich panoply   pranced in their pride
Gallant their galloping,   strong was their stride.
The day was just breaking   and freighted with fruits
The world was awaking   and quickened with shoots
Spread under God's weather   His wisdom unfurled,
Men talking together   went guests in this world,
Their dress never dim   and pleasure prevailed.
My ship in good trim   sallied and sailed
Over ocean askim,   fair winds never failed.
Rank and degree   and high heaps of treasure
Belonged then to me   in no meager measure.
Brave riders and bold   set out on their steeds
To gape at the gold   a nobleman needs.
I joyed not in vain,   my hopes were all grounded,
Well-founded my reign   with allies surrounded.
I held the high seat   my might was my word,
Earth's bounty replete   bonds of kinship secured.
The year was not loath   with gifts but abounded,
Men honored their oath,   the harp-strings resounded.
The wellspring of woe   was stopped at its source,
Its faltering flow   curbed on its course.
Plectrums would pluck   the high-voiced harp

hlude hlynede,   hleoþor dynede,
sweglrad swinsade,   swiþe ne minsade.
30 Burgsele beofode,   beorht hlifade,
ellen eacnade,   ead beacnade,
freaum frodade,   fromum godade,
mod mægnade,   mine fægnade,
treow telgade,   tir welgade,
35 blæd blissade,
gold gearwade,   gim hwearfade,
sinc searwade,   sib nearwade.
From ic wæs in frætwum,   freolic in geatwum;
wæs min dream dryhtlic,   drohtað hyhtlic.
40 Foldan ic freoþode,   folcum ic leoþode,
lif wæs min longe,   leodum in gemonge,
tirum getonge,   teala gehonge.
Nu min hreþer is hreoh,   **heofsiþum** sceoh,
nydbysgum neah;   gewiteð nihtes in fleah
45 se ær in dæge wæs dyre.   Scriþeð nu deop in **feore**
brondhord geblowen,   breostum in forgrowen,
flyhtum toflowen.   Flah is geblowen
miclum in gemynde;   modes gecynde
greteð ungrynde   grorn efenpynde,
50 bealofus byrneð,   bittre toyrneð.
Werig winneð,   widsið onginneð,
sar ne sinniþ,   sorgum cinnið,
blæd his blinnið,   blisse **linnið**,

That keenly struck cried clear and sharp;
Loudly resounding brightly it sang
With music abounding the firmament rang.
The tune never ended lilting and long,
While lofty and splendid the hall shook with song.
Daring deeds were rewarded with glimmer of gold.
Wisdom was lorded, the best were the bold.

Heart and mind both grew glad and great,
Trusted was troth and good name its mate.
I flourished in fame all through the land
All the gold I could claim lay ready to hand,
Peerless my pleasure hale my health.
But tricky is treasure deceitful is wealth
Kith and kin pressure by steel and by stealth.
In tackle for battle in royal array
My might and my mettle were firm in the fray.
Duly defended the land was secured
Faithfully friended the good folk endured.
Such was my story: long living among
My people; my glory sure-rooted and strong.

Now heavy my heart and faded with fear;
Woe won't depart, but ever draws near.
Things dear by day and loved in the light
Flee far away in nebulous night.
Deep in my chest the treasure-hoards burn
And grant me no rest: I toss and I turn.
Wickedness waxes and blooms in the brain
Evil attacks burning with bane,
Bottomless trouble, the heart's heavy pondering.
Weary with struggle I start the far wandering
Unending anguish begets ceaseless sorrow,
Good names languish joy has no morrow,

listum linneð,   lustum ne tinneð.

55 Dreamas swa her gedreosað,   dryhtscype gehreosað,
lif her men forleosað,   leahtras oft geceosað;
treowþrag is to trag,   seo untrume genag,
steapum eatole misþah,   ond eal stund genag.
Swa nu world wendeþ,   wyrde sendeþ,
60 ond hetes henteð,   hæleþe scyndeð.
Wercyn gewiteð,   wælgar sliteð,
flahmah fliteþ,   flan mon hwiteð,
borgsorg biteð,   bald ald þwiteþ,
wræcfæc wriþað,   wraþ að smiteþ,
65 **singryn** sidað,   **searofearo** glideþ,
gromtorn græfeþ,   græft hafað,
searohwit solaþ,   sumurhat colað,
foldwela fealleð,   feondscipe wealleð,
eorðmægen ealdaþ,   ellen colað.
70 Me þæt wyrd gewæf,   ond **gewyrht** forgeaf,
þæt ic grofe græf,   ond þæt grimme græf
flean flæsce ne mæg,   þonne flanhred dæg
nydgrapum nimeþ,   þonne seo **neaht** becymeð
seo me eðles **ofonn**   ond mec her **eardes** onconn.
75 þonne lichoma ligeð,   lima wyrm friteþ,
ac him wenne gewigeð   ond þa wist geþygeð,
oþþæt beoþ þa ban   an,
ond æt nyhstan nan   nefne se neda tan
balawun her **gehloten**.   Ne biþ se hlisa adroren.

Skill has left, freedom flies.
Dream-bereft, nobility dies.
Here men lose life and sin quickens
A season of strife, while faith sickens
And hope descends, withered and wan.
The world wends the fortune of man:
Unfurling fate and dogged doom
To hound him with hate unto the tomb.
Companions once cherished chiefly contend
Pierced and perished friend by friend
The spear snickers, the wicked arrow
Narrowly flickers and nicks the marrow.
Oaths are hard-bitten, faith ill-afforded,
The aged wrath-smitten, the bold are thwarted.
No rest from rancor: the ship of fools
Weighs its anchor. Hot summer cools.
False fouls the fair the grave carves,
Foeships flare, the harvest starves.
Earth's great strength grows frail and old,
Loath at length, all zeal goes cold.
Upon its loom Fate weaves my doom:
The narrow room, the gaping tomb,
No flesh may flee the grim rift.
That day for me comes arrow-swift
With deadly aim as it approaches,
And just the same the night encroaches
That won't condone my tenant's terms,
Abode of bone. Wassailing worms
Feast afresh where limbs lie slain
Devouring flesh: only bones remain.
Body bereft, the frame rotted,
Naught is left but what fate's allotted.

80 ær þæt eadig geþenceð,   he hine þe oftor swenceð,
   byrgeð him þa bitran synne,   hogaþ to þære betran wynne,
   gemon morþa lisse,   þær sindon miltsa blisse
   hyhtlice in heofona rice.   Uton nu halgum gelice
   scyldum biscyrede   scyndan generede,
85 wommum biwerede,   wuldre generede,
   þær moncyn mot   for meotude rot
   soðne god geseon,   ond aa in sibbe gefean.

His fame remains who soon repents
Sin's bitter banes for better intents,
Keeping his mind on heaven's word
On mercy's kind and sweet reward.
So let us haste to join the saints
Where no bale wastes and no blame taints,
Where Mankind saved by Glory's sword
Stands unenslaved before the Lord
Rejoicing for ever in brotherhood
Before the very face of God.

The Rune Poem

ᚠ (Feoh) byþ frofur   fira gehwylcum.
Sceal ðeah manna gehwylc   miclun hyt dælan
gif he wile for drihtne   domes hleotan.

ᚢ (Ur) byþ anmod   and oferhyrned,
5   felafrecne deor,   feohteþ mid hornum,
mære morstapa;   þæt is modig wuht.

ᚦ (Thorn) byþ ðearle scearp;   ðegna gehwylcum
anfeng ys yfyl,   ungemetun reþe
manna gehwylcun   ðe him mid resteð.

10   ᚩ (Os) byþ ordfruma   ælcre spræce,
wisdomes wraþu   and witena frofur,
and eorla gehwam   eadnys and tohiht.

ᚱ (Rad) byþ on recyde   rinca gehwylcum
sefte, and swiþhwæt   ðam ðe sitteþ on ufan
15   meare mægenheardum   ofer milpaþas.

ᚳ (Cen) byþ cwicera gehwam   cuþ on fyre,
blac and beorhtlic,   byrneþ oftust
ðær hi æþelingas   inne restaþ.

The Rune Poem

James Harpur

Wealth brings leisure
but share it freely if you really
want God's pleasure.

Aurochs is wild and very savage
and it fights with great long horns;
Aurochs is proud and full of courage
as it strides across the moors.

Thorn is incredibly sharp
to the hand of any thane;
people who sit on them start
with the shock of searing pain.

Mouth is the font of words
consoles the wise
delights the earls
and brings hope to their eyes.

Riding seems like a pleasant thing
to warriors indoors
but tests a man who's galloping
upon a sturdy horse.

Torch is a dazzling blaze
which always burns inside
where princes like to laze.

ᚷ (Gifu) gumena byþ   gleng and herenys,
20 wraþu and wyrþscype,   and wræcna gehwam
ar and ætwist   ðe byþ oþra leas.

ᚹ (Wynn) bruceþ   ðe can weana lyt,
sares and **sorge**,   and him sylfa hæfþ
blæd and blysse   and eac byrga geniht.

25 ᚻ (Haegl) byþ hwitust corna;   hwyrft hit of heofones lyfte,
wealcaþ hit windes **scuras**,   weorþeþ hit to wætere syððan.

ᚾ (Nyd) byþ nearu on breostan,   weorþeþ hi ðeah oft niþa bearnum
to helpe and to hæle gehwæþre,   gif hi his hlystaþ æror.

ᛁ (Is) byþ oferceald,   ungemetum slidor,
30 glisnaþ glæshluttur,   gimmum gelicust,
flor forste **geworuht**,   fæger ansyne.

ᛄ (Ger) byþ gumena hiht,   ðon god læteþ,
halig heofones cyning,   hrusan syllan
beorhte bleda   beornum and ðearfum.

35 ᛇ (Eoh) byþ utan   unsmeþe treow,
heard, hrusan fæst,   hyrde fyres,
wyrtrumun underwreþyd,   **wyn** on eþle.

Generosity
honors you and me;
it gives the poor a crust
when all they have is dust.

Joy comes to those who do not know
the things that make you sad or sore,
to those who revel in success
and all those fortresses galore.

Hail, hail, the whitest grain
swirling down from God's domain
for blustery winds to slaughter
transmuting it to water.

Need falls upon us with a thud
but is the saving of our children
if they can nip her in the bud.

Ice is so slippery, cold,
glitters like glass or gems
fashions a floor of frost—
Marvelous thing to behold!

Spring fills us with the sun
when God the holy king
allows the earth to bring
bright fruits to everyone.

Yew is a tree that has rough bark
stands firm in earth
protects the hearth
rooted so deep, it lights up parks.

ᚹ (Peorth) byþ symble   plega and hlehter
wlancum   ðar wigan sittaþ
40 on beorsele   bliþe ætsomne.

ᛉ (Eolh) **secg eard** hæfþ   oftust on fenne,
wexeð on wature,   wundaþ grimme,
blode breneð   beorna gehwylcne
ðe him ænigne   onfeng gedeð.

45 ᛋ (Sigil) semannum   symble biþ on hihte,
ðonn hi hine feriaþ   ofer fisces beþ,
oþ hi brimhengest   bringeþ to lande.

ᛏ (Tir) biþ tacna sum,   healdeð trywa wel
wiþ æþelingas,   a biþ on færylde,
50 ofer nihta genipu   næfre swiceþ.

ᛒ (Beorc) byþ bleda leas,   bereþ efne swa ðeah
tanas butan tudder,   biþ on telgum wlitig,
heah on helme   hrysted fægere,
geloden leafum,   lyfte getenge.

55 ᛖ (Eh) byþ for eorlum   æþelinga wyn,
hors hofum wlanc,   ðær him **hæleþ ymbe**,
welege on wicgum,   wrixlaþ spræce,
and biþ unstyllum   æfre frofur.

Dicing is always fun to play
where warriors' cheer is drinking beer
Passing the time of day.

Elk-sedge is found in the marshes
loves water and can inflict
the most horrible bloodiest gashes
on any man grasping it.

Sun is the seaman's hope and friend
when sailing on the fishes' bath
before their sea-steeds take the path
back home and to the journey's end.

Tir is a star that keeps its faith
with noblemen; a guiding light,
it never fails to keep its course
above the blanket mists of night.

Birch has no fruits
but grows new shoots
without the help of seeds;
with crown so high
it hits the sky
and shakes its dress of leaves.

Horse is—for warriors—a must,
a steed that revels in its shapely hooves;
rich riders chat about it, and it proves
a joy to those with wanderlust.

ᛗ (Man) byþ on myrgþe   his magan leof;
60   sceal þeah anra gehwylc   **oðrum** swican,
     for ðam dryhten wyle   dome sine
     þæt earme flæsc   eorþan betæcan.

ᛚ (Lagu) byþ leodum   langsum geþuht,
     gif hi sculun **neþan**   on nacan tealtum,
65   and hi sæyþa   swyþe bregaþ,
     and se brimhengest   bridles ne **gymeð**.

ᛝ (Ing) wæs ærest   mid Eastdenum
     gesewen secgun,   oþ he siððan **eft**
     ofer wæg gewat,   wæn æfter ran;
70   ðus heardingas   ðone hæle nemdun.

ᛟ (Ethel) byþ oferleof   æghwylcum men,
     gif he mot ðær **rihtes**   and gerysena on
     brucan on **bolde**   bleadum oftast.

ᛞ (Daeg) byþ drihtnes sond,   deore mannum,
75   mære metodes leoht,   myrgþ and tohiht
     eadgum and earmum,   eallum brice.

ᚨ (Ac) byþ on eorþan   elda bearnum
     flæsces fodor,   fereþ gelome
     ofer ganotes bæþ;   garsecg fandaþ
80   hwæþer ac hæbbe   æþele treowe.

ᚨ (Aesc) biþ oferheah,   eldum dyre,
     stiþ on staþule,   stede rihte hylt,
     ðeah him feohtan on   firas monige.

Man full of joy delights his brother;
yet we are doomed by laws God gave
to ultimately fail each other
when we're committed to the grave.

Sea can appear to stretch forever
when wind and gales attack your sails,
your sea-steed rushing hell-for-leather.

Ing first appeared to the eastern Danes
then vanished east across the waves
a wagon followed him behind
Ing was his name among the thanes.

Home is a man's most valuable possession
if there he can pursue
his rights and what is due,
and he maintains a prosperous profession.

Day is God's message, gives great joy
and hope to all who see its glory—
the elite and the hoi polloi.

Oak feeds the pigs that feed our bairns,
oak moves across the gannet's bath
and sea finds out if oak will last
and not let down our noble thanes.

Ash rises high, a cherished tree;
it's keeps in line and stands its ground
when charged at by the enemy.

ᛉ (Yr) byþ æþelinga   and eorla gehwæs
85 wyn and wyrþmynd,   byþ on wicge fæger,
fæstlic on færelde,   **fyrdgeatewa** sum.

ᛡ (Iar) byþ **eafix**,   and ðeah a bruceþ
fodres on **foldan**,   hafaþ fægerne eard,
wætre beworpen,   ðær he wynnum leofaþ.

90 ᛠ (Ear) byþ egle   eorla gehwylcun,
ðonn fæstlice   flæsc onginneþ,
hraw colian,   hrusan ceosan
blac to gebeddan;   bleda gedreosaþ,
wynna gewitaþ,   wera geswicaþ.

Bow is for the nobility a source
of pride and joy—it's splendid on a horse
and handy on a journey and in wars.

Iar is a river-fish
that gets its food
on terra firma;
in realms of water
its life is good
its home is very swish.

Grave fills all nobles with grim repugnance.
How quickly does the body spoil,
grow pale—a bedmate of the soil!
Then it's bye-bye to our joy and our covenants.

Maxims II

Cyning sceal rice healdan.   Ceastra beoð feorran gesyne,
orðanc enta geweorc,   þa þe on þysse eorðan syndon,
wrætlic weallstana geweorc.   Wind byð on lyfte swiftust,
þunar byð þragum hludast.   þrymmas syndan Cristes myccle,
5 wyrd byð swiðost.   Winter byð cealdost,
lencten hrimigost   (he byð lengest ceald),
sumor sunwlitegost   (swegel byð hatost),
hærfest hreðeadegost,   hæleðum bringeð
geres wæstmas,   þa þe him god sendeð.
10 Soð bið **switolost**,   sinc byð deorost,
gold gumena gehwam,   and gomol snoterost,
fyrngearum frod,   se þe ær feala gebideð.
Weax bið wundrum clibbor.   Wolcnu scriðað.
Geongne æþeling sceolan   gode gesiðas
15 byldan to beaduwe   and to beahgife.
Ellen sceal on eorle,   ecg sceal wið hellme
hilde gebidan.   Hafuc sceal on glofe
wilde gewunian,   wulf sceal on bearowe,
earm anhaga,   eofor sceal on holte,

Maxims II

Rachel Hadas

A king must reign over his realm.
From a distance cities loom,
Built by giants, hewn from stone.
Wind is fleetest; thunder roars
When it is thunder's time of year.
  Christ's power is great;
  Strongest is Fate.
Winter is coldest. Spring brings rime
And stays chill for the longest time.
Summer is rich with the sun's heat;
Bounteous autumn pours forth fruit,
The harvest that God sends to men.
On truth do not at all depend.
Treasure is precious, costly gold;
The man who knows the most is old,
Schooled by years now in the past.
Grief clutches us and holds us fast.
Clouds roll on. A fledgling prince
Must learn two things from his good friends:
How to make war and how to share
Out his wealth. A warrior
Must have courage; a sword must seek
Battle, and clash against a helm.
The hawk, wild creature, has to learn
To perch on a glove. The wolf, alone,
Must lurk within a forest glade.
Safe in the strength his tusks provide,
The boar must dwell within the wood.

20 toðmægenes trum.   Til sceal on eðle
    domes wyrcean.   Daroð sceal on handa,
    gar golde fah.   Gim sceal on hringe
    standan steap and geap.   Stream sceal on yðum
    mencgan mereflode.   Mæst sceal on ceole,
25 segelgyrd seomian.   Sweord sceal on bearme,
    drihtlic isern.   Draca sceal on hlæwe,
    frod, frætwum wlanc.   Fisc sceal on wætere
    cynren cennan.   Cyning sceal on healle
    beagas dælan.   Bera sceal on hæðe,
30 eald and egesfull.   Ea of dune sceal
    flodgræg feran.   Fyrd sceal ætsomne,
    tirfæstra getrum.   Treow sceal on eorle,
    wisdom on were.   Wudu sceal on foldan
    blædum blowan.   Beorh sceal on eorþan
35 grene standan.   God sceal on heofenum,
    dæda demend.   Duru sceal on healle,
    rum recedes muð.   Rand sceal on scylde,
    fæst fingra gebeorh.   Fugel uppe sceal
    lacan on lyfte.   Leax sceal on wæle
40 mid sceote scriðan.   Scur sceal on heofenum,
    winde geblanden,   in þas woruld cuman.
    þeof sceal gangan þystrum wederum.   þyrs sceal on fenne gewunian
    ana innan lande.   Ides sceal dyrne cræfte,
    fæmne hire freond gesecean,   gif heo nelle on folce geþeon
45 þæt hi man beagum gebicge.   Brim sceal sealte weallan,

A good man in his own land
Must win his honor. In the hand
The javelin fits, spear rich with gold.
A gem on a ring stands bright and bold.
A river must flow into the sea;
On a ship a mast must stay
Upright. A sword in the lap must lie,
As in its barrow the dragon, sly,
Guarding its hoard. Fish must spawn.
In his high hall the king must share
Out rings to all. The aged bear
Must live on the heath, a thing to fear.
Gushing with foam, downhill the river
Must flow. Men must stick together,
Each in the band a glory seeker.
To truth the warrior must cleave,
Mortals to wisdom. Trees must bear leaves
And flowers. Green the hill must stand,
Firmly rooted in the land.
　Heaven is God's house
　Who judges us.
Every hall must have a door,
Mouth of the building. A shield must bear
A boss to keep the fingers safe.
A bird must freely fly aloft.
Deep in a pool salmon must swim,
Glide with the trout. Wind stirs a storm
Out of the welkin down to earth.
The thief must walk in dirty weather.
In lonely marshes dwells the monster.
A maid must see her lover on the sly,
Lest people pay her dowry
With rings. Salt swells the roiling sea.

lyfthelm and laguflod   ymb ealra landa gehwylc,
flowan firgenstreamas.   Feoh sceal on eorðan
tydran and tyman.   Tungol sceal on heofenum
beorhte scinan,   swa him bebead meotud.
50 God sceal wið yfele,   geogoð sceal wið yldo,
lif sceal wið deaþe,   leoht sceal wið þystrum,
fyrd wið fyrde,   feond wið oðrum,
lað wið laþe   ymb land sacan,
synne stælan.   A sceal snotor hycgean
55 ymb þysse worulde gewinn,   wearh hangian,
fægere ongildan   þæt he ær facen dyde
manna cynne.   Meotod ana wat
hwyder seo sawul sceal   syððan hweorfan,
and ealle þa gastas   þe for gode hweorfað
60 æfter deaðdæge,   domes bidað
on fæder fæðme.   Is seo forðgesceaft
digol and dyrne;   drihten ana wat,
nergende fæder.   Næni eft cymeð
hider under hrofas,   þe þæt her for soð
65 mannum secge   hwylc sy meotodes gesceaft,
sigefolca gesetu,   þær he sylfa wunað.

Everywhere mighty streams must flow
With tide and cloud and winds that blow.
Cattle must breed and multiply;
The star must shine bright in the sky
As God ordained. Evil fights good;
Youth struggles with decrepitude;
Life against death, light against gloom,
One army against another one.
Enemy with enemy contends,
Struggling together over land,
Blaming each other for spilt blood.
On these wars a sage must brood.
The criminal must expiate his crime,
Hanged for the damage he has done.
Where do souls go? The Lord alone
Knows the destination
Of those who die and go to God,
Awaiting judgment's final word.
Of God's creation none can tell,
Where the conquering heroes dwell,
And God dwells too. No man comes back
To tell us here what Heaven's like.

The Gifts of Men

Fela bi∂ on foldan   for∂gesynra
geongra geofona,   þa þa gæstberend
wega∂ in gewitte,   swa her weoruda god,
meotud meahtum swi∂,   monnum dæle∂,
5 syle∂ sundorgiefe,   sende∂ wide
agne spede,   þara æghwylc mot
dryhtwuniendra   dæl onfon.
Ne bi∂ ænig þæs   earfo∂sælig
mon on moldan,   ne þæs medspedig,
10 lytelhydig,   ne þæs læthydig,
þæt hine se argifa   ealles biscyrge
modes cræfta   oþþe mægendæda,
wis on gewitte   oþþe on wordcwidum,
þy læs ormod sy   ealra þinga,
15 þara þe he geworhte   in woruldlife,
geofona gehwylcre.   Næfre god deme∂
þæt ænig eft   þæs earm geweor∂e.
Nænig eft þæs swiþe   þurh snyttrucræft
in þeode þrym   þisses lifes
20 for∂ gestige∂,   þæt him folca weard
þurh his halige giefe   hider onsende
wise geþohtas   ond woruldcræftas,
under anes meaht   ealle forlæte,
þy læs he for wlence   wuldorgeofona ful,
25 mon mode swi∂   of gemete hweorfe
ond þonne forhycge   heanspedigran;
ac he gedæle∂,   se þe ah domes geweald,
missenlice   geond þisne middangeard

The Gifts of Men

Major Jackson

Behold God's prevailing gifts on earth, discernible
to all souls! His unique powers are bestowed
and apportioned widely to every woman and man.
None are so wretched, unfortunate, or feeble-minded
to believe that the Giver of all has not endowed them
at least with a living breath, speech, and a smart mind
to appreciate their worldly abilities in this life.
God does not apportion misery to any soul,
nor would He allow any one woman or man to rise up on
this glorious earth, to bear all His wisdom and power, lest
that servant become too high and mighty,
neglectful of the least fortunate of His flock. Rather,
God exercises superb prudence and wisdom and broadly confers

leoda leoþocræftas londbuendum.
30 **Sumum** her ofer eorþan æhta onlihð,
woruldgestreona.   Sum bið wonspedig,
heardsælig hæle,   biþ hwæþre gleaw
modes cræfta.   Sum mægenstrengo
furþor onfehð.   Sum freolic bið
35 wlitig on wæstmum.   Sum biþ woðbora,
giedda giffæst.   Sum biþ gearuwyrdig.
Sum bið on huntoþe   hreðeadigra
deora dræfend.   Sum dyre bið
woruldricum men.   Sum bið wiges heard,
40 beadocræftig beorn,   þær bord stunað.
Sum in mæðle mæg   modsnottera
folcrædenne   forð gehycgan,
þær witena biþ   worn ætsomne.
Sum mæg wrætlice   weorc **ahycgan**
45 heahtimbra gehwæs;   hond bið gelæred,
wis ond gewealden,   swa bið wyrhtan ryht,
sele asettan,   con he sidne ræced
fæste gefegan   wiþ færdryrum.
Sum mid hondum mæg   hearpan gretan,
50 ah he gleobeames   gearobrygda list.
Sum bið rynig,   sum ryhtscytte,
sum leoða gleaw,   sum on londe snel,
feþespedig.   Sum **on** fealone wæg
stefnan steoreð,   streamrade con,
55 weorudes wisa,   ofer widne holm,
þonne særofe   snelle mægne
arum bregdað   yðborde neah.
Sum bið syndig,   sum searocræftig
goldes ond gimma,   þonne him gumena weard
60 hateð him to mærþum   maþþum renian.
Sum mæg wæpenþræce,   wige to nytte,

skills to those who inhabit His land. To those on earth,
He grants wealth, treasures from around the globe.

One is poor, unfortunate, but smart.
One is gifted with bodily strength.
One is marvelously philanthropic.
One is a moving songwriter.
One is quick to argue a cause.
One is quick to hunt animals.
One is beloved by world leaders.
One is a fierce combat fighter, ready for deployment
    when called by superiors.
One is a visionary statesman and effective member of the parliament.
One is a master architect of high-ceilinged buildings, a deft hand,
    disciplined and judicious, drafting expansive halls that last.
One skillfully plays a harp.
One flies swiftly around the track, one makes a good shot,
    one is limber, and one swift, first to finish a foot race.
One maneuvers a ship over harrowing waves.
One knows waterways well.
One pilots merchant vessels over dangerous seas, where ships
    come under attack by pirates who pull alongside and overpower
    with such might as to seize control of precious cargo.
One is a swimmer.
One masters the making of jewelry and gold out of a love
    for beauty and precision, and not merely for commission
    from the leaders of men.
One has a mind for warfare, and makes tools for use in war—

modcræftig smið   monige gefremman,
þonne he gewyrceð   to wera hilde
helm oþþe hupseax   oððe heaþubyrnan,
65 scirne mece   oððe scyldes rond,
fæste **gefeged**   wið flyge gares.
Sum bið arfæst   ond ælmesgeorn,
þeawum geþyde.   Sum bið þegn gehweorf
on meoduhealle.   Sum bið meares gleaw,
70 **wicgcræfta** wis.   Sum gewealdenmod
þafað in geþylde   þæt he þonne sceal.
Sum domas con,   þær dryhtguman
ræd eahtiað.   Sum bið hrædtæfle.
Sum bið gewittig   æt winþege,
75 beorhyrde god.   Sum bið bylda til
ham to **hebbanne**.   Sum bið heretoga,
fyrdwisa from.   Sum biþ folcwita.
Sum biþ æt **þearfe**   þristhydigra
þegn mid his þeodne.   Sum geþyld hafað,
80 fæstgongel ferð.   Sum bið fugelbona,
hafeces cræftig.   Sum bið to horse hwæt.
Sum bið swiðsnel,   hafað searolic gomen,
gleodæda gife   for gumþegnum,
leoht ond leoþuwac.   Sum bið leofwende,
85 hafað mod ond word   monnum geþwære.
Sum her geornlice   gæstes þearfe
mode bewindeþ,   ond him metudes **est**
ofer eorðwelan   ealne geceoseð.
Sum bið deormod   deofles gewinnes,
90 bið a wið firenum   in gefeoht gearo.
Sum cræft hafað   circnytta fela,
mæg on lofsongum   lifes waldend
hlude hergan,   hafað healice
beorhte stefne.   Sum bið boca gleaw,

an able smith, hammering swords, helmets, and coats
   of mail to protect from flying spears.
Honorable, virtuous, and obedient, one eagerly makes large donations to
   the poor.
One returns after military service to a town hall.
One trains horses for equestrian events.
One is ruled by the mind, exercises patience when the occasion calls.
One shows good judgment during an assembly.
One throws the dice and beats the odds.
One is a connoisseur of fine wines.
One brews a delicious beer.
One is a noted building contractor, able to construct any home.
One is a noted general in the armed forces.
One is a well-sought counselor.
One is known for heroic deeds and staunch faith in the Lord.
One possesses a determined spirit and shows great patience.
One hunts game birds and breeds hawks.
One is gallant on a horse.
One, humorous and quick-witted, has a gift of performing for audiences,
   possessing a light heart.
One is endearing, an ability to charm and enchant the people.
One readily perceives in mind needs of the spirit
   and the abundance of God is chosen over earthly wealth.
One is courageous and steadfast in the face of the devil's temptations
   and resists his sins.
One serves avidly as a church deacon and praises the Lord in elevated tones.
One is well-read on books of folklore.

95 larum leoþufæst.   Sum biþ listhendig
   to awritanne   wordgeryno.
   Nis nu ofer eorþan   ænig monna
   mode þæs cræftig,   ne þæs mægeneacen,
   þæt hi æfre anum   ealle weorþen
100 gegearwade,   þy læs him gilp sceððe,
   oþþe fore þære mærþe   mod astige,
   gif he hafaþ ana   ofer ealle men
   wlite ond wisdom   ond weorca blæd;
   ac he missenlice   monna cynne
105 gielpes styreð   ond his giefe bryttað,
   sumum on cystum,   sumum on cræftum,
   sumum on wlite,   sumum on wige,
   sumum he syleð monna   milde heortan,
   þeawfæstne geþoht,   sum biþ þeodne hold.
110 Swa weorðlice   wide tosaweð
   dryhten his duguþe.   A þæs dom age,
   leohtbære lof,   se us þis lif giefeð
   ond his milde mod   monnum cyþeð.

Another is clever at writing word games.

Presently, no one on earth is so brilliant
or talented as to accomplish all of these things, lest
vanity wound, fame cause the head to swell,
convinced that one might outshine all mankind in beauty,
judgment, and superb works. But God invariably discourages
mankind from self-importance, and with grace bequeaths gifts
to one in honor, to the other in influence, to one in splendor, to one
in battle; to one He gives a peaceful heart, a moral character,
and one is faithful to a master. So commendably does He broadly
broadcast His gifts. Thus, let Him bear our light-filled praises,
He who confers life and reveals to all mankind His gentle heart.

Precepts

ðus frod fæder   freobearn lærde,
modsnottor **mon**,   maga cystum eald,
wordum wisfæstum,   þæt he wel þunge:
"Do a þætte duge,   deag þin gewyrhtu;
5 god þe biþ symle   goda gehwylces
frea ond fultum,   feond þam oþrum
wyrsan gewyrhta.   Wene þec þy betran,
efn elne þis   a þenden þu lifge.
Fæder ond modor   freo þu mid heortan,
10 maga gehwylcne,   gif him sy meotud on lufan.
Wes þu þinum yldrum   arfæst symle,
fægerwyrde,   ond þe in ferðe læt
þine lareowas   leofe in mode,
þa þec geornast   to gode trymmen."
15 Fæder eft his sunu   frod gegrette
oþre siþe: "Heald elne þis!
Ne freme firene,   ne næfre freonde þinum,
mæge man ne geþafa,   þy læs þec meotud oncunne,
þæt þu sy wommes gewita.   He þe mid wite gieldeð,
20 swylce þam oþrum   mid eadwelan."
ðriddan syþe   þoncsnottor guma
breostgehygdum   his bearn lærde:
"Ne gewuna wyrsa,   widan feore,
ængum eahta,   ac þu þe anne genim
25 to gesprecan symle   spella ond lara
rædhycgende.   Sy ymb rice swa hit mæge."

Precepts

Jay Parini

So did the father, shrewd himself, experienced in choices,
teach his gentle son with words of hard-won truth,
and wishing him to grow in wisdom's ways:

Do good works always, and your work will prosper.

God will protect you, as he aids the virtuous;
the Devil will confound the works of others.

Teach yourself what's right, and do this bravely to the end of time.

Love both your parents, kith and kin, if they love God.

Be faithful to your elders, kind in words; think well of teachers,
and of those who would instruct you in the ways of virtue.

Now the wise old father spoke again:

Obey me now! Do nothing wrong.
Condone no sinfulness in friends or family;
the Ruler will believe you're an accomplice if you do,
and he will punish you, absolving others, who will surely prosper.

Once again, a third time, this wise father taught his child in heartfelt ways:

Never associate with those beneath you in their virtue.
Choose to be with those bountiful in good and sound suggestions,
wise in parables. Pay no attention to their rank or station.

Feorþan siðe   fæder eft lærde
modleofne magan,   þæt he gemunde þis:
"Ne aswic sundorwine,   ac a symle geheald
30 ryhtum gerisnum.   Ræfn elne þis,
þæt þu næfre fæcne **weorðe**   freonde þinum."
Fiftan siþe   fæder eft ongon
breostgeþoncum   his bearn læran:
"Druncen beorg þe   ond dollic word,
35 man on mode   ond in muþe lyge,
yrre ond æfeste   ond idese lufan.
Forðon sceal æwiscmod   oft siþian,
se þe gewiteð   in wifes lufan,
fremdre meowlan.   þær bið a firena wen,
40 laðlicre scome,   long nið wið god,
geotende gielp.   Wes þu a giedda wis,
wær wið willan,   worda hyrde."
Siextan siþe   swæs eft ongon
þurh bliðne geþoht   his bearn læran:
45 "Ongiet georne   hwæt sy god oþþe yfel,
ond toscead simle   scearpe mode
in sefan þinum   ond þe a þæt selle geceos.
A þe bið gedæled;   gif þe deah hyge,
wunað wisdom in,   ond þu wast geare
50 ondgit yfles,   heald þe elne wið,
feorma þu symle   in þinum ferðe god."
Seofeþan siþe   his sunu lærde
fæder, frod guma,   sægde fela **geongum**:
"Seldan snottor guma   sorgleas blissað,
55 swylce dol seldon   drymeð sorgful
ymb his forðgesceaft,   nefne he fæhþe wite.
Wærwyrde sceal   wisfæst hæle
breostum hycgan,   nales breahtme hlud."

A fourth time he addressed his child, to emphasize his point:

Stick by your friends, don't let them down.
Obey this strictly.
You must not deceive those who stay close.

Then a fifth time he regaled his child with heartfelt wisdom:

Avoid all drunkenness and foolish comments,
sinful heart-thoughts, spoken lies.
Beware of anger, spite, and lustfulness for women.
Often those who fall for stranger, exotic women will regret it,
and will leave ashamed.
In such relations sinfulness takes root, as well as hatefulness of God,
and arrogance as well. Be careful
what you say, and watchful of desires: guard all your words.

*Now again, a sixth time, this good man spoke to his son
with kindly feelings:*

Be quick to separate all good from evil.
Be clever as you do, and favor goodness over evil.
Sharp minds know one from the other,
and with sure perception opt for goodness.

Now a seventh time the father spoke, teaching his young son what to do:

A wise man will encounter sorrows, too.
But fools will rarely mix real pleasure with a sense of foresight—
not unless they know the enemy quite well.
A man of good will must be careful with his words
and, quietly, consider all his options carefully in every way.

Eahtoþan siþe   eald fæder ongon
60 his mago monian   mildum wordum:
"Leorna lare   lærgedefe,
wene þec in wisdom,   weoruda scyppend
hafa þe to hyhte,   haligra gemynd,
ond a soð to syge,   þonne þu secge hwæt."
65 Nigeþan siþe   nægde se gomola,
eald uðwita   sægde eaforan worn:
"Nis nu fela folca   þætte fyrngewritu
healdan wille,   ac him hyge brosnað,
ellen colað,   idlað þeodscype;
70 ne habbað wiht for þæt,   þeah hi wom don
ofer meotudes bibod.   Monig sceal ongieldan
sawelsusles.   Ac læt þinne sefan healdan
forð fyrngewritu   ond frean domas,
þa þe her on mægðe gehwære   men forlætaþ
75 swiþor asigan,   þonne him sy sylfum ryht."
Teoþan siþe   tornsorgna ful,
eald eft ongon   eaforan læran:
"Snyttra bruceþ   þe fore sawle lufan
warnað him wommas   worda ond dæda
80 on sefan symle   ond soþ fremeð;
bið him geofona gehwylc   gode geyced,
meahtum spedig,   þonne he mon flyhð.
Yrre ne læt þe   æfre gewealdan,
heah in hreþre,   heoroworda grund
85 wylme bismitan,   ac him warnað þæt
on geheortum hyge.   Hæle sceal wisfæst
ond gemetlice,   modes snottor,
gleaw in gehygdum,   georn wisdomes,
swa he wið ælda mæg   eades hleotan.

234

And again, another time he spoke,
this father saying kind words for his young son:

Learn what is taught, and faithfully obey.
Instruct yourself in wisdom.
Put your trust in heaven and its saints.
And speak the truth whenever you would speak.

A ninth time, now, the wise old father showed his wisdom:

So many in our time eschew all scriptures,
and their thoughts will often be corrupt, their zeal restrained.
They grow undisciplined and hollow.
They pay no heed to what the Ruler says.
And some will suffer torment for their sins.
But turn yourself back always to the scriptures
and the Lord's clear judgments.
Often people will ignore them—and betray themselves.

A tenth time, full of worry and real fear, the old man spoke to his dear son:

The man who guards himself against all sins of word and deed
makes use of wisdom and advances truth, always in aid of his own soul.
God will increase his talents by degrees.
Whenever he rejects a form of sin, his strength increases.

Do not let anger overwhelm you, even when it rises in your soul.
Let no sharp cutting words disgrace you.
A wise man girds himself against such things.
He should be shrewd and moderate as well,
a modest man, prudent by nature, eager to excel in wisdom always.
Thus he will secure his share of happiness among the rest.

90 Ne beo þu no to tælende,   ne to tweospræce,
    ne þe on mode læt   men to fracoþe,
    ac beo leofwende,   leoht on gehygdum
    ber breostcofan.   Swa þu, min bearn, gemyne
    frode fæder lare   ond þec a wið firenum geheald."

Never be quick to slander others, and beware of flattery.

Be slow to judge the worth of others,
and enjoy their good will toward yourself.
Be cheerful always, spirited, and loving.

In these ways, son, heed my advice, your father's wisdom,
keeping pure, remaining virtuous in every way.

The Order of the World

Wilt þu, fus hæle,   fremdne monnan,
wisne woðboran   wordum gretan,
fricgan felageongne   ymb forðgesceaft,
biddan þe gesecge   sidra gesceafta
5   cræftas cyndelice   cwichrerende,
þa þe **dogra** gehwam   þurh dom godes
bringe wundra fela   wera cneorissum!
Is þara anra gehwam   orgeate tacen,
þam þurh wisdom   woruld ealle con
10   behabban on hreþre,   hycgende mon,
þæt geara iu,   gliwes cræfte,
mid gieddingum   guman oft wrecan,
rincas rædfæste;   cuþon ryht sprecan,
þæt a fricgende   fira cynnes
15   ond secgende   searoruna gespon
a gemyndge mæst   monna wiston.
Forþon scyle ascian,   se þe on elne leofað,
deophydig mon,   dygelra gesceafta,
bewritan in gewitte   wordhordes cræft,
20   fæstnian ferðsefan,   þencan forð teala;
ne sceal þæs aþreotan   þegn modigne,
þæt he wislice   woruld fulgonge.
Leorna þas lare.   Ic þe lungre sceal
meotudes mægensped   maran gesecgan,
25   þonne þu hygecræftig   in hreþre mæge
mode gegripan.   Is **sin** meaht forswiþ.

A Song of the Cosmos

Daniel Tobin

Hard-striving soul, greet the wayfaring stranger,
To the keen-sighted singer give welcoming words,
Question the questing one of all the worlds before,
Implore him to tell of incalculable creations,
The innate artful forces forever quickening
That day after day under God's dominion
Bring wonders laid bare to faring generations.
Day to day each makes its mark manifest
To one who with wisdom beholds the world whole
In the mind's clasp—the one who contemplates
What others gave voice to long ago
In thrumming rhythms and wide-reckoning songs:
Those kinsmen whose ken was strong, who with glee
And searching wit—with their bearing witness—
Drew forth common humankind's fullest measure,
Full mindful themselves of the weave of mysteries.

To live therefore a probing and emboldened life
One should fathom the world-trove's buried ends,
Should scribe into mind the word-hoard's might and skill,
Make thought a strong march and meditate steadfastly
So the noble servant will never grow way-worn,
Tholling in wisdom through each earthly arrival.

School yourself in these sciences! Now let me sing
Of the Given's glory, that like wind through sedge
Outstrips your art, though the heart grasps it
By staying steady—is your soul's heft stout enough?

Nis þæt monnes gemet   moldhrerendra,
þæt he mæge in hreþre   his heah geweorc
furþor aspyrgan   þonne him frea sylle
30 to ongietanne   godes agen bibod;
ac we sculon þoncian   þeodne mærum
awa to ealdre,   þæs þe us se eca cyning
on gæste wlite   forgiefan wille
þæt we eaðe magon   upcund rice
35 forð gestigan,   gif us on ferðe geneah
ond we willað healdan   heofoncyninges bibod.
Gehyr nu þis herespel   ond þinne hyge gefæstna.
Hwæt, on frymþe gescop   fæder ælmihtig,
heah hordes weard,   heofon ond eorðan,
40 sæs sidne grund,   sweotule gesceafte,
þa nu in þam þream   þurh þeodnes hond
heaþ ond hebbaþ   þone halgan blæd.
Forþon eal swa teofanade,   se þe teala cuþe,
æghwylc wiþ oþrum;   sceoldon eal beran
45 stiþe stefnbyrd,   swa him se steora bibead
missenlice gemetu   þurh þa miclan gecynd.
Swa hi to worulde   wlite forþ berað
dryhtnes duguþe   ond his dæda þrym,
lixende lof   in þa longan tid,
50 fremmaþ fæstlice   frean ece word
in þam frumstole   þe him frea sette,
hluttor heofones weard,   healdað georne
mere gemære;   meaht forð tihð
heofoncondelle   ond holmas mid,
55 laþað ond lædeþ   lifes agend
in his anes fæþm   ealle gesceafta.
Swa him wideferh   wuldor stondeþ,

It is not with human scales, inconstant scud of dust,
That one weighs the portion his wit strains to grasp
Of the most-high work: the code of God's design.
For we shall thank the Chief of All, Unbounded,
From always back to Nil so the everlasting King
May astonish with radiance, shearing off all want,
So that, knuckled-down, we may scale the high walls
Choosing as hand holds the heavenly King's word.

Take hold of what you are! Hear my song of marvels!
Listen! In the creation's quick the almighty Father,
The cosmic hoard's Keeper, authored heaven and earth,
The sea's breadth and depth, and everything one sees
That at this moment lifts up its thrum of praise,
The gathered consort held in the holiest Hands.

In this way, with the windward of his forethought,
God assembles all together, the whole ensemble—
Oarsmen tuned strictly to the Steersman's many measures—
So the realms bear up, bear onward through all becoming.

So through time's tides the great Lord's noble throng
Carry across to the world His fulgent emanations,
His works' eminence, his glory's dawn-mantle;
Steadfastly they mount the Master's endless Song
From thrones first fashioned by Heaven's utter Guardian.
With all they are they hold gladly the splendid course.
His rowing is mighty. It quickens the welkin's candles,
Begets the teeming oceans—with one gesture,
Prolific, He holds and calls and leads all life
Who harbors in his breast the abundant womb of All.

So never-ending He abides, Abounding Splendor,

ealra demena   þam gedefestan,
þe us þis lif gescop,   ond þis leohte beorht
60 cymeð morgna gehwam   ofer misthleoþu
wadan ofer wægas   wundrum gegierwed,
ond mid ærdæge   eastan snoweð
wlitig ond wynsum   wera cneorissum;
lifgendra gehwam   leoht forð biereð
65 bronda beorhtost,   ond his brucan mot
æghwylc on eorþan,   þe him eagna gesihð
sigora soðcyning   syllan wolde.
Gewiteð þonne mid þy wuldre   on westrodor
forðmære tungol   faran on heape,
70 oþþæt on æfenne   ut garsecges
grundas pæþeð,   glom oþer cigð;
niht æfter cymeð,   healdeð nydbibod
halgan dryhtnes.   Heofontorht swegl
scir gescyndeð   in gesceaft godes
75 under foldan fæþm,   farende tungol.
Forþon nænig fira   þæs frod leofað
þæt his mæge æspringe   þurh his ægne sped **witan**,
hu geond grund færeð   goldtorht sunne
in þæt wonne genip   under wætra geþring,
80 oþþe hwa þæs leohtes   londbuende
brucan mote,   siþþan heo ofer brim hweorfeð.
Forþon swa teofenede,   se þe teala cuþe,
dæg wiþ nihte,   deop wið hean,
lyft wið lagustream,   lond wiþ wæge,
85 flod wið flode,   fisc wið yþum.
Ne waciað þas geweorc,   ac he **hi** wel healdeð;
stondað stiðlice   bestryþed fæste

Of all judges most gentle, mercy's full measure,
Who forges life in us. And this lightsome shimmer
Moves morning to morning through night's misty slopes,
Passing over waters wondrously adorned,
And from dawn's east it hastens luminously west,
Brilliant and beguiling to each new generation.
For everything living it engenders its light,
Brightest of torches through which all may flourish,
Each one of us on earth given the eyes to see,
Being entrusted with sight by victory's true King.
Then together with its train the star's blinding brilliance
Dies away beyond the western door, exalted star
Whose sail skirts the ether like a shining shire,
Until with dim descent the gloaming summons night
From ocean's depths—a second shadowing
That holds in store the Master's adamant command,
So the wayfaring sun follows along God's course
And bends to the bosom of the earth's embrace.

No one, therefore, with all mind's precious wisdom,
Can discern while they live the living Font from which
This flow glories forth, from where the gold-reined sun
Fares forward beyond earth into darkening mists,
Descending deeper under waters' thronging waves,
Or who of those who dwell in light and on land
Call themselves content after it roams over the brim.

So therefore the One who knows full well the way
To fix together daytime, nighttime, depth and height,
Sky-road and river, the waves and solid land,
Floodtides and fields, the fish and all their waters—
His works do not weaken. Upheld by healing Hands,
They stand steadfast, fastened unbreakably

miclum meahtlocum   in þam mægenþrymme
mid þam sy ahefed   heofon ond eorþe.
90 Beoð þonne eadge   þa þær in wuniað,
hyhtlic is þæt **heorðwerud.**   þæt is herga mæst,
eadigra unrim,   engla þreatas.
Hy geseoð symle   hyra sylfra cyning,
eagum on wlitað,   habbað æghwæs genoh.
95 Nis him wihte won,   þam þe wuldres cyning
geseoþ in swegle;   him is symbel ond dream
ece unhwylen   eadgum to frofre.
Forþon scyle mon gehycgan   þæt he meotude hyre;
æghwylc ælda bearna   forlæte idle lustas,
100 læne lifes wynne,   fundige him to lissa blisse,
forlæte heteniþa   gehwone sigan
mid synna fyrnum,   fere him to þam sellan rice.

By a net of bonds through the Bright Abounding
That leavens and sustains the heavens and the earth.
They are rife with blessedness who bide in that estate,
Those who crowd beside the hearth, the hallowed—
I am mute to say—those numberless angelic throngs.
What they see with their eyes is an everlasting feast,
Their King encompassing the circuit of their gaze
So that each one forever has forever enough
For in Him there is no scintilla of shadow
For they perceive plainly in sonorous resplendence
The King of All Wonders. So ecstasy and peace
Befit the joyous in the plenty of time's Plenitude.

Everyone born should remember this therefore:
Keep earshot of the measure made deathless by the One,
Forget Life's idle longings, its lissome delights,
Let it draw you, striving, to that utmost loving Bliss
One finds when one fares to the Excellent Kingdom;
Leave behind isolation, self-born suffering,
Forsake your harbored malice—let them all drift away.

from Solomon and Saturn

Salomon cwæð:
"Dol bið se ðe gæð   on deop wæter,
se ðe sund nafað   ne gesegled scip
235 ne fugles flyht,   ne he mid fotum ne mæg
grund geræcan;   huru se godes cunnað
full dyslice,   dryhtnes meahta."
Saturnus cuæð:
"Ac hwæt is se dumba,   se ðe on sumre dene resteð?
240 Swiðe snyttrað,   hafað seofon tungan;
hafað tungena gehwylc   XX orda,
hafað orda gehwylc   engles snytro,
ðara ðe wile anra hwylc   uppe bringan,
ðæt ðu ðære gyldnan gesiehst   Hierusalem
245 weallas blican   and hiera winrod lixan,
soðfæstra segn.   Saga hwæt ic mæne."
Salomon cuæð:
"Bec sindon breme,   bodiað geneahhe
weotodne willan   ðam ðe wiht hygeð.
250 Gestrangað hie and gestaðeliað   staðolfæstne geðoht,
amyrgað modsefan   manna gehwylces
of ðreamedlan   ðisses lifes."
Saturnus cwæð:
"Bald bið se ðe onbyregeð   boca cræftes;
255 symle bið ðe wisra   ðe hira geweald hafað."

Two passages from
The Second Dialogue of Solomon and Saturn
Fiona Sampson

1.

Solomon said—
He's a fool who goes out on deep water
unable to swim, without a boat's sails
or bird's wings, unable to touch bottom
with his foot. And he tests God's power
most unwisely.

Saturn said—
But what dumb creature settles in some valley,
gathering wisdom: seven-tongued,
each tongue with twenty buds,
each bud with the wisdom of an angel?
Only it can lift you up
to see golden Jerusalem,
her walls gleaming and her victorious cross shining,
a sign of enduring truth. Say what I mean—

Solomon said—
Books are revered. They proclaim
the divine order to whoever listens a little.
They strengthen and restore reason,
cheer each human heart
through life's miseries.

Saturn said—
He who tastes books' insight is bold;
he who takes on their power always the wiser.

Salomon cuæð:

"Sige hie onsendað   soðfæstra gehwam,
hælo hyðe,   ðam ðe hie lufað."

Saturnus cwæð:

260 "An wise is   on woroldrice
ymb ða me fyrwet bræc   L wintra
dæges and niehtes   ðurh deop gesceaft;
geomrende gast   deð nu gena swa,
ærðon me geunne   ece dryhten
265 ðæt me geseme   snoterra monn."

Salomon cwæð:

"Soð is ðæt ðu sagast;   seme ic ðe recene
ymb ða wrætlican wiht.   Wilt ðu ðæt ic ðe secgge?
An fugel siteð   on **Filistina**
270 middelgemærum;   munt is hine ymbutan,
geap gylden weall.   Georne hine healdað
witan Filistina,   wenað ðæs ðe naht is,
ðæt hiene him scyle eall ðeod   on genæman
wæpna ecggum;   hie ðæs wære cunnon,
275 **healdað** hine niehta gehwylce   norðan and suðan
on twa healfa   tu hund wearda.
Se fugel hafað   IIII heafdu
medumra manna,   and he is on middan hwælen;
geowes he hafað fiðeru   and griffus fet,
280 ligeð lonnum fæst,   locað unhiere,
swiðe swingeð   and his searo hringeð,
gilleð geomorlice   and his gyrn sefað,
wylleð hine on ðam wite,   wunað unlustum,
singgeð syllice;   seldum æfre
285 his leoma licggað.   Longað hine hearde,

Solomon said—
Each of these truth-tellers brings victory,
salvation's safekeeping, to those who love them.

Saturn said—
Curiosity has pressed me for fifty winters,
day and night, through direst destiny,
about one thing on this earth.
Now, when the Eternal Ruler allows
a wiser man to answer me,
the desire to know remains.

Solomon said—
What you say is true. I can tell you now
about that complex creature you'd like me to speak of.
A bird sits amid the Philistines,
at the heart of their territory. There's a mound around it,
a gapped golden wall holding it fast.
The Philistines' wise men falsely believe
that a tribe of foreigners will abduct it
by force; reckoning on this
they keep it prisoner, nightly dividing
two hundred guards to north and south.
The bird has four heads,
each like a normal man's, and a whale's torso.
It has vulture feathers and griffin's feet.
It lies chained up, glaring fiercely,
thumping loudly and jangling its fetters;
shrieks mournfully and wheezes-out misery
it wishes on the wise man. It lives without wanting to,
limbs stiffly extended,
constantly sending strange cries into the Hall;

ðynceð him ðæt sie ðria XXX   ðusend wintra
ær he domdæges   dynn gehyre.

Nyste hine on ðære foldan   fira ænig
eorðan cynnes,   ærðon ic hine ana onfand
290 and hine ða **gebendan** het   ofer brad wæter,
ðæt hine se modega heht   Melotes bearn,
Filistina fruma,   fæste gebindan,
lonnum belucan   wið leodgryre.
ðone fugel hatað   feorbuende,
295 Filistina **fruman,**   uasa mortis."
Saturnus cwæð:
"Ac hwæt is ðæt wundor   ðe geond ðas worold færeð,
styrnenga gæð,   staðolas beateð,
aweceð wopdropan,   winneð oft hider?
300 Ne mæg hit steorra ne stan   ne se steapa gimm,
wæter ne wildeor   wihte beswican,
ac him on hand gæð   heardes and hnesces,
micles **and** mætes;   him to mose sceall
gegangan geara gehwelce   grundbuendra,
305 lyftfleogendra,   laguswemmendra,
ðria ðreoteno   ðusendgerimes."
Salomon cuæð:
"Yldo beoð on eorðan   æghwæs cræftig;
mid hiðendre   hildewræsne,
310 rumre racenteage,   ræceð wide,
langre linan,   lisseð eall ðæt heo wile.
Beam heo abreoteð   and bebriceð telgum,
astyreð **standendne**   stefn on siðe,
afilleð hine on foldan;   friteð æfter ðam
315 wildne fugol.   Heo oferwigeð wulf,
hio oferbideð stanas,   heo oferstigeð style,

imagines three times thirty thousand winters
before the din of doomsday.
It was known to no one,
not one human being, until I discovered it
and ordered it to be brought captive across the wide sea.
The proud son of Melot, chief of the Philistines,
commanded that it be bound fast,
locked in chains to counter the people's terror.
Distant civilizations, the ancestors of the Philistines,
call that bird The Instrument of Death.

Saturn said—
But what wonder travels this world
unstoppably, razing foundations,
starting tears, often victorious?
Neither star nor stone nor ostentatious gem,
water nor wild beast, can deflect it one whit,
but into its hand go hard and soft,
small and big. Into it
every single earth-dweller, air-skimmer, sea-swimmer—
three times thirteen thousand of them—
is sure to sink.

Solomon said—
On earth, age overpowers everything
with press-gang prison-irons.
That great chain yaws wide,
a long line capturing all it desires.
It uproots trees and breaks branches,
shakes the standing stem,
gorges on soil, then gobbles down
the wild bird; it overwhelms the wolf.
It outlives stones, it outstays steel,

hio abiteð iren mid ome, deð usic swa."

. . . .

Saturnus cwæð:

"Saga ðu me, Salomon cyning, sunu Dauides,
355 hwæt beoð ða feowere fægæs rapas?"
Salomon cuæð:

"Gewurdene wyrda,
ðæt beoð ða feowere fæges rapas."
Saturnus cwæð:

360 "Ac hwa demeð ðonne dryhtne Criste
on domes dæge, ðonne he demeð eallum gesceaftum?"
Salomon cwæð:

"Hwa dear ðonne dryhtne deman, ðe us of duste geworhte,
365 nergend of niehtes wunde? Ac sæge me hwæt nærende wæron."
Saturnus cwæð:

"Ac forhwon ne mot seo sunne side gesceafte
scire geondscinan? Forhwam besceadeð heo
muntas and moras and monige ec
370 weste stowa? Hu geweorðeð ðæt?"
Salomon cuæð:

"Ac forhwam næron **eorðwelan** ealle **gedæled**
leodum gelice? Sum to lyt hafað,
godes grædig; hine god seteð
ðurh geearnunga eadgum to ræste."
375 Saturnus cwæð:

it eats up iron with rust: does the same to us.

2.

Saturn said—
Tell me, King Solomon, Son of David,
what are the four ropes that condemn a man?

Solomon said—
That which has happened:
those are the four ropes that condemn a man.

Saturn said—
Then who judges Christ the Lord
on Doomsday, when he judges all creation?

Solomon said—
Who dares judge God the Savior, who made us from dust,
out of night's wound?   Tell me, what was but was not?

Saturn said—
Why can't the sun shine through all creation
and light it: why does it darken
mountains, moors and much waste ground?
How does that happen?

Solomon said—
Why isn't earthly reward shared-out
equally? One has too little
and longs for good things; through his merit,
God places him at rest among the Blessed Ones.

Saturn said—

"Ac forhwan beoð ða gesiðas   somod ætgædre,
wop and hleahtor?   Full oft hie weorðgeornra
sælða toslitað;   hu gesæleð ðæt?"
Salomon cuæð:
380 "Unlæde bið and ormod   se ðe a wile
geomrian on gihðe;   se bið gode fracoðast."
Saturnus cwæð:
"Forhwon ne moton we ðonne ealle   mid onmedlan
gegnum gangan   in godes rice?"
385 Salomon cwæð:
"Ne mæg fyres feng   ne forstes cile,
snaw ne sunne   somod eardian,
aldor geæfnan,   ac hira sceal anra gehwylc
onlutan and onliðigan   ðe hafað læsse **mægn**."
Saturnus cwæð:
390 "Ac forhwon ðonne leofað   se wyrsa leng?
Se wyrsa ne wat   in woroldrice
on his mægwinum   maran are."
Salomon cwæð:
395 "Ne mæg mon **forildan**   ænige hwile
ðone deoran sið,   ac he hine adreogan sceall."
Saturnus cwæð:
"Ac hu gegangeð ðæt?   Gode oððe yfle,
ðonne hie beoð ðurh ane   idese acende,
400 twegen getwinnas,   ne bið hira tir gelic.
Oðer bið unlæde on eorðan,   oðer bið eadig,
swiðe leoftæle   mid leoda duguðum;

Why do crying and laughter come together
like companions? They often destroy high-minded contentment—
how does that happen?

Solomon said—
He who likes to worry and grumble
is miserable and cowardly: he disgusts God most.

Saturn said—
Why can't we all go
proudly into God's kingdom?

Solomon said—
Neither fire's embrace and frost's chill
nor snow and sun can live together,
nor can age be stirred up. Whatever has less power
must bend and yield.

Saturn said—
Why do the worst live long?
They haven't found greater friendship or family favor
in this world.

Solomon said—
Man cannot avoid the hard journey
through aging, but must endure it.

Saturn said—
But how do good and evil happen?
When twins are born from the same woman
their success is unequal.
One is unlucky on earth; the other lucky,
popular with leaders.

oðer leofað   lytle hwile,
swiceð on ðisse sidan gesceafte,   and ðonne eft mid sorgum
gewiteð.
405 Fricge ic ðec, hlaford Salomon,   hwæðres bið hira folgoð betra?"
Salomon cuæð:
"Modor ne rædeð,   ðonne heo magan cenneð,
hu him weorðe geond worold   widsið sceapen.
Oft heo to bealwe   bearn afedeð,
410 seolfre to sorge,   siððan dreogeð
his earfoðu   orlegstunde.
Heo ðæs afran sceall   oft and gelome
grimme greotan,   ðonne he geong færeð,
hafað wilde mod,   werige heortan,
415 sefan sorgfullne,   slideð geneahhe,
werig, wilna leas,   wuldres bedæled,
hwilum higegeomor   healle weardað,
leofað leodum feor;   locað geneahhe
fram ðam unlædan   **agen** hlaford.
420 Forðan nah seo modor geweald,   ðonne heo magan cenneð,
bearnes blædes,   ac sceall on gebyrd faran
an æfter anum;   ðæt is eald **gesceaft**."

The one lives for a short while,
wanders about this wide creation, then leaves it sadly.
I ask you, Lord Solomon, which has the better lot?

Solomon said—
When she conceives, a mother doesn't decide
what shape the baby's journey will take through the wide world.
She often raises a child to harm,
bringing grief to herself: she suffers
at the harshness of his fate.
Often she keens unstoppably
over that son, when he sets out on some journey
with a restless mind, a weary heart,
a sad soul, slipping easily
into weariness and loss of will. Deprived of honors,
sometimes this grief-struck ghost avoids the Hall,
living far from people, miserable and anxious.
His only lord glances quickly away from him.
So a mother has no power over the child's destiny
when she conceives, but from birth
one thing follows another, as is the way of the world.

Third
Riddle-Hoard

Riddle 28

Biþ foldan dæl   fægre gegierwed
mid þy heardestan   ond mid þy scearpestan
ond mid þy grymmestan   gumena gestreona,
corfen, sworfen,   cyrred, þyrred,
5   bunden, wunden,   blæced, wæced,
frætwed, geatwed,   feorran læded
to durum dryhta.   Dream biŏ in innan
cwicra wihta,   clengeŏ, lengeŏ,
þara þe ær lifgende   longe hwile
10   wilna bruceŏ   ond no wiŏ spriceŏ,
ond þonne æfter deaþe   deman onginneŏ,
meldan mislice.   Micel is to hycganne
wisfæstum menn,   hwæt seo wiht sy.

A Part of Earth Is Made Fairer

Gail Holst–Warhaft

A part of earth is made fairer
by man's hardest treasure.
Fierce at first, it's softened,
shaped, soaked scrubbed,
bound, burnished, bedecked
and brought, strung to the step.
Joy quivers in it for the living
in the halls. It lingers, clinging,
lengthening the revelers' mirth.
Don't censure them—in death
it speaks to one and all;
the wise know what it's called.

Riddle 29

Ic wiht geseah   wundorlice
hornum bitweonum   huþe lædan,
lyftfæt leohtlic,   listum gegierwed,
huþe to þam ham   of þam heresiþe;
5 walde hyre on þære byrig   bur **atimbran**,
searwum asettan,   gif hit swa meahte.
ða cwom wundorlicu wiht   ofer wealles hrof,
seo is eallum cuð   eorðbuendum,
ahredde þa þa huþe   ond to ham **bedraf**
10 wreccan ofer willan,   gewat hyre west þonan
fæhþum feran,   forð **onette**.
Dust stonc to heofonum,   deaw feol on eorþan,
niht forð gewat.   Nænig siþþan
wera gewiste   þære wihte sið.

I Watched a Wonder, a Bright Marauder

Molly Peacock

I watched a wonder,   a bright marauder,
bearing its booty   between its horns.
An etched ship of air,   a silver sky-sliver,
it lugged a month's loot   from its raid on time
to build a great bower   from all it brought back
—if only it might   make plunder into art.

Climbing the sky-cliffs   rose another wonder
its dazzle known   to all dwellers on earth.
It seized the spoils   and drove the silver creature
with all its wrecked wishes   off to the west
(hurling back insults   as it hurried home).

Dust rose to heaven.   Dew fell on earth.
Night went forth.   Nothing afterward then.
No man knew how   to map its path.

Riddle 30

Ic eom legbysig,   lace mid winde,
bewunden mid wuldre,   wedre gesomnad,
fus forðweges,   fyre gebysgad,
bearu blowende,   byrnende gled.
5 Ful oft mec gesiþas   sendað æfter hondum,
þæt mec weras ond wif   wlonce cyssað.
þonne ic mec onhæbbe,   ond hi **onhnigaþ** to me
monige mid miltse,   þær ic monnum sceal
ycan upcyme   eadignesse.

I Dance like Flames

David Constantine

I dance like flames, I lend the winds
Glorious shapes, the fire in me
Eager for exit, feels for the lightning
And breathes me away down the wind. Or you
Cup me in hands from lip to lip
From man to woman, from woman to man
Kiss by kiss or you raise me up
For luck in the house in winter, lit.

Riddle 31

Is þes middangeard   missenlicum
wisum gewlitegad,   wrættum gefrætwad.
Ic seah sellic þing   singan on ræcede;
wiht wæs **nower**   werum on gemonge,
5   sio hæfde wæstum   wundorlicran.
Niþerweard   wæs neb hyre,
fet ond folme   fugele gelice;
no hwæþre fleogan mæg   ne fela gongan,
hwæþre feþegeorn   fremman onginneð,
10   gecoren cræftum,   cyrreð geneahhe
oft ond gelome   eorlum on gemonge,
siteð æt symble,   sæles bideþ,
hwonne ær heo cræft hyre   cyþan mote
werum on wonge.   Ne heo þær wiht þigeð
15   þæs þe him æt blisse   beornas **habbað**.
Deor domes georn,   hio dumb wunað;
hwæþre hyre is on fote   fæger hleoþor,
wynlicu woðgiefu.   Wrætlic me þinceð,
hu seo wiht mæge   wordum lacan
20   þurh fot neoþan,   frætwed hyrstum.
Hafað hyre on halse,   þonne hio hord warað,
bær, beagum deall,   broþor sine,
mæg mid mægne.   Micel is to hycgenne
wisum woðboran,   hwæt **sio** wiht sie.

Wondrous Is This World, Incomparable
David Wojahn

Wondrous is this world, incomparable
Its trappings and adornments.
And in a house I watch a strange thing singing.
Bizarre beyond words is its form
And unearthly is this creature's shape.
Strange bird—though her beak sags down
Her feet and talons bristle upward.
Though she cannot take wing or waddle,
She puffs herself up, and attends to her work,
Her specialty. All the men have gathered
And among them she circles. Beside them as they feast,
She roosts and waits her turn. And then,
How artfully her talents entrance them,
These drunken thanes and earls. But not
A bite of food or drink will pass her lips.
Sly, ambitious, yearned-for, she keeps her mouth shut.
But from her *foot* a melody arises:
Ravishing is her gift for song. How wondrous
Strange it is—that jeweled foot singing!
And now her brothers come, supplicants,
Adorning with baubles and ringlets her white
Naked neck. Tell me poets, you who so smugly
Proclaim your vast powers of invention,
What manner of creature is she?

Riddle 33

Wiht cwom æfter wege   wrætlicu liþan,
cymlic from ceole   cleopode to londe,
hlinsade hlude;   **hleahtor** wæs gryrelic,
egesful on earde,   ecge wæron scearpe.
5 Wæs hio hetegrim,   hilde to sæne,
biter beadoweorca;   bordweallas grof,
heardhiþende.   Heterune bond,
sægde searocræftig   ymb hyre sylfre gesceaft:
"Is min modor   **mægða** cynnes
10 þæs deorestan,   þæt is dohtor min
eacen up liden,   swa þæt is ældum cuþ,
firum on folce,   þæt seo on foldan sceal
on ealra londa gehwam   lissum stondan."

A Sea Monster Came Sailing

James McGonigal

A sea monster came sailing   amazing the very waves   she moved upon
and called out to the shore: "Am I not spectacular?"   That voice was
deafening   and then laughter echoed   atrociously miles inland.
Her flanks were so sharp   they could cut you up.   Malignant, I'd say.
It was difficult to make her   turn and fight   but she was merciless
when battle commenced.   Indomitable.   She crushed in our sides.
And spoke in riddles   —black magic not white—   these cunning words:
"My mother sprung   from a race of pure women   becomes my daughter
in the fullness of time.   As everyone knows   throughout the earth
she is happy to reach   your farthest shore."

Riddle 34

Ic wiht geseah   in wera burgum,
seo þæt feoh fedeð.   Hafað fela toþa;
nebb biþ hyre æt nytte,   niþerweard gongeð,
hiþeð holdlice   ond to ham tyhð,
5   wæþeð geond weallas,   wyrte seceð;
aa heo þa findeð,   þa þe fæst ne biþ;
læteð hio þa wlitigan,   wyrtum fæste,
stille stondan   on staþolwonge,
beorhte blican,   blowan ond growan.

At Rest, Laborers Lean on Me

Gary Soto

At rest, laborers lean on me,
Then lead me to the barn
To pitch feed at drooling cattle.
I'm both tooth and nose,
A hurtful thing if you're a barking dog.
I herd chicken droppings to the fence,
Scratch the garden's terraced rows,
And drag the fields for an early summer harvest.
On my prongs, I lift wheat into a golden pile.
A hero to the laborer,
I return home riding on his shoulder!
If you look closely, you'll see smeared bee and moth,
Maybe an errant flower,
Just past blooming.

Riddle 35

Mec se wæta wong,   wundrum freorig,
of his innaþe   ærist cende.
Ne wat ic mec beworhtne   wulle flysum,
hærum þurh heahcræft,   hygeþoncum min.
5 Wundene me ne beoð wefle,   ne ic wearp hafu,
ne þurh þreata geþræcu   þræd me ne hlimmeð,
ne æt me hrutende   hrisil scriþeð,
ne mec ohwonan   sceal **am** cnyssan.
Wyrmas mec ne awæfan   wyrda cræftum,
10 þa þe geolo godwebb   geatwum frætwað.
Wile mec mon hwæþre seþeah   wide ofer eorþan
hatan for hæleþum   hyhtlic gewæde.
Saga soðcwidum,   searoþoncum gleaw,
wordum wisfæst,   hwæt þis **gewæde** sy.

Dank Earth, Dealing Dumbfounding Chill

Robert B. Shaw

Dank earth, dealing dumbfounding chill,
first brought me forth, fostered my breaking
clear of its clutching inner keep.
My musing mind mulls over my nature:
wrought not of wool of ram or wether
nor of the hairs of wild beasts hunted
and closely woven with wondrous craft.
No woof, no warp, no weaving made me.
No taut thread hummed as I took form,
no shuttle sang me its rasping song,
no treadle thumped, keeping time with the tune.
Those exquisitely embroidering worms
whose caches of yellow silk crowd cocoons,
who spin their skeins with the skill of Fates,
forbore to fashion me of their fabric.
Even so, to every end of the earth,
with worthy experts offering witness,
people proclaim me the kind of apparel
a man can count on in a tight corner.
Might and mettle meet in my mesh.
You, whose wit can winnow this welter,
culling out clues, now use your cunning
to reach the answer this riddle requires:
lay out language to label this garment.

Riddle 36

Ic wiht geseah   on wege feran,
seo wæs wrætlice   wundrum gegierwed.
Hæfde feowere   fet under wombe
ond ehtuwe   ufon on hrycge;
5   hæfde tu fiþru   ond twelf eagan
ond siex heafdu.   Saga hwæt hio wære.
For flodwegas;   ne wæs þæt na fugul ana,
ac þær wæs æghwylces   anra gelicnes
horses ond monnes,   hundes ond fugles,
10   ond eac wifes wlite.   þu wast, gif þu const,
to gesecganne,   þæt we soð witan,
hu þære wihte   wise gonge.

Riddle 37

Ic þa wihte geseah;   womb wæs on hindan
þriþum aþrunten.   þegn folgade,
mægenrofa man,   ond micel hæfde
gefered þæt hit felde,   fleah þurh his eage.
5   Ne swylteð he symle,   þonne syllan sceal
innað þam oþrum,   ac him eft cymeð
bot in bosme,   blæd biþ ar. ræred;
he sunu wyrceð,   bið him sylfa fæder.

It Was a Creature Traveling with Pendulum Motion
Jacqueline Jones LaMon

It was a creature traveling with pendulum motion
Dressed for the occasion in flamboyant wonder:
Four feet beneath its belly, eight springing from its back
Two wings, twelve eyes, six bobbing heads. Tell me.
It traveled where night is fluid, not the ways of birds,
but reminiscent of horse and of man, of hound and fowl together.
And then too, of a woman. Tell me. Tell me how it moves.

I Saw This Creature, His Belly Arseways
Paddy Bushe

I saw this creature, his belly arseways,
Bloated to bejasus. He had a heavy,
A macho guy, who with some almighty
Huffing and puffing blew his eye out.
He'll never snuff it; what he spreads around
He calls in, kiss of life. Full of himself,
He's his own seed, breed and generation.

Riddle 38

Ic þa wiht geseah   wæpnedcynnes,
geoguðmyrþe grædig;   him on gafol forlet
ferðfriþende   feower wellan
scire sceotan,   on gesceap þeotan.
5   Mon maþelade,   se þe me gesægde:
    "Seo wiht, gif hio gedygeð,   duna briceð;
    gif he tobirsteð,   bindeð cwice."

I Watched This Big Well-Hung Young Laddie

Edwin Morgan

I watched this big well-hung young laddie
As he grabbed the four bright fountains
His mother had set gushing for him.
An onlooker said: "Living, he'll turn
The furrows to loam, and dead,
He'll catch us with belts and whips too.
And all this is well—
For both use and joy
Meet in this boy."

Poems
about Dying

Bede's Death Song: West Saxon Version

For þam nedfere   næni wyrþeþ
þances snotera,   þonne him þearf sy
to gehicgenne   ær his heonengange
hwæt his gaste   godes oþþe yfeles
5   æfter deaþe heonon   demed weorþe.

Bede's Dying Words

Anthony Cronin

Before the inevitable hour looms
When, however unwilling,
You must face the final court
You cannot give enough thought
To the state of your account,
Its balance of good and evil,
For when that hour arrives
It will be too late
To add or subtract,
Regret or amend.

The Fortunes of Men

Ful oft þæt gegongeð,   mid godes meahtum,
þætte wer ond wif   in woruld cennað
bearn mid gebyrdum   ond mid bleom gyrwað,
tennaþ ond tætaþ,   oþþæt seo tid cymeð,
5   gegæð gearrimum,   þæt þa geongan leomu,
liffæstan leoþu,   geloden weorþað.
Fergað swa ond feþað   fæder ond modor,
giefað ond gierwaþ.   God ana wat
hwæt him weaxendum   winter bringað!
10   Sumum þæt gegongeð   on geoguðfeore
þæt se endestæf   earfeðmæcgum
wealic weorþeð.   Sceal hine wulf etan,
har hæðstapa;   hinsiþ þonne
modor bimurneð.   Ne bið swylc monnes geweald!
15   Sumne sceal hungor ahiþan,   sumne sceal hreoh fordrifan,
sumne sceal gar agetan,   sumne guð abreotan.
Sum sceal leomena leas   lifes neotan,
folmum ætfeohtan,   sum on feðe lef,
seonobennum seoc,   sar cwanian,
20   murnan meotudgesceaft   mode gebysgad.
Sum sceal on holte   of hean **beame**
fiþerleas feallan;   bið on flihte seþeah,
laceð on lyfte,   oþþæt lengre ne bið
westem wudubeames.   þonne he on wyrtruman
25   sigeð sworcenferð,   sawle bireafod,
fealleþ on foldan,   feorð biþ on siþe.
Sum sceal on feþe   on feorwegas
nyde gongan   ond his nest beran,

The Fortunes of Men

Kelly Cherry

Thanks be to God, two become three,
Caring for their child from cradle through youth,
But only God knows the grown man's fate.
Parental guidance prepares him for manhood—
The child is clothed in colorful costumes,
Is taught to walk and talk and obey,
Adored, encouraged, and ever praised.
Yet—mourned by their mothers—some men die young,
As savage wolves separate out and surround
This lad or that, attack, and dismember
His small body limb by motionless limb.
Mere people cannot prevent or alter
The events prepared by purpose divine.
Some men starve, or storms bury them
At sea, and some by spears are slain
In war. A blinded man worries his way
through life, groping. Another, lame,
Becomes bitter and curses his circumstance.
One falls from a tree in a forest, waving
His arms like wings but they are not wings.
His spirit survives to ascend, perhaps,
Or fly far away. And far away,
Estranged or exiled, enduring the opprobrium

tredan uriglast   elþeodigra,
30 frecne foldan;   ah he feormendra
lyt lifgendra,   lað biþ æghwær
fore his wonsceaftum   wineleas hæle.
Sum sceal on geapum   galgan ridan,
seomian æt swylte,   oþþæt sawlhord,
35 bancofa blodig,   abrocen weorþeð.   .
þær him hrefn nimeþ   heafodsyne,
sliteð salwigpad   sawelleasne;
noþer he þy facne mæg   folmum biwergan,
laþum lyftsceaþan,   biþ his lif scæcen,
40 ond he feleleas,   feores orwena,
blac on beame   bideð wyrde,
bewegen wælmiste.   Bið him werig noma!
Sumne on bæle sceal   brond **aswencan**,
fretan frecne **lig**   fægne monnan;
45 þær him lifgedal   lungre weorðeð,
read reþe gled;   reoteð meowle,
seo hyre bearn gesihð   brondas þeccan.
Sumum meces ecg   on meodubence
yrrum ealowosan   ealdor oþþringeð,
50 were winsadum;   bið ær his worda to hræd.
Sum sceal on beore   þurh byreles hond
meodugal mæcga;   þonne he gemet ne con
gemearcian his muþe   mode sine,
ac sceal ful earmlice   ealdre linnan,
55 dreogan dryhtenbealo   dreamum biscyred,
ond hine to sylfcwale   secgas nemnað,
mænað mid muþe   meodugales gedrinc.
Sum sceal on geoguþe   mid godes meahtum
his earfoðsiþ   ealne forspildan,
60 ond on yldo eft   eadig weorþan,
wunian wyndagum   ond welan þicgan,

Of those fearful of the unfamiliar,
Someone's lost son slumps beneath the burdens
Of hardship, homesickness, hellish loneliness,
Perceived as the bearer of ruinous luck.
Some men will swing slowly from the gallows
Till dead, whereupon darksome birds
Steal the sightless eyes and shred the bodies—
Which cannot fend off these flying thieves,
Which feel nothing, neither hope nor warmth—
Ghostly pale and pirouetting pointlessly
In demon air, their dread names now
Imprecations, unholy and calamitous.
Some are sentenced to be consumed by fire,
Rabid flames flaring red and wild,
Women weeping, watching sons cremated alive,
Charred remains like ashen coals.
Drink swallows others: diabolic reversal,
It maddens men to mindless volubility
And vehemence, provoking swift swords,
Or, if not, it dazes them night and day
And they drink away their drear, reduced lives,
Slow suicide for sure say those who knew them,
Though some will save themselves in time
To prosper and take pleasure in a separate peace,

maþmas ond meoduful   mægburge on,
þæs þe ænig fira mæge   **forð** gehealdan.
Swa missenlice   meahtig dryhten
65 geond eorþan sceat   eallum dæleð,
scyreþ ond scrifeð   ond gesceapo healdeð,
sumum eadwelan,   sumum earfeþa dæl,
sumum geogoþe glæd,   sumum guþe blæd,
gewealdenne wigplegan,   sumum wyrp oþþe scyte,
70 torhtlicne tiir,   sumum tæfle cræft,
bleobordes gebregd.   Sume boceras
weorþað wisfæste.   Sumum wundorgiefe
þurh goldsmiþe   gearwad **weorþað**;
ful oft he gehyrdeð   ond gehyrsteð wel,
75 brytencyninges beorn,   ond he him brad syleð
lond to leane.   He hit on lust þigeð.
Sum sceal on heape   hæleþum cweman,
blissian æt beore   bencsittendum;
þær biþ drincendra   dream se micla.
80 Sum sceal mid hearpan   æt his hlafordes
fotum sittan,   feoh þicgan,
ond a snellice   snere wræstan,
lætan scralletan   **sceacol**, se þe hleapeð,
nægl **neomegende**;   biþ him neod micel.
85 Sum sceal wildne fugel   wloncne atemian,
heafoc on honda,   oþþæt seo heoroswealwe
wynsum weorþeð;   deþ he wyrplas on,
fedeþ swa on feterum   fiþrum dealne,
lepeþ lyftswiftne   lytlum gieflum,
90 oþþæt se wælisca   wædum ond dædum
his ætgiefan   eaðmod weorþeð
ond to hagostealdes   honda gelæred.
Swa wrætlice   weoroda **nergend**
geond middangeard   monna cræftas

Encircled by family and serene as the sun
Till the last light of a long day.
Almighty God administers
Just so his godly justice to all,
Meting out our fortunes meager or great.
Such is our human and honorable estate.
A happy childhood to him here; glory
In triumphant battle to that one there;
Great skill in hunting, shrewdness at dice,
Championship swiftly achieved
At chess, to others. Some crave knowledge,
Becoming scholars, discoursing wisely.
And God shall give the gift of working
In gold to him who hammers the metal
For a king's mail-coat and the king will thank him
With acres of land (accepted at once).
A charming fellow cheers on a crowd
Of rowdy ale-guzzlers ranged on benches.
What revelry, what roisterous joy!
At his king's feet one calls forth music
From the lyre's strings, skipping lightly
Through lovely and lively, lissome moods.
—Songs that fetch a fine fee.
One teaches a hawk to trust his arm,
And the proud creature that plies the skies
Bows to the coaxing, courteous hand
That teaches the hawk to take the scraps
Offered, and bide its time in fetters.
His *master's* hand. Multitudes of men
Move over the earth in manifold ways,

95 sceop ond scyrede   ond gesceapo ferede
    æghwylcum on eorþan   eormencynnes.
    Forþon him nu ealles þonc   æghwa secge,
    þæs þe he fore his miltsum   monnum scrifeð.

Their diverse dispositions designed by God,
Each as carefully carved and placed
As a chess piece on the chessboard.
Therefore must we admit our God
The Master of men, Deity who determines
The fortunes of men.

from Soul and Body I

Huru, ðæs behofað   hæleða æghwylc
þæt he his sawle **sið**   sylfa geþence,
hu þæt bið deoplic   þonne se deað cymeð,
asyndreð þa sybbe   þe ær samod wæron,
5 lic ond sawle!   Lang bið syððan
þæt se gast nimeð   æt gode sylfum
swa wite swa wuldor,   swa him on worulde ær
efne þæt eorðfæt   ær geworhte.
Sceal se gast cuman   geohðum hremig,
10 symble ymbe seofon niht   sawle findan
þone lichoman   þe hie ær lange wæg,
þreo hund wintra,   butan ær þeodcyning,
ælmihtig god,   ende worulde
wyrcan wille,   weoruda dryhten.
15 Cleopað þonne swa cearful   cealdan reorde,
spreceð grimlice   se gast to þam duste:
"Hwæt, druh ðu dreorega,   to hwan drehtest ðu me,
eorðan fulnes   eal forwisnad,
lames gelicnes!   Lyt ðu gemundest
20 to hwan þinre sawle þing   siðþan wurde,
syððan of lichoman   læded wære!
Hwæt, wite **ðu** me, weriga!   Hwæt, ðu huru wyrma gyfl
lyt geþohtest,   þa ðu lustgryrum eallum
ful **geeodest**,   hu ðu on eorðan scealt
25 wyrmum to wiste!   Hwæt, ðu on worulde ær
lyt geþohtest   hu þis is þus lang hider!
Hwæt, þe la engel   ufan of roderum
sawle onsende   þurh his sylfes hand,

The Damned Soul Addresses the Body

Maurice Riordan

Make no mistake, a man should bear in mind
The fateful journey his soul will face
After death, how dangerous it will be
When those siblings who were always linked,
The body and soul, are pulled asunder.
Then time passes, while either pain or pleasure
Is doled out to the soul, as God decides,
In accordance with that man's deeds on earth.
The ghost will come, grieving in its plight,
One night in every seven to seek out
The corpse which once wrapped it close.
This will happen for three hundred winters
Unless God meanwhile ends the world.
It speaks in a voice devoid of breath,
Uttering grim words, the ghost to the dust:

"Listen, mudball, how come you abused me?
You skinbag, all shriveled up at last,
You paid little heed, in your hunt for pleasure,
To the hard future in store for your soul
Once it had been banished from the body.
Am I the offender? Isn't it you, worm-fodder?
Who alive paid no heed to what lay ahead,
To the angel who presented you with a soul,
Handing it down to you from heaven's door,

meotod ælmihtig,   of his mægenþrymme,

30 ond þe gebohte   blode þy halgan,
ond þu me mid þy heardan   hungre gebunde
ond gehæftnedest   helle witum!
Eardode ic þe on innan.   Ne meahte ic ðe of cuman,
flæsce befangen,   ond me fyrenlustas

35 þine geþrungon.   þæt me þuhte ful oft
þæt hit **wære XXX**   þusend wintra
to þinum deaðdæge.   A ic uncres gedales onbad
earfoðlice.   Nis nu huru se ende to **god**!
Wære þu þe wiste wlanc   ond wines sæd,

40 þrymful þunedest,   ond **ic** ofþyrsted wæs
godes lichoman,   gastes drynces.
Forðan þu ne hogodest   her on life,
syððan ic ðe on worulde   wunian sceolde,
þæt ðu wære þurh flæsc   ond þurh fyrenlustas

45 strange gestryned   ond gestaðolod þurh me,
ond ic wæs gast on ðe   fram gode sended.
Næfre ðu me **wið** swa heardum   helle witum
ne generedest   þurh þinra **nieda** lust.
Scealt ðu minra gesynta   sceame þrowian

50 on ðam myclan dæge   þonne eall manna cynn
se **ancenneda**   ealle gesamnað.
Ne eart ðu þon leofra   nænigum lifigendra
men to gemæccan,   ne meder ne fæder
ne nænigum gesybban,   þonne se swearta hrefen,

55 syððan ic ana of ðe   ut siðode
þurh þæs sylfes hand   þe ic ær onsended wæs.
Ne **magon** þe nu heonon adon   hyrsta þa readan
ne gold ne seolfor   ne þinra goda nan,
ne þinre bryde beag   ne þin **boldwela**,

60 ne nan þara goda   þe ðu iu ahtest,
ac her sceolon onbidan   ban bereafod,

And that it was the Almighty in His majesty
Who'd bartered for it with His holy blood.
But you punished me with pangs of hunger,
Kept me like a convict in hell's confines.
I was stuck inside you, I couldn't escape,
Locked up in flesh, where your fiery lusts
Were torture to me. I thought my sentence
Would last thirty thousand winters
Until the day you died. I couldn't wait
For my release. Little good that did me!
You'd grown fat with food, bloated with beer,
Stupefied with pride, while I was parched,
Starved of communion, the soul's drink.
The idea never hit you, while alive here,
Not once since I came to stay in the world,
That you were made of flesh by the fire of lust,
Kept standing upright only by my strength,
The soul lodged inside you by the Lord.
You didn't protect me from hell's punishments,
But indulged instead your own desires.
You'll be the accused, held to account for my state,
On that great day when the Only-Begotten
Calls upon the dead to get up from their graves.
No better partner have you proved to others,
No more luck than the black raven have you brought
To your father and mother, and faithful cousins,
Since the day I departed, left to fend for myself
By that same hand which sent me here.
Your bright rubies won't rectify this,
Nor gold nor silver nor any of your goods,
Not your wife's wedding band, nor the big house,
Not all the property you once possessed.
But here your trimmed bones shall tarry,

besliten synum,   ond þe þin sawl sceal
minum **unwillum**   oft gesecan,
wemman þe mid wordum,   swa ðu worhtest to me.
65 Eart ðu nu dumb ond deaf,   ne synt þine dreamas awiht.
Sceal ic ðe nihtes swa þeah   nede gesecan,
synnum gesargod,   ond eft sona fram þe
hweorfan on hancred,   þonne halige men
lifiendum gode   lofsang doð,
70 secan þa hamas   þe ðu me her scrife,
ond þa arleasan   eardungstowe,
ond þe sculon her moldwyrmas   manige ceowan,
slitan sarlice   swearte wihta,
gifre ond grædige.   Ne synt þine æhta awihte
75 þe ðu her on moldan   mannum eowdest.
Forðan þe wære selre   swiðe mycle
þonne þe wæron ealle   eorðan speda,
(butan þu hie gedælde   dryhtne sylfum),
þær ðu wurde æt frymðe fugel   oððe fisc on sæ,
80 oððe on eorðan neat   ætes tilode,
feldgangende   feoh butan snyttro,
oððe on westenne   **wildra** deora
þæt wyrreste,   þær swa god wolde,
ge þeah ðu wære   **wyrma** cynna
85 þæt grimmeste,   þær swa god wolde,
þonne ðu æfre on moldan   man gewurde
oððe æfre fulwihte   onfon sceolde.
þonne ðu for unc bæm   andwyrdan scealt
on ðam miclan dæge,   þonne mannum beoð
90 wunda onwrigene,   þa ðe on worulde ær
fyrenfulle men   fyrn geworhton,
ðonne wyle dryhten sylf   dæda gehyran
hæleða gehwylces,   heofena scippend,
æt ealra manna gehwæs   muðes reorde

Stripped of their sinews. Here your soul shall come,
Unwillingly, to pinpoint your whereabouts
And speak rough words—for the wrongs you've done me.
You're dumb and deaf now, your revels ended.
Yet stung by sins I make my midnight visit,
Then quit again quickly before the cock crows,
When the holy monks abandon their beds
To chant lauds in praise of the living God.
I go to that kip to which you've consigned me,
The dungeon where sinners gather in disgrace.
Meanwhile here the mould-worm does his work,
The black beetles gnaw into your bones,
Guzzling and eager. Those earthly goods
You once gloated over are worthless now.
So it would have benefited you better,
More than all the wealth the world offers
(Unless you'd given it away for God's work),
If you'd been born a bird or a fish in the sea,
Or if you'd only lived the life of an ox
And foraged for food on the ground,
Grazed with the cattle carefree in the fields.
Or had you been the basest of the wild beasts,
If God wished it so, bred in the wilderness,
Even though a despised poisonous snake,
That would have proved a preferable fate
Than to be born man and been baptized.
When asked to answer for us both,
On that great day when God's wounds are displayed,
The wounds which felons long ago inflicted,
Then the Lord will demand account of every man,
The Creator will want to hear the words
From each man's mouth, one by one,
About the repayments they've made for his pain.

95 wunde wiðerlean.   Ac hwæt wylt ðu þær

on þam domdæge   dryhtne secgan?

þonne ne bið nan na to þæs lytel lið   on lime aweaxen,

þæt ðu ne scyle for anra   gehwylcum onsundrum

riht agildan,   þonne reðe bið

100 dryhten æt þam dome.   Ac hwæt do wyt unc?

Sculon wit þonne eft ætsomne   siððan brucan

swylcra yrmða,   swa ðu unc her ær scrife!"

Fyrnað þus þæt flæschord,   sceall þonne feran onweg,

secan hellegrund,   nallæs heofondreamas,

105 dædum gedrefed.   **Ligeð** dust þær hit wæs,

ne mæg him ondsware   ænige gehatan,

geomrum gaste,   geoce oððe frofre.

Bið þæt heafod tohliden,   handa toliðode,

geaglas toginene,   goman toslitene,

110 sina beoð asocene,   swyra becowen,

fingras tohrorene.

Rib reafiað   reðe wyrmas,

beoð hira tungan totogenne   on tyn healfa

hungregum to frofre;   forþan hie ne magon huxlicum

115 wordum wrixlian   wið þone werian gast.

Gifer hatte se wyrm,   þe þa eaglas beoð

nædle scearpran.   Se genydde **to**

ærest eallra   on þam eorðscræfe,

þæt he þa tungan totyhð   ond þa teð þurhsmyhð

120 ond þa eagan þurheteð   ufan on þæt heafod

ond to ætwelan   oðrum gerymeð,

wyrmum to wiste,   þonne þæt werie

lic acolod bið   þæt **he** lange ær

werede mid wædum.   Bið þonne wyrma gifel,

125 æt on eorþan.   þæt mæg æghwylcum

men to gemynde,   modsnotra gehwam!

How will you answer the Lord on the Last Day?
There's no bone in your body so small
For which you won't have to pay the price,
The exact amount due on each item.
You'll have no voice, when the Lord gives his verdict.
We will endure together for eternity
The torments you've earned for us on earth."

Thus it berates the carcase—then rushes off
To hell's hovel, not the vault of heaven,
Doomed by how things are. The dust remains unmoved.
It can't give any answer or assistance
Or offer succor to its forsaken soul.
Its head is broken in, its hands disjointed,
The jaws lie gaping, the gums fester,
The fingers have already fallen off.
Wriggling worms are raiding the rib cage,
Their tongues active in ten directions
Struggling to satisfy the hungry horde.
They don't pause to bandy words and pleasantries.
Guzzler is the name of that general,
The wriggler in charge with the razor teeth,
Who in the grave leads the frontline.
He attacks the tongue, bores into the jawbone,
He eats the lids over the eyes
And opens a path to the prime meat.
He burrows a way through to the worms' banquet.
Barely has the body, long accustomed to luxury,
Gone cold than it becomes itself a tasty dish,
Food for worms. Let this serve as a fair warning,
A reminder to men, who want wisdom.

The Ruin

Wrætlic is þes wealstan,   wyrde gebræcon;
burgstede burston,   brosnað enta geweorc.
Hrofas sind gehrorene,   hreorge torras,
hrungeat berofen,   hrim on lime,
5   scearde scurbeorge   scorene, gedrorene,
ældo undereotone.   Eorðgrap hafað
waldend wyrhtan   forweorone, geleorene,
heardgripe hrusan,   oþ hund cnea
werþeoda gewitan.   Oft þæs wag gebad
10 ræghar ond readfah   rice æfter oþrum,
ofstonden under stormum;   steap geap gedreas.
Wonað giet se   . . . num geheapen,
fel on . . . . . .
grimme gegrunden . . . . . .
15 . . . scan   heo . . .
    . . . g orþonc   ærsceaft . . .
    . . . g   lamrindum beag
mod mo . . .   . . . yne swiftne gebrægd
hwætred in hringas,   hygerof gebond
20 weallwalan wirum   wundrum togædre.
Beorht wæron burgræced,   burnsele monige,
heah horngestreon,   heresweg micel,
meodoheall monig   ᛗ dreama full,
oþþæt þæt onwende   wyrd seo swiþe.
25 Crungon walo wide,   cwoman woldagas,

The Ruin

Yusef Komunyakaa

Look at the elaborate crests chiseled into this stone wall
shattered by fate, the crumbled city squares,
and the hue and cry of giants rotted away.
There are caved-in roofs, towers in shambles,
rime on the limy mortar,
a storm-wall tilted and scarred,
half-fallen, slumped by time.
An earthly embrace holds the royal architects
rotting in their graves and lost to the cruel grip
of the ground, while a hundred generations
passed away. This wall, mapped and veined by lichen,
stained with red, outlasted one kingdom
after another, long stood upright after storms:
lofty and broad, it has fallen. The rampart
hewn and wedged together, sharpened roughly
and polished, an ancient structure well-worked by men . . .
ringed with encrustations of soil
still prods the brain and draws up a fiery clue.
Clever in the forging of chains,
some bold-minded man bound together the ribs
of the wall with amazing cables.

There were bright city plots linked by bathhouses,
a wealth of high, towering gables,
much clamor of the multitude,
many mead halls filled with revelry,
until a mighty Lot changed that.
Far and wide people fell dead:

swylt eall fornom   **secgrofra** wera;
wurdon hyra wigsteal   westen staþolas,
brosnade burgsteall.   Betend crungon
hergas to hrusan.   Forþon þas hofu dreorgiað,
30 ond þæs teaforgeapa   tigelum sceadeð
hrostbeages **hrof.**   Hryre wong gecrong
gebrocen to beorgum,   þær iu beorn monig
glædmod ond goldbeorht   gleoma **gefrætwed,**
wlonc ond wingal   wighyrstum scan;
35 seah on sinc, on sylfor,   on searogimmas,
on ead, on æht,   on eorcanstan,
on þas beorhtan burg   bradan rices.
Stanhofu stodan,   stream hate wearp
widan wylme;   weal eall befeng
40 beorhtan bosme,   þær þa baþu wæron,
hat on hreþre.   þæt wæs hyðelic.
Leton þonne geotan . . . . . .
ofer harne stan   hate streamas
un . . . . . .
45 . . . þþæt hringmere   hate . . .
. . . . . . þær þa baþu wæron.
þonne is . . . . . .
. . . re;   þæt is cynelic þing,
huse . . . . . .   burg. . . .

days of pestilence ran rampant
and death clobbered ranks of the infamous swordsmen.
Their fortress became a tomb; the city rotted away:
those who should have braced it up, the multitudes,
were bones on the ground. Then, the courts knelt in dust
and the wide red roof of vaulted beams was left shedding tiles.
This ritual-place fell into ruin and piled-up heaps,
where once stood those lighthearted with gold,
clothed in splendor, proud and lifted by wine,
shorn in war-gear, and gazed upon a treasure
of silver and inlaid-plated gems,
on wealth and property, on precious stones
and this glorious citadel of a stout kingdom;
and the stone courts stood upright,
and the warming stream spouted its whole surge,
and a wall hugged everything to its bosom,
where the baths were steamy in its heart.
Streams poured across hot gray stones
until the round pool heated. . . .
It is still a fitting thing for this city.

Fourth
Riddle-Hoard

Riddle 39

Gewritu secgað   þæt seo wiht sy
mid moncynne   miclum tidum
sweotol ond gesyne.   Sundorcræft hafað
maran micle,   þonne hit men witen.
5 Heo wile gesecan   sundor æghwylcne
feorhberendra,   gewiteð eft feran on weg.
Ne bið hio næfre   niht þær oþre,
ac hio sceal wideferh   wreccan laste
hamleas hweorfan;   no þy heanre biþ.
10 Ne hafað hio fot ne **folme**,   ne æfre foldan hran,
ne **eagena**   ægþer twega,
ne muð hafaþ,   ne wiþ monnum spræc,
ne gewit hafað,   ac gewritu secgað
þæt seo sy earmost   ealra wihta,
15 þara þe æfter gecyndum   cenned wære.
Ne hafað hio sawle ne feorh,   ac hio siþas sceal
geond þas wundorworuld   wide dreogan.
Ne hafaþ hio blod ne ban,   hwæþre bearnum wearð
geond þisne middangeard   mongum to frofre.
20 Næfre hio heofonum hran,   ne to helle mot,
ac hio sceal wideferh   **wuldorcyninges**
larum lifgan.   Long is to secganne
hu hyre ealdorgesceaft   æfter gongeð,
woh wyrda gesceapu;   þæt **is** wrætlic þing
25 to gesecganne.   Soð is æghwylc
þara þe ymb þas wiht   wordum becneð;
ne hafað **heo** ænig lim,   leofaþ efne seþeah.
Gif þu mæge reselan   recene gesecgan
soþum wordum,   saga hwæt hio hatte.

It Is Written in Scriptures

Saskia Hamilton

It is written in scriptures that this
creature appears plainly to us
when the hour calls,
while its singular power compels
and confounds our knowing.
It seeks us out, one by one,
following its own way; fares on,
with its stranger's step, never
there a second night, native
to no place; moves according
to its nature. It has no hands,
no feet, has never touched the ground,
no mouth to speak of,
nor mind. Scriptures say
it is the least of anything made.
It has no soul, no life, but travels
widely among us in this world;
no blood nor bone, but
consoles all the children of men.
It hasn't reached heaven,
it won't touch hell,
but takes instruction from
the king of glory. The whole story
of its fate—limbless as it is,
animate—is too obscure to tell.
And yet all the words we find
to describe it are just and true.
If you can say it, call it
by its rightful name.

Riddle 40

Ece is se scyppend,   se þas eorþan nu
wreðstuþum **wealdeð**   ond þas world healdeð.
Rice is se reccend   ond on ryht cyning
ealra anwalda,   eorþan ond heofones,
5 healdeð ond wealdeð,   swa he ymb þas utan hweorfeð.
He mec wrætlice   worhte æt frymþe,
þa he þisne ymbhwyrft   ærest sette,
heht mec wæccende   wunian longe,
þæt ic ne slepe   siþþan æfre,
10 ond mec semninga   slæp ofergongeþ,
beoð eagan min   ofestum betyned.
þisne middangeard   meahtig dryhten
mid his onwalde   æghwær styreð;
swa ic mid waldendes   worde ealne
15 þisne ymbhwyrft   utan ymbclyppe.
Ic eom to þon bleað,   þæt mec bealdlice mæg
gearu gongende   grima abregan,
ond eofore eom   æghwær cenra,
þonne he gebolgen   bidsteal giefeð;
20 ne mæg mec oferswiþan   segnberendra
ænig ofer eorþan,   nymþe se ana god
se þisne hean heofon   healdeþ ond wealdeþ.
Ic eom on stence   strengre **micle**
þonne ricels   oþþe rose sy,
25 on eorþan tyrf
wynlic weaxeð;   ic eom wræstre þonne heo.
þeah þe lilie sy   leof moncynne,
beorht on blostman,   ic eom betre þonne heo;

Forever Is the Creator

David Wojahn

Forever is the Creator, and still He guides our world & the firmament, still
      He governs every precinct of this earth.
All powerful sovereign, He commands and reigns—heaven & earth
      are orbs within His hands.
& from the beginning I was there. Marvel at me: my radiance & watchfulness
      predate the world. He ordered

that I never sleep. But sleep will always overtake me & my eyes snap shut.
      All knowingly the Master rules
& He grants me dominion over all this planet. So timid am I
      that a fleeting ghost can bring me
to my knees in terror. Yet I am bolder than the wild boar bristling at bay,
      so fearful no hunter can subdue me.

Only to God I answer, Master of earth and heaven. My fragrance
      surpasses frankincense, surpasses
the rose-petal & . . . its scent from the greensward oozing.
      Immense is my delicacy.
Although the lily is beloved of men, bedazzling in blossom,
      I am more delicate by far.

swylce ic nardes stenc   nyde oferswiþe
30 mid minre swetnesse   symle æghwær,
ond ic fulre eom   þonne þis fen swearte
þæt her yfle   adelan stinceð.
Eal ic under heofones   hwearfte recce,
swa me leof fæder   lærde æt frymþe,
35 þæt ic þa mid ryhte   reccan moste
þicce ond þynne;   þinga gehwylces
onlicnesse   æghwær healde.
Hyrre ic eom heofone,   hateþ mec heahcyning
his deagol þing   dyre bihealdan;
40 eac ic under eorþan   eal sceawige
wom wraðscrafu   wraþra gæsta.
Ic eom micle yldra   þonne ymbhwyrft **þes**
oþþe þes middangeard   meahte geweorþan,
ond ic giestron wæs   geong acenned
45 mære to monnum   þurh minre modor hrif.
Ic eom fægerre   frætwum goldes,
þeah hit mon awerge   wirum utan;
ic eom wyrslicre   þonne þes wudu fula
oððe þis waroð   þe her aworpen ligeð.
50 Ic eorþan eom   æghwær brædre,
ond widgielra   þonne þes wong grena;
folm mec mæg bifon   ond fingras þry
utan eaþe   ealle ymbclyppan.
Heardra ic eom ond caldra   þonne se hearda forst,
55 hrim heorugrimma,   þonne he to hrusan cymeð;
ic eom Ulcanus   up irnendan
leohtan leoman   lege hatra.
Ic eom on goman   gena swetra
þonne þu beobread   blende mid hunige;
60 swylce ic eom wraþre   þonne wermod sy,
þe her on hyrstum   heasewe stondeþ.

My sweetness is everywhere, more aromatic than the spikenard.
      Yet I also reek of the stagnant swap.
Over the firmament I stand guard, enjoined by the Father to govern
      all that is under heaven,
the weak & the strong alike. A shape-shifter, I can take the form
      of any thing. I rise above heaven

& the Great King bids me to behold His secret nature.
      & the underworld—
I see its every pit & crater, the damned crying out from its depths.
      I am older than the firmament,
older than the human world, yet only yesterday I sprang
      from my mother's womb,

mankind's hope. I shine like golden ornaments, my filigree
      turned in awestruck hands.
But I'm also moldering wood. I'm kelp flung up by sea-spray
      to the shore. Broader
than the earth I am, wider than this vast green world. Yet I fit
      within a palm, a button

guided through its hole by three deft fingers. I am also
      the harsh biting frost,
the grim rime that whitens the fields, yet hotter than the sparks
      flaring up from Vulcan's forge.
& sweeter am I than bread slathered yellow with honey. Yet also
      I'm the bitterness of wormwood,

Ic mesan mæg   meahtelicor
ond efnetan   ealdum **þyrse,**
ond ic gesælig mæg   symle lifgan
65 þeah ic ætes ne sy   æfre to feore.
Ic mæg fromlicor   fleogan þonne pernex
oþþe earn oþþe hafoc   æfre meahte;
nis zefferus,   se swifta wind,
þæt swa fromlice mæg   feran æghwær;
70 me is snægl swiftra,   **snelra** regnwyrm
ond fenyce   fore hreþre;
is þæs gores sunu   gonge hrædra,
þone we wifel   wordum nemnað.
Hefigere ic eom micle   þonne se hara stan
75 oþþe unlytel   leades clympre,
leohtre ic eom micle   þonne þes lytla wyrm
þe her on **flode** gæð   fotum dryge.
Flinte ic eom heardre   þe þis fyr drifeþ
of þissum strongan   style heardan,
80 hnescre ic eom micle   halsrefeþre,
seo her on winde   wæweð on lyfte.
Ic eorþan eom   æghwær brædre
ond widgelra   þonne þes wong grena;
ic uttor **eaþe**   eal ymbwinde,
85 wrætlice gewefen   wundorcræfte.
Nis under me   ænig oþer
wiht waldendre   on worldlife;
ic eom ufor   ealra gesceafta,
þara þe worhte   waldend user,
90 se mec ana mæg   ecan meahtum,
geþeon þrymme,   þæt ic **onþunian** ne sceal.
Mara ic eom ond strengra   þonne se micla hwæl,
se þe garsecges   grund bihealdeð
sweartan syne;   ic eom swiþre þonne he,

its spikes gray & ashen on the hillsides. My appetite's
        insatiable, a hunger
more greedy than that of the giants of yore. In any contest,
        I can eat them under the table.
Happily ever after I will always live & never does a bite
        of any food touch my lips.

Pheasant, eagle, hawk—I fly faster by far. I outrun the zephyr
        & the gale & neither
can range as I do, my cold breath filling all the quadrants of this earth.
        But the snail, the earthworm,
the fen-frog—all slither and hop more quickly than I.
        & the weevil, burrowing through

the shit that spawned him, always shall outpace me. I'm
        a lichen-studded boulder,
an ingot of lead, but lighter than the water strider skittering
        the surface of a pond.
I'm the hard flint sparking fire as it rears against the adamant
        steel blade. I'm downy feathers

afloat & scattered in a breeze. Broader than the earth I am, wider
        than the vast green world.
I embrace all. I contain multitudes. My loom braids everything
        with wondrous skill.
Over all the firmament I stand watch; all creatures bow down before me.
        Yet the great Creator

holds my pride in thrall. How puny is the whale compared to me,
        a speck who scavenges
the dim ocean floor. His strength is nothing compared to mine.
        Yet I'm scarcely as muscled

95 swylce ic eom on mægene   minum læsse
þonne se hondwyrm,   se þe hæleþa bearn,
secgas searoþoncle,   seaxe delfað.
Nu hafu ic in heafde   hwite loccas
wræste gewundne,   ac ic eom wide calu;
100 ne ic breaga ne bruna   brucan moste,
ac mec bescyrede   scyppend eallum;
nu me wrætlice   weaxað on heafde
þæt me on gescyldrum   scinan motan
ful wrætlice   wundne loccas.
105 Mara ic eom ond fættra   þonne amæsted swin,
bearg bellende,   þe on bocwuda,
won wrotende   wynnum lifde
þæt he

Riddle 41

edniwu;
þæt is moddor   monigra cynna,
þæs selestan,   þæs sweartestan,
þæs deorestan   þæs þe dryhta bearn
5 ofer foldan sceat   to gefean agen.
Ne magon we her in eorþan   owiht lifgan,
nymðe we brucen   þæs þa bearn doð.
þæt is to geþencanne   þeoda gehwylcum,
wisfæstum werum,   hwæt seo wiht sy.

as a bloated tick, pried out with a knife by skillful hands.
        No curly blond locks for me:

I'm bald from head to toe. Eyebrows & eyelids I have none—
        they were snipped by the Creator
eons ago. Yet when I wish it, sultry golden tresses sprout lightning-
        quick from out my scalp.
Down past my shoulders they shimmer. Behold how I root & grunt,
        The fattest of swine,

Greedily feasting in the beech wood forest, so that I. . . .

But When Renewal Comes

David Constantine

                    . . . but when
Renewal comes she visits us here
In many appearances, bright, dark,
All beautiful, the best of blessings
Humans are given in the folds of the earth
And no good life can we live unless
We receive her numerous children well
And use them kindly. Understand this
Or die.

Riddle 42

Ic seah wyhte   wrætlice twa
undearnunga   ute plegan
hæmedlaces;   hwitloc anfeng
wlanc under wædum,   gif þæs weorces **speow**,
5   fæmne fyllo.   Ic on flette mæg
þurh runstafas   rincum secgan,
þam þe bec witan,   bega ætsomne
naman þara wihta.   þær sceal Nyd wesan
twega oþer   ond se torhta æsc
10   an an linan,   Acas twegen,
Hægelas swa some.   Hwylc **þæs** hordgates
cægan cræfte   þa clamme onleac
þe þa rædellan   wið rynemenn
hygefæste heold   heortan bewrigene
15   orþoncbendum?   Nu is undyrne
werum æt wine   hu þa wihte mid us,
heanmode twa,   hatne sindon.

I Saw, at Foreplaying, Two Wondrous Ones

Marcia Karp

I saw, at foreplaying, two wondrous ones,
      at large, laid out for the looking.

The fairheaded fair will (under her whatnot) grow great
      if the work of their playing went well.

Now, by rounding my fresh-from-my-forge runic staves
      into the halls of your hearing

      (you wits of words and their works),
may I be sounding the names of these two to your knowing.

      Take from the CORN only its first crunch of sound.
      Take it twice. Take it thrice.

      Quit sitting. Quick. Pick INCUBATE's gift.

      One mate is complete with what AUSPICE can offer.

      With a CHIRP, the match (the set of the game) is dispatched.

Has anyone caught from my staves the key
      and been able to bear it
            to the guardings on the gates of the hoard
               and open the fastness as if flimsy hoarding
          then run through the ruin
      and bedevil the bonds round the heart of my riddle
which never before has lain bare?

      Now, we-at-our-wine can name
the foul-minded company we keep.

Riddle 43

Ic wat indryhtne   æþelum deorne
giest in geardum,   þam se grimma ne mæg
hungor sceððan   ne se hata þurst,
yldo ne adle.   Gif him arlice
5   esne þenað,   se þe agan sceal
on þam siðfate,   hy gesunde æt ham
findað witode him   wiste ond blisse,
cnosles unrim,   care, gif se esne
his hlaforde   hyreð yfle,
10   frean on fore.   Ne wile forht wesan
broþor oþrum;   him þæt bam sceðeð,
þonne hy from bearme   begen hweorfað
anre magan   ellorfuse,
moddor ond sweostor.   Mon, se þe wille,
15   cyþe cynewordum   hu se cuma hatte,
eðþa se esne,   þe ic her ymb sprice.

A Noble Guest of Brave Lineage

David Cavanagh

A noble guest of brave lineage
dwells within. Neither fierce hunger
nor fiery thirst can harm him,
nor age nor illness. If the servant attends
honorably to this ruler on their travels,
they will find at journey's end
a fate of feasting and of bliss;
countless sorrows will be their brood
if the servant ill obeys his lord
along the way and does not fear
for him as for a brother. Then both
will suffer from the split as they turn
to leave their one kinswoman,
the mother and sister who nurtured them.
Let him with fitting words to name
this guest and servant reveal them now.

Riddle 43

Ic wat indryhtne   æþelum deorne
giest in geardum,   þam se grimma ne mæg
hungor sceððan   ne se hata þurst,
yldo ne adle.   Gif him arlice
5 esne þenað,   se þe agan sceal
on þam siðfate,   hy gesunde æt ham
findað witode him   wiste ond blisse,
cnosles unrim,   care, gif se esne
his hlaforde   hyreð yfle,
10 frean on fore.   Ne wile forht wesan
broþor oþrum;   him þæt bam sceðeð,
þonne hy from bearme   begen hweorfað
anre magan   ellorfuse,
moddor ond sweostor.   Mon, se þe wille,
15 cyþe cynewordum   hu se cuma hatte,
eðþa se esne,   þe ic her ymb sprice.

A King Who Keeps to Himself Dwells

Elizabeth Spires

A king who keeps to himself dwells
in a humble house with his sole servant.
While his body–man eats, drinks, feels fever
and chills, and plucks gray hairs from his head,
his master knows nothing of thirst or hunger,
illness or age. They set out together, but whether
fortune or misfortune awaits them on the world's
wide road depends on the servant's whim, faithful
or unfaithful to his king. Along the way, a kinswoman,
mother and sister to them both, offers them a room,
a meal, but they soon press on, until the old servant
can go no farther. He stumbles, falls, and cannot
rise again. Then the king, without a glance backward,
continues on to a country we shall all come to know.
Whoever knows this pair, say their names.

Riddle 44

Wrætlic hongað   bi weres þeo,
frean under sceate.   Foran is þyrel.
Bið stiþ ond heard,   stede hafað godne;
þonne se esne   his agen hrægl
5   ofer cneo hefeð,   wile þæt cuþe hol
mid his hangellan   heafde gretan
þæt he efenlang ær   oft gefylde.

Riddle 45

Ic on wincle gefrægn   **weaxan** nathwæt,
þindan ond þunian,   þecene hebban;
on þæt banlease   bryd grapode,
hygewlonc hondum,   hrægle þeahte
5   þrindende þing   þeodnes dohtor.

A Curious Thing Dangles by Man's Thigh

Peter Constantine

A curious thing dangles by man's thigh,
peeking out from under his mantle,
a hole in its tip. Stiff and hard,
it stands up well to use.
Man lifts his mantle above his knee
to slide its hovering head into a hole
that it has filled so often: a perfect fit.

I Saw in a Corner Something Swelling

Richard Wilbur

I saw in a corner   something swelling,
Rearing, rising   and raising its cover.
A lovely lady,   a lord's daughter,
Buried her hands   in that boneless body,
Then covered with a cloth   the puffed-up creature.

Riddle 47

Moððe word fræt.   Me þæt þuhte
wrætlicu wyrd,   þa ic þæt wundor gefrægn,
þæt se wyrm forswealg   wera gied sumes,
þeof in þystro,   þrymfæstne cwide
5 ond þæs strangan staþol.   Stælgiest ne wæs
wihte þy gleawra,   þe he þam wordum swealg.

Riddle 48

Ic gefrægn **for** hæleþum   hring endean,
torhtne butan tungan,   tila þeah he hlude
stefne ne cirmde,   strongum wordum.
Sinc for secgum   swigende cwæð:
5 "Gehæle mec,   helpend gæsta."
Ryne ongietan   readan goldes
guman galdorcwide,   gleawe **beþencan**
hyra hælo to gode,   swa se hring gecwæð.

A Moth Ate Words

Jane Hirshfield

A moth ate words—
I thought it strange to hear,
and a wonder of fate,
that a worm in darkness
can thieve a man's fine riddle,
swallow his song,
sip eloquence and feast on its foundation.
And yet that stealthy guest
who dines on stolen words will leave no wiser.

I Heard of a Circle that Spoke before Men

Lia Hills

I heard of a circle that spoke before men,
a bright and tongueless treasure,
it did not shout or say a strong word,
but, powerful in its silence, said:
"Save me, helper of souls."
Let men understand the mystery
of the red gold, its incantation, and in their wisdom
entrust their souls to God, as the circle said.

Biblical Stories
and Lives of Saints

Genesis A: chapters one and two

I.

Us is riht micel   ðæt we rodera weard,
wereda wuldorcining,   wordum herigen,
modum lufien!   He is mægna sped,
heafod ealra   heahgesceafta,

5   frea ælmihtig.   Næs him fruma æfre,
or geworden,   ne nu ende cymþ
ecean drihtnes,   ac he bið a rice
ofer heofenstolas.   Heagum þrymmum
soðfæst and **swiðfeorm**   sweglbosmas heold,

10   þa wæron gesette   wide and side
þurh geweald godes   wuldres bearnum,
gasta weardum.   Hæfdon gleam and dream,
and heora ordfruman,   engla þreatas,
beorhte blisse.   Wæs heora blæd micel!

15   þegnas þrymfæste   þeoden heredon,
sægdon lustum lof,   heora liffrean
demdon, drihtenes   dugeþum wæron
swiðe gesælige.   Synna ne cuþon,
firena fremman,   ac hie on friðe lifdon,

20   ece mid heora aldor.   Elles ne ongunnon
ræran on roderum   nymþe riht and soþ,
ærðon engla weard   for oferhygde
dwæl on gedwilde.   Noldan dreogan leng
heora selfra ræd,   ac hie of siblufan

25   godes ahwurfon.   Hæfdon gielp micel
þæt hie wið drihtne   dælan meahton
wuldorfæstan wic   werodes þrymme,

from Genesis A: The Fall of the Rebel Angels and the First Day

Harvey Shapiro

I.

It is right that heaven's guardian,
man's Glory-King, should receive our words of praise
and the love of our hearts for His strength is so great
and He heads a great host of angelic beings,
Lord almighty, who commanded us from the beginning
nor will His rule ever end over the thrones of heaven.
Just and majestic, steadfast in truth,
He entrusted broad heaven to the guardian angels
where they abound in bliss, without knowledge of sin,
royal servants, praising their Prince.
These spirits took joy in truth and right.
They shone in their bliss. They wanted nothing.
To celebrate the Lord of Life was all their pleasure.
But the peace of heaven was broken and a sin committed
when a portion of the angels, sunk into error,
followed their prideful and envious chief
who declared the right to part of God's kingdom,
a home and a throne in the northern region.
Then pain came upon them born of envy and pride,
the special pride of that angel who first proposed evil.

sid and swegltorht.   Him þær sar gelamp,
æfst and oferhygd,   and þæs engles mod

30   þe þone unræd ongan   ærest fremman,
wefan and weccean,   þa he worde cwæð,
niþes ofþyrsted,   þæt he on norðdæle
ham and heahsetl   heofena rices
agan wolde.   þa wearð yrre god

35   and þam werode wrað   þe he ær wurðode
wlite and wuldre.   Sceop þam werlogan
wræclicne ham   weorce to leane,
helleheafas,   hearde niðas.
Heht þæt witehus   wræcna bidan,

40   deop, dreama leas,   drihten ure,
gasta weardas,   þa he hit geare wiste,
synnihte beseald,   susle geinnod,
geondfolen fyre   and færcyle,
rece and reade lege.   Heht þa geond þæt rædlease hof

45   weaxan witebrogan.   Hæfdon hie wrohtgeteme
grimme wið god gesomnod;   him þæs grim lean becom!
Cwædon þæt heo rice,   reðemode,
agan woldan,   and swa eaðe meahtan.
Him seo wen geleah,   siððan waldend his,

50   heofona heahcining,   honda arærde,
hehste wið þam herge.   Ne mihton hygelease,
mæne wið metode,   mægyn **bryttigan,**
ac him se mæra   mod getwæfde,
bælc forbigde.   þa he gebolgen wearð,

55   besloh synsceaþan   sigore and gewealde,
dome and dugeðe,   and dreame benam
his feond, friðo   and gefean ealle,
torhte tire,   and his torn gewræc
on gesacum swiðe   selfes mihtum

60   strengum stiepe.   Hæfde styrne mod,

328

They turned aside from God with their great boasting
that they should share in the heavenly bright mansion.
Then God grew angry that those He had made glorious
should abjure His bounty and turn from His will.
With the howlings of hell, God furnished them a home.
Into miserable exile He violently thrust them.
This was the reward rebellion had brought them.
When the house of punishment was ready for them,
deep in hell, bereft of pleasure,
our God surrounded this band of rebels
with perpetual night and burning sulfur,
in a place of red fire and intense cold.
Fear of further torments spread through the host.
for they were now serial sinners and could expect the worst
from a God whose vengeance would match their crimes.
Still they desired dominion and primed by their anger
said they would have it. But as before
they were struck by surprise when the High King and Ruler
against that host raised His powerful hand.
Fools they lacked force to effect their evil,
to exercise power along with their Ruler.
God in his rage stripped them of arrogance,
broke their pride, crushed their spirit.
He laid them low like a defeated army.
Gone were their dreams of joy and glory
along with any hope of peace or security.

gegremed grymme,   grap on wraðe
faum folmum,   and him on fæðm gebræc
yrre on mode;   æðele bescyrede
his wiðerbrecan   wuldorgestealdum.
65 **Sceof** þa and scyrede   scyppend ure
oferhidig cyn   engla of heofnum,
wærleas werod.   Waldend sende
laðwendne here   on langne sið,
geomre gastas;   wæs him gylp forod,
70 beot forborsten,   and forbiged þrym,
wlite gewemmed.   Heo on wrace syððan
seomodon swearte,   siðe ne þorfton
hlude hlihhan,   ac heo helltregum
werige wunodon   and wean cuðon,
75 sar and sorge,   susl þrowedon
þystrum beþeahte,   þearl æfterlean
þæs þe heo ongunnon   wið gode winnan.
þa wæs soð swa ær   sibb on heofnum,
fægre freoþoþeawas,   frea eallum leof,
80 þeoden his þegnum;   þrymmas weoxon
duguða mid drihtne,   dreamhæbbendra.

II.

Wæron þa gesome,   þa þe swegl **buað**,
wuldres eðel.   Wroht wæs asprungen,
oht mid englum   and orlegnið,
85 siððan herewosan   heofon ofgæfon,
leohte belorene.   Him on laste setl,
wuldorspedum welig,   wide stodan
gifum growende   on godes rice,
beorht and geblædfæst,   buendra leas,
90 siððan wræcstowe   werige gastas
under hearmlocan   heane geforan.

God was unrelenting, violent in His resolve
to be avenged for the wrongs done to Him by his adversaries.
Bitterly provoked, He grasped them fiercely
and crushed them in His hostile hands.
Thus were they judged and separated out,
this proud and faithless army, from among the other angels
and banished from their home. The Creator sent the miserable host
on a long journey, their bragging broken,
their brightness blotted, their strength humiliated.
At the end of the long fall, they hovered darkly,
silent in their torment, heavy in their grief.
There is no loud laughter in the precincts of hell.
There is only exhaustion and terror, pain and sorrow.
This was retribution for their struggle with God.
In heaven, as before, peace prospered.
The heavenly hosts, as noblemen to prince,
gently and reverently served their Lord
and through Him their joy grew along with their glory.

II.

Then the angels inhabiting heaven
enjoyed perfect peace endowed as they were
with splendor and glory. Enmity was no more.
Warfare was ended because the rebels
had left the kingdom and were deprived of the light.
After their departure, their rich thrones were empty.
There was an abundance of grace, a superfluity of splendor,
now that the miserable rebels were down in hell's dungeon.

þa þeahtode   þeoden ure

modgeþonce,   hu he þa mæran gesceaft,

eðelstaðolas   eft gesette,

95   swegltorhtan seld,   selran werode,

þa hie gielpsceaþan   ofgifen hæfdon,

heah on heofenum.   Forþam halig god

under roderas feng,   ricum mihtum,

wolde þæt him eorðe   and uproder

100 and sid wæter   **geseted** wurde

woruldgesceafte   on wraðra gield,

þara þe forhealdene   of hleo sende.

Ne wæs her þa giet   nymþe heolstersceado

wiht geworden,   ac þes wida grund

105 stod deop and dim,   drihtne fremde,

idel and unnyt.   On þone eagum wlat

stiðfrihþ cining,   and þa stowe beheold,

dreama lease,   geseah deorc gesweorc

semian sinnihte   sweart under roderum,

110 wonn and weste,   oðþæt þeos woruldgesceaft

þurh word gewearð   wuldorcyninges.

Her ærest gesceop   ece drihten,

helm eallwihta,   heofon and eorðan,

rodor arærde,   and þis rume land

115 gestaþelode   strangum mihtum,

frea ælmihtig.   Folde wæs þa gyta

græs ungrene;   garsecg þeahte

sweart synnihte,   side and wide,

wonne wægas.   þa wæs wuldortorht

120 heofonweardes gast   ofer holm boren

miclum spedum.   Metod engla heht,

lifes brytta,   leoht forð cuman

ofer rumne grund.   Raþe wæs gefylled

heahcininges hæs;   him wæs halig leoht

So God considered how to refurbish
His glorious creation, His heavenly bright dwellings,
abandoned as they were in the high places.
Whereupon, holy God, with His great power,
conceived of an earth under the firmament,
with its own sky and wide water,
a created world to replace
the host no longer under His protection.
At this point nothing existed save the shadow of darkness.
The Lord looked on an abyss, deep and dim,
empty and unused, strange to His sight.
The resolute King, surveying this desolation,
saw darkness, saw perpetual night
hovering under the firmament
until a created world came to be
out of the Word of the Glory-King.
Here the Lord, eternal protector
of all living things, first created
by His great might heaven and earth,
raised the heaven, established the broad earth.
Earth was not yet grass-green.
Instead, there was ocean, wild and wide,
black waves looming like limitless night.
Then bright with glory, the guardian of heaven
lay His spirit over the deep.
God of the angels, giver of life
decreed light shine on all that black surface.
The High-King's bidding was quickly done.
Holy light covered the nothingness

ofer westenne,   swa se wyrhta bebead.
      þa gesundrode   sigora waldend
      ofer laguflode   leoht wið þeostrum,
      sceade wið sciman.   Sceop þa bam naman,
      lifes brytta.   Leoht wæs ærest
130 þurh drihtnes word   dæg genemned,
      wlitebeorhte **gesceaft**.   Wel licode
      frean æt frymðe   forþbæro tid,
      dæg æresta;   geseah deorc sceado
      sweart swiðrian   geond sidne grund.

as the Creator had commanded it to.
When God over the waters then parted light from shade.
the brilliance from the darkness, He named them both.
First light, bright with beauty, the Life-Giver called day.
God was pleased with this creative moment,
this beginning, the first day,
as the dark shadow slid from the vast abyss.

Genesis A: from chapter 41

þa þæs rinces   se rica ongan
cyning costigan,   cunnode georne
hwilc þæs æðelinges   ellen wære,
stiðum wordum   spræc him stefne to:
2850 "Gewit þu ofestlice,   Abraham, feran,
lastas lecgan   and þe læde mid
þin agen bearn.   þu scealt Isaac me
onsecgan, sunu ðinne,   sylf to tibre.
Siððan þu gestigest   steape dune,
2855 hrincg þæs hean landes,   þe ic þe heonon getæce,
up þinum agnum fotum,   þær þu scealt ad gegærwan,
bælfyr bearne þinum,   and blotan sylf

from **Genesis A: Offering of Isaac**
David Ferry

Then the Lord wanted to know
How steadfast was His man,

So He said, in the Lord's stern voice,
"Abraham, Abraham, you

Must take your belovèd child,
Your own, your only son,

And go with him to where
I will show you what to do.

A place there is, high in the hills.
You must climb up there on foot.

The two of you together,
Around you only nothing,

Only the mountain peaks
Around you witnessing.

And there make ready a fire,
A bale-fire for your bairn,

And then, you must, yourself,
Take up the sword you carry,

sunu mid sweordes ecge,   and þonne sweartan lige
leofes lic forbærnan   and me lac bebeodan."
2860 Ne forsæt he þy siðe,   ac sona ongann
fysan to fore.   Him wæs **frean** engla
word ondrysne   and his **waldend** leof.
þa se eadga   Abraham sine
nihtreste ofgeaf.   Nalles nergendes
2865 hæse wiðhogode,   ac hine se halga wer
gyrde grægan sweorde,   cyðde þæt him gasta weardes
egesa on breostum wunode.   Ongan þa his esolas bætan

And kill him with its edge,
And burn his dear body black

In the flames you have set going
And present what you have done,

A burnt offering to Me."
Abraham heard the Lord

And did not put off the journey.
At once he made his way,

Determined and intent,
On the task that he had been

Commanded to undertake.
He was in awe of the Word

Of the Lord God of angels.
He was the Lord's servant,

Eager to please his Master.
Blessèd was Abraham.

Without any night-rest
He got up from his bed.

He obeyed without any question
The commandment of the Lord.

He girded on his sword,
Fear of the Lord's Word

gamolferhð goldes brytta,   heht hine geonge twegen

men mid siðian.   Mæg wæs his agen þridda

2870 and he feorða sylf.   þa he fus gewat

from his agenum hofe   Isaac lædan,

bearn unweaxen,   swa him bebead metod.

Efste þa swiðe   and onette

forð foldwege,   swa him frea tæhte

2875 wegas ofer westen,   oðþæt wuldortorht,

dæges þriddan up   ofer deop wæter

ord aræmde.   þa se eadega wer

geseah hlifigan   hea dune

swa him sægde ær   swegles aldor.

2880 ða Abraham spræc   to his ombihtum:

Continual in his breast.
That good old man, the giver

Of rings to his followers,
He harnessed and bridled his asses,

And selected from his household
Two young men, and told them

To go with him on his journey.
Isaac his half-grown son

Was the third one of the party.
He was himself the fourth.

So together they went to do
The bidding of the Lord,

Hastening on their way
Across the deserted landscape,

Until, on the third day,
The bright light of the morning

Rose up from the deep water,
Where everything begins.

There, then, the blessèd man
Looked up and saw the high

Mountain that the Lord
Had told him they were to go to.

"Rincas mine,   restað incit
her on þissum wicum.   Wit eft cumað,
siððan wit ærende   uncer twega
gastcyninge   agifen habbað."
2885 Gewat him þa se æðeling   and his agen sunu
to þæs gemearces   þe him metod tæhte,
wadan ofer wealdas.   Wudu bær sunu,
fæder fyr and sweord.   ða þæs fricgean ongann
wer wintrum geong   wordum Abraham:
2890 "Wit her fyr and sweord,   frea min, habbað;
hwær is þæt tiber,   þæt þu torht gode
to þam brynegielde   bringan þencest?"

Abraham spoke to the two
Retainers and said, "My men,

Stay here where we have camped.
We will return when we

Have carried out what the King
Of souls has told us to do."

Then Abraham left them and went
Up onto the high mountain,

Climbing through woods and groves,
Taking his own son with him.

The son carried the wood,
The father carried the fire,

And was carrying the sword.
Then his belovèd son,

Trudging beside his father,
Said to his father, "Father,

We're carrying the wood,
The fire, and the sword,

To do what the bright Lord
Asks us to do, but where

Is the sacrificial victim?
Where is the offering

Abraham maðelode   (hæfde on an gehogod
þæt he **gedæde**   swa hine drihten het):
2895 "Him þæt soðcyning   sylfa findeð,
moncynnes weard,   swa him gemet þinceð."
Gestah þa stiðhydig   steape dune
up mid his eaforan,   swa him se eca bebead,
þæt he on hrofe gestod   hean landes
2900 on þære **stowe**   þe him se stranga to,
wærfæst metod   wordum tæhte.
Ongan þa ad hladan,   æled weccan,
and gefeterode   fet and honda
bearne sinum   and þa on bæl ahof

To put upon the fire"?
His father, who was steadfast,

Faithful to what the Creator
Had told him to do, replied

"He, who is the true
King, the Guardian,

Protector of His people,
He will find what is right

And what is fitting for this."
Then, obedient, resolute,

Steadfast, he went on climbing
Up the steep mountain with

His only son beside him,
Until they came to the top,

To the place to which the Lord
Had told him He would show him,

And there he took the sticks
Of wood his son had carried

And with them made ready the fire,
Only the mountains around,

Witnessing what they were doing.
Hand and foot he bound

2905 Isaac geongne,   and þa ædre gegrap
     sweord be gehiltum,   wolde his sunu cwellan
     folmum sinum,   fyre **scencan**
     mæges dreore.   þa metodes ðegn,
     ufan engla sum,   Abraham hlude
2910 stefne cygde.   He stille gebad
     ares spræce   and þam engle oncwæð.
     Him þa ofstum to   ufan of roderum
     wuldorgast godes   wordum mælde:
     "Abraham leofa,   ne sleah þin agen bearn,
2915 ac þu cwicne abregd   cniht of ade,
     eaforan þinne!   Him an wuldres god!
     Mago Ebrea,   þu medum scealt
     þurh þæs halgan hand,   heofoncyninges,
     soðum sigorleanum   selfa onfon,

His own, his only son,
Young half-grown Isaac,

And lifted his own child up
And laid him on the pyre,

And took up the sword in his hand
And stood there ready to kill him,

And for the thirsty fire
To drink the blood of his boy.

Then suddenly from above
An angel of the Lord

Called out to Abraham
In a loud voice, "Abraham!"

Abraham stood still,
He stood stock-still and listened

And heard the words of the angel.
"Abraham, do not kill

Your own, your only son.
Take him up, lift him away

From the pyre you have put him upon.
The Lord has granted him

Great honor, and you, great scion,
And patriarch of the Hebrews

2920 ginfæstum gifum.   þe wile gasta weard
      lissum gyldan   þæt þe wæs **leofre** his
      sibb and hyldo   þonne þin sylfes bearn."
      Ad stod onæled.   Hæfde Abrahame
      metod moncynnes,   mæge Lothes,
2925 breost geblissad,   þa he him his bearn forgeaf,
      Isaac cwicne.   ða se eadega bewlat,
      rinc ofer exle,   and him þær rom geseah
      unfeor þanon   ænne standan,
      broðor Arones,   brembrum fæstne.
2930 þone Abraham genam   and hine on ad ahof
      ofestum miclum   for his agen bearn.

Will be given many rewards
By the Guardian of Souls,

Because you were willing to
Sacrifice your son,

Your belovèd only son,
In obedience to the Lord

And for the love of Him."
The fire went on burning.

The Creator of Mankind
Had so approved the heart

Of Abraham, Lot's kinsman,
That God gave him back his bairn

In safety, and alive.
Then Abraham, the brother

Of Haran, turned his head,
And looked back over his shoulder,

And saw, not far away,
A ram caught in the brambles.

Then he took hold of the ram
And quickly lifted it up

Onto the burning pyre
And took his sword and killed it,

Abrægd þa mid þy bille,   brynegield onhread,
reccendne weg   rommes blode,
   onbleot þæt lac gode,   sægde leana þanc
2935 and ealra þara **sælða**   þe he him sið and ær,
   gifena drihten,   forgifen hæfde.

In place of his own son,
There on the smoking altar

Stained with the blood of the ram.
He offered to the Lord

The burnt offering
In gratitude for the gifts

He had given them and would give
Forever and ever after.

from Exodus

Hof ða for hergum   hlude stefne
lifigendra **leod**,   þa he to leodum spræc:
"Hwæt, ge nu eagum to   on lociað,
folca leofost,   færwundra sum,
280 hu ic sylfa sloh   and þeos swiðre hand
grene tacne   garsecges deop.
Yð up færeð,   ofstum wyrceð
wæter **wealfæsten**.   Wegas syndon dryge,
haswe herestræta,   holm gerymed,
285 ealde staðolas,   þa ic ær ne gefrægn
ofer middangeard   men geferan,
fage feldas,   þa forð heonon
in ece **tid**   yðe þeahton,
sælde sægrundas.   Suðwind fornam
290 bæðweges blæst,   **brim** is areafod,
sand sæcir **spaw**.   Ic wat soð gere
þæt eow mihtig god   miltse gecyðde,
eorlas ærglade.   Ofest is selost
þæt ge of feonda   fæðme weorðen,
295 nu se agend   up arærde
reade streamas   in randgebeorh.
Syndon þa foreweallas   fægre gestepte,
wrætlicu wægfaru,   oð wolcna hrof."
æfter þam wordum   werod eall aras,
300 modigra mægen.   Mere stille bad.
Hofon herecyste   hwite linde,

from **Exodus: The Israelites Cross the Red Sea**
David Curzon

In the fore of the troops   the lord of the living
lifted his voice loud,   spoke to the people:

"Watch now! You,   the chosen nation,
with your own eyes will witness   a quick miracle:
how I myself   by the Strong Right Hand
have struck with a living stick   the deep ocean.
A rising wave   rapidly fashions
water into bulwark,   leaving dry roads,
gray highways,   suited to an army.
The sea has opened   ancient foundations
I have never heard   men walked before,
and gleaming plains   overspread with waves
an eternal time.   A south wind swept
the storm waters away   from the sea's secret floor;
the ocean is cleaved;   the receding sea
has ceded sands.   This truth I seize:
Almighty God   granted you mercy,
and grace makes glad.   Speed is best
so you may escape   your enemies' clench
now God, who owns them,   has banked red waters,
a shield to protect you.   These retaining walls
are piled as high   as the sky's ceiling,
a wonderful walkway   between waves."

Hearing these words   the whole host rose,
an army of ardor.   The sea stayed still.
The squads of the chosen   raised on the shore   shields and standards.

segnas on sande.   Sæweall astah,
uplang gestod   wið Israhelum
andægne fyrst.   Wæs seo eorla gedriht
305   anes modes,
fæstum fæðmum   freoðowære heold.
Nalles hige gehyrdon   haliges lare,
siððan leofes leoþ   læste near
sweg swiðrode   and sances bland.
310   þa þæt feorðe cyn   fyrmest eode,
wod on wægstream,   wigan on heape,
ofer grenne grund,   Iudisc feða
on orette   **on** uncuð gelad
for his mægwinum.   Swa him mihtig god
315   þæs dægweorces   deop lean forgeald,
siððan him gesælde   sigorworca hreð,
þæt he ealdordom   agan sceolde
ofer cynericu,   cneowmaga blæd.
Hæfdon him to segne,   þa hie on sund stigon,
320   ofer bordhreoðan   beacen aræred
in þam garheape,   gyldenne **leon**,
drihtfolca mæst,   deora cenost.
Be þam herewisan   hynðo ne woldon
be him lifigendum   lange þolian,
325   þonne hie to guðe   garwudu rærdon
ðeoda ænigre.   **þracu** wæs on ore,
heard handplega,   hægsteald modige
wæpna wælslihtes,   wigend unforhte,
bilswaðu blodige,   beadumægnes ræs,
330   grimhelma gegrind,   þær Iudas for.
æfter þære fyrde   flota modgade,
Rubenes sunu.   Randas bæron

The rampart of the sea   arched upward,
stood straight for Israel   a day's duration.
That company of men   had one will,
clove to the Covenant   with a close embrace.
They did not disdain   the holy man's dictate
when, following him,   their song of salvation,
the harmony of their psalm,   grew strong.

Then the fourth tribe   went to the forefront,   pressed on in the sea;
a throng of warriors   crossed the green sea-floor.
One soldier of the house of Judah   hurried along
that weird road   before his folk.
Almighty God therefore   gave him great reward
for that day's act   when by valor's glory
victory was his: he'd have dominion
over kingdoms,   increase of offspring.

The standard they carried   as they marched seaward,
the banner above   the phalanx of shields
of that lance-armed troop,   was a gold lion,
the bravest of beasts   for the greatest of peoples.
Because of their war leader   they were not willing
to long endure   life in dishonor
when with lifted spears   they deployed against goyim.
At the head of where   Judah went
was hand-to-hand combat   by brave young troops,
warriors uncowed   by weapons' carnage,
bloody sword gashes,   the force of battle's attack,   smashed helmets.

After that army   came the proud sons of Reuben.

sæwicingas ofer sealtne mersc,
manna menio; micel angetrum
335 eode unforht. He his ealdordom
synnum aswefede, þæt he siðor for
on leofes last. Him on leodsceare
frumbearnes riht freobroðor oðþah,
ead and æðelo; he wæs gearu swa þeah.
340 þær **forð** æfter him folca þryðum
sunu Simeones sweotum comon;
þridde þeodmægen (þufas wundon
ofer garfare) guðcyste onþrang
deawig sceaftum. Dægwoma becwom
345 ofer **garsecge**, godes beacna sum,
morgen mæretorht; mægen forð gewat.
þa þær folcmægen for æfter oðrum,
isernhergum. An wisode
mægenþrymmum mæst, þy he mære wearð,
350 on forðwegas folc æfter wolcnum,
cynn æfter cynne. Cuðe æghwilc
mægburga riht, swa him Moises bead,
eorla æðelo. Him wæs an fæder,
leof leodfruma, landriht geþah,
355 frod on ferhðe, freomagum leof.
Cende cneowsibbe cenra manna
heahfædera sum, halige þeode,
Israela cyn, onriht godes,
swa þæt orþancum ealde reccað
360 þa þe mægburge mæst gefrunon,
frumcyn feora, fæderæðelo gehwæs.

Those sea-rovers,   a mariner multitude,
carried their shields   across the salt fen.
The huge battalion   resolutely advanced.
His ascendance was wrecked   by sin, and so
he was placed farther back   in the wake of the favorite.
His own brother   had taken over
the firstborn's right   to noble wealth
yet Reuben was   at the ready.

Behind them came   the sons of Simeon;
the host of their folk   trod on with their troops.
The third tribal power,   flags fluttering above them,
pressed ahead in regiment   with wet spear-shafts.
The portent of day   rose over the ocean,   a beacon of God.
Morning gleamed from the sea.   The army marched forward.

Every tribe   progressed in succession
in iron-clad contingents   each with one man
who was known to all   guiding his mighty host
along the paths,   the pillar of cloud
leading the people,   tribe following tribe.
They knew in truth   the tribal hierarchy
since Moses had taught them   their own lineage.
All had one father,   a loved ruler,
a sage of the spirit   of his noble kinsmen,
who had been granted   his title to land.
The patriarch progeny   were courageous men,
a holy nation,   the kindred of Israel,
the fit folk of God,   as the ancients, those
who know most   of the origin of peoples,
of each person's paternity,   recount with skill.

. . . .

Folc wæs afæred,   flodegsa becwom
gastas geomre,   geofon deaðe hweop.
Wæron beorhhliðu   blode bestemed,
450 holm heolfre spaw,   hream wæs on yðum,
wæter wæpna ful,   wælmist astah.
Wæron Egypte   eft oncyrde,
flugon forhtigende,   fær ongeton,
woldon herebleaðe   hamas findan,
455 gylp wearð gnornra.   Him ongen genap
atol yða gewealc,   ne ðær ænig becwom
herges to hame,   ac behindan beleac
wyrd mid wæge.   þær ær wegas lagon,
mere modgode,   mægen wæs adrenced.
460 Streamas stodon,   storm up gewat
heah to heofonum,   herewopa mæst.
Laðe cyrmdon,   (lyft up geswearc),
fægum stæfnum,   flod blod gewod.

. . . .

Egypt's people were fearful,   a terror of the flood
subdued their spirits   threatened with death by the deep.
That wall of water   was smeared with blood,
the sea spat gore,   clamor was in the waves,
a water dense with weapons,   an ascending spume of death.
Egypt retreated,   felt panic
fled in fear.   Their coward wish
was to wander home,   their boasting became sorrow.
The dread swirl of waves   drew darkness on them;
not one of that army   would come home;
fate cut them off   by the flood behind them.
Ocean seethed where paths had been;   torrent swamped that army.
A confusion climbed   right to the skies,
the cry of despair   of the mighty army.
The aggressors called   with dying voices;
air darkened above them,   blood spread in the flood.

from Judith

           ða wearð Holofernus,
    goldwine gumena,   on gytesalum,
    hloh ond hlydde,   hlynede ond dynede,
    þæt mihten fira bearn   feorran gehyran
25 hu se stiðmoda   styrmde ond gylede,
    modig ond medugal,   manode geneahhe
    bencsittende   þæt hi gebærdon wel.
    Swa se inwidda   ofer ealne dæg
    dryhtguman sine   drencte mid wine,
30 swiðmod sinces brytta,   oðþæt hie on swiman lagon,
    oferdrencte his duguðe ealle,   swylce hie wæron deaðe geslegene,
    agotene goda gehwylces.   Swa het se gumena aldor
    fylgan fletsittendum,   oðþæt fira bearnum
    nealæhte niht seo þystre.   Het ða niða geblonden
35 þa eadigan mægð   ofstum fetigan
    to his bedreste   beagum gehlæste,
    hringum gehrodene.   Hie hraðe fremedon,
    anbyhtscealcas,   swa him heora ealdor bebead,
    byrnwigena brego,   bearhtme stopon
40 to ðam gysterne,   þær hie Iudithðe
    fundon ferhðgleawe,   ond ða fromlice
    lindwiggende   lædan ongunnon
    þa torhtan mægð   to træfe þam hean,
    þær se rica hyne   reste on symbel
45 nihtes inne,   nergende lað,
    Holofernus.   þær wæs eallgylden
    fleohnet fæger   **ymbe** þæs folctogan
    bed ahongen,   þæt se bealofulla
    mihte wlitan þurh,   wigena baldor,
50 on æghwylcne   þe ðær inne com

from Judith: Beheading Holofernes

Peter Constantine

Infernal Holofernes, illustrious king,
wild with wine raged and roared,
hollered and howled, unruly in carousing.
Far and wide the sons of man heard
his stalwart storming haughtily summoning
his warriors to raise their horns of wine.
The stern strewer of treasures drowned
his warriors in wine till they sank into stupor,
the wicked fiend plying them with drink
till they lay as in death, shedding their spirits.
Thus the king goaded his valiant warriors,
the children of man, late into darkness.
Steeped in evil, he ordered the maiden
with rings and bracelets brought to his bed.
And the shield-bearers did as their evil king bade,
entering the tent where Judith lingered,
wisest of women, and the warriors took
the most beautiful of maidens to where Holofernes,
despised by our Savior, rested at night.
A wondrous fly-net, all of gold
covered the bed of the mighty king,
so he could look on every man
but no son of man could look on him,

hæleða bearna,   ond on hyne nænig
monna cynnes,   nymðe se modiga hwæne
niðe rofra   him þe near hete
rinca to rune gegangan.   Hie ða on reste gebrohton
55 snude ða snoteran idese;   eodon ða stercedferhðe,
hæleð heora hearran cyðan   þæt wæs seo halige meowle
gebroht on his burgetelde.   þa wearð se brema on mode
bliðe, burga ealdor,   þohte ða beorhtan idese
mid widle ond mid womme besmitan.   Ne wolde þæt wuldres dema
60 geðafian, þrymmes hyrde,   ac he him þæs ðinges gestyrde,
dryhten, dugeða waldend.   Gewat ða se deofulcunda,
galferhð gumena ðreate
bealofull his beddes neosan,   þær he sceolde his blæd forleosan
ædre binnan anre nihte;   hæfde ða his ende gebidenne
65 on eorðan unswæslicne,   swylcne he ær æfter worhte,
þearlmod ðeoden gumena,   þenden he on ðysse worulde
wunode under wolcna hrofe.   Gefeol ða wine swa druncen
se rica on his reste middan,   swa he nyste ræda nanne
on gewitlocan.   Wiggend stopon
70 ut of ðam inne   ofstum miclum,
weras winsade,   þe ðone wærlogan,
laðne leodhatan,   læddon to bedde
nehstan siðe.   þa wæs nergendes
þeowen þrymful,   þearle gemyndig
75 hu heo þone atolan   eaðost mihte
ealdre benæman   ær se unsyfra,
womfull, onwoce.   Genam ða wundenlocc
scyppendes mægð   scearpne mece,
scurum heardne,   ond of sceaðe abræd
80 swiðran folme;   ongan ða swegles weard
be naman nemnan,   nergend ealra
woruldbuendra,   ond þæt word acwæð:
"Ic ðe, frymða god   ond frofre gæst,
bearn alwaldan,   biddan wylle

unless the lord commanded him closer.
Swiftly they brought wise Judith to his bed
and went, stouthearted, to tell their lord
the holy woman was now in his lair.
The resplendent ruler rejoiced in triumph
eager to stain the radiant maiden
with foul filth and terrible sin.
But our Celestial Judge, our Glorious Shepherd,
God our King, would not consent.
The lustful lord arrived with his warriors,
seeking in evil his bed of death.
A terrible end awaited the king,
toward which he had striven all his life
walking beneath the roof of clouds.
Senseless with drink he fell on his bed,
and the wine-sated warriors marched from the tent,
leaving the mighty false-faithed king,
the tyrannical torturer, in his last place of rest.
Now our Great God's glorious maiden
resolved to destroy the filthy fiend
before he awoke in foul lust.
God's true servant with braided locks
seized from its sheath a shining sword
sharpened in the clash of storming battles,
and called upon the Great Guardian of Heaven,
naming His name, Lord of all
who dwell on earth, and uttered these words:
"God of Creation, Spirit of Comfort,
All-Powerful Son, Triumphant Trinity,

85 miltse þinre   me þearfendre,
ðrynesse ðrym.   þearle ys me nu ða
heorte onhæted   ond hige geomor,
swyðe mid sorgum gedrefed.   Forgif me, swegles ealdor,
sigor ond soðne geleafan,   þæt ic mid þys sweorde mote
90 geheawan þysne morðres bryttan;   geunne me minra gesynta,
þearlmod þeoden gumena.   Nahte ic þinre næfre
miltse þon maran þearfe.   Gewrec nu, mihtig dryhten,
torhtmod tires brytta,   þæt me ys þus torne on mode,
hate on hreðre minum."   Hi ða se hehsta dema
95 ædre mid elne onbryrde,   swa he deð anra gehwylcne
herbuendra   þe hyne him to helpe seceð
mid ræde ond mid rihte geleafan.   þa wearð hyre rume on mode,
haligre hyht geniwod;   genam ða þone hæðenan mannan
fæste be feaxe sinum,   teah hyne folmum wið hyre weard
100 bysmerlice,   ond þone bealofullan
listum alede,   laðne mannan,
swa heo ðæs unlædan   eaðost mihte
wel gewealdan.   Sloh ða wundenlocc
þone feondsceaðan   fagum mece,
105 heteþoncolne,   þæt heo healfne forcearf
þone sweoran him,   þæt he on swiman læg,
druncen ond dolhwund.   Næs ða dead þa gyt,
ealles orsawle;   sloh ða eornoste
ides ellenrof   oðre siðe
110 þone hæðenan hund,   þæt him þæt heafod wand
forð on ða flore.   Læg se fula leap
gesne beæftan,   gæst ellor hwearf
under neowelne næs   ond ðær genyðerad wæs,
susle gesæled   syððan æfre,
115 wyrmum bewunden,   witum gebunden,
hearde gehæfted   in hellebryne
æfter hinsiðe.

364

I crave Your mercy in my hour of need.
Fiery flames rage in my heart
but my thoughts are heavy with grief and gloom.
Grant me, Great Lord, victory and faith,
that I may cut down this bringer of death.
Grant me deliverance, Mighty Grim God,
Great Giver of Glory, avenge the evil
grieving my mind and burning my heart."
And our highest Judge filled her with courage,
as with all on earth who seek His help
praying in wise and humble faith.
Renewed with hope, her spirit soared,
and she seized the heathen by the hair
drawing him toward her to his shame,
skillfully placing the miserable man,
the fiendish foe, for her deadly deed.
Then Judith of the braided locks
struck the ruthless robber, formidable foe,
with flashing sword, slicing his neck.
Senseless and stunned, wine-drunk and wounded,
he was not dead, not wholly lifeless,
so the unwavering woman struck again,
brought down her sword on the idolatrous dog
and his head went rolling over the ground.
The king's coarse carcass lay unstirring
as his spirit tumbled down death's sharp cliff,
hampered and humbled, tortured and tormented,
forever fettered in a tangle of serpents,
trapped in the eternal fires of Hell.

Dream of the Rood

Hwæt! Ic swefna cyst   secgan wylle,
hwæt me gemætte   to midre nihte,
syðþan reordberend   reste wunedon!
þuhte me þæt ic gesawe   syllicre treow
5 on lyft lædan,   leohte bewunden,
beama beorhtost.   Eall þæt beacen wæs
begoten mid golde.   Gimmas stodon
fægere æt foldan sceatum,   swylce þær fife wæron
uppe on þam eaxlegespanne.   Beheoldon þær engel dryhtnes ealle,
10 fægere þurh forðgesceaft.   Ne wæs ðær huru fracodes gealga,
ac hine þær beheoldon   halige gastas,
men ofer moldan,   ond eall þeos mære gesceaft.
Syllic wæs se sigebeam,   ond ic synnum fah,
forwunded mid wommum.   Geseah ic wuldres treow,
15 wædum geweorðode,   wynnum scinan,
gegyred mid golde;   gimmas hæfdon
bewrigene weorðlice   **wealdendes** treow.
Hwæðre ic þurh þæt gold   ongytan meahte
earmra ærgewin,   þæt hit ærest ongan
20 swætan on þa swiðran healfe.   Eall ic wæs mid **sorgum** gedrefed,
forht ic wæs for þære fægran gesyhðe.   Geseah ic þæt fuse beacen
wendan wædum ond bleom;   hwilum hit wæs mid wætan bestemed,
beswyled mid swates gange,   hwilum mid since gegyrwed.
Hwæðre ic þær licgende   lange hwile
25 beheold hreowcearig   hælendes treow,
oððæt ic gehyrde   þæt hit hleoðrode.
Ongan þa word sprecan   wudu selesta:

The Vision of the Cross

Ciaran Carson

Listen, until I relate the wondrous dream
that came to me at dead of night, when those
who have the gift of speech were sound asleep.
I thought I saw a tree above all trees,
uplifted high and shimmering—
so bright a beam, that veritable beacon
was ablaze with gold, and precious stones
begemmed its base. Five gleamed upon
the shoulder-span. The hallowed of the Lord,
made beautiful for all eternity,
watched over it. No common gallows this,
for it was gazed upon by angels and by men,
and by all creatures marvelously made.

The tree of victory was radiant, and I
was stained with sin and riddled through with guilt.
I saw the shining shaft and crossbeam, tree of glory,
gear of gold bedecked with precious stones,
yet I perceived beyond its aureole
the age-old strife of wretches, when it first began
to sweat blood from its right side.
I was soaked in sorrow, fearful at the sight
of that live beacon changing form and hue
from teeming blood to glittering with gems.
For all that, I lay there a long while
deeply troubled, gazing on the Healer's Tree,
until I heard it boom aloud.
The beam of wood began to speak these words:

"þæt wæs geara iu,   (ic þæt gyta geman),
þæt ic wæs aheawen   holtes on ende,
30 astyred of stefne minum.   Genaman me ðær strange feondas,
geworhton him þær to wæfersyne,   heton me heora wergas hebban.
Bæron me ðær beornas on eaxlum,   oððæt hie me on beorg asetton,
gefæstnodon me þær feondas genoge.   Geseah ic þa frean mancynnes
efstan elne mycle   þæt he me wolde on gestigan.
35 þær ic þa ne dorste   ofer dryhtnes word
bugan oððe berstan,   þa ic bifian geseah
eorðan sceatas.   Ealle ic mihte
feondas gefyllan,   hwæðre ic fæste stod.
Ongyrede hine þa geong hæleð,   (þæt wæs god ælmihtig),
40 strang ond stiðmod.   Gestah he on gealgan heanne,
modig on manigra gesyhðe,   þa he wolde mancyn lysan.
Bifode ic þa me se beorn ymbclypte.   Ne dorste ic hwæðre bugan to
   eorðan,
feallan to foldan sceatum,   ac ic sceolde fæste standan.
Rod wæs ic aræred.   Ahof ic ricne cyning,
45 heofona hlaford,   hyldan me ne dorste.
þurhdrifan hi me mid deorcan næglum.   On me syndon þa dolg
   gesiene,
opene inwidhlemmas.   Ne dorste ic hira nænigum sceððan.
Bysmeredon hie unc butu ætgædere.   Eall ic wæs mid blode bestemed,
begoten of þæs guman sidan,   siððan he hæfde his gast onsended.
50 Feala ic on þam beorge   gebiden hæbbe
wraðra wyrda.   Geseah ic weruda god
þearle þenian.   þystro hæfdon
bewrigen mid wolcnum   wealdendes hræw,
scirne sciman,   sceadu forðeode,
55 wann under wolcnum.   Weop eal gesceaft,
cwiðdon cyninges fyll.   Crist wæs on rode.

Years ago, I still remember it,
they hewed me from a forest. I was cut off
from my roots and taken by determined foes
who made a laughingstock of me, a hoist
for criminals. Men shouldered me and set me on a hill.
That gang of foes secured me there. And then I saw the Lord
courageously approach to climb on high on me.
I dared not burst nor shiver into bits
against his word, although I saw
the earth quake. I could have felled all his foes,
but stood fast instead.

This man of mettle—God Almighty—then stripped off
for battle; stern and strong, he climbed the gallows,
brave before the throng, that he might free mankind.
I trembled when the warrior embraced me,
but dared not bow to earth. I had to stand fast.
I was the cross they raised. I lifted up a mighty king,
Lord of the Firmament, and dared not keel over.
They drove dark nails into me, scars still to be seen,
seething with malice. And I dared not harm them.
They mocked us both and I was bathed with blood
that streamed from him when he had given up the ghost.

I suffered much upon that hill.
Foul deeds and cruel acts. I saw the Sovereign of Armies
racked and stretched. Darkness dimmed
with clouds the shining body
of the Conqueror. A shadow flitted forth
beneath the sombre sky. The whole world mourned
that regal fall. Christ was on the Cross.

Hwæðere þær fuse   feorran cwoman
to þam æðelinge.   Ic þæt eall beheold.
Sare ic wæs mid **sorgum** gedrefed,   hnag ic hwæðre þam secgum to
    handa,
60 eaðmod elne mycle.   Genamon hie þær ælmihtigne god,
ahofon hine of ðam hefian wite.   Forleton me þa hilderincas
standan steame bedrifenne;   eall ic wæs mid strælum forwundod.
Aledon hie ðær limwerigne,   gestodon him æt his lices heafdum,
beheoldon hie ðær heofenes dryhten,   ond he hine ðær hwile reste,
65 meðe æfter ðam miclan gewinne.   Ongunnon him þa moldern wyrcan
beornas on banan gesyhðe;   curfon hie ðæt of beorhtan stane,
gesetton hie ðæron sigora wealdend.   Ongunnon him þa sorhleoð galan
earme on þa æfentide,   þa hie woldon eft siðian,
meðe fram þam mæran þeodne.   Reste he ðær mæte weorode.
70 Hwæðere we ðær **greotende**   gode hwile
stodon on staðole,   syððan **stefn** up gewat
hilderinca.   Hræw colode,
fæger feorgbold.   þa us man fyllan ongan
ealle to eorðan.   þæt wæs egeslic wyrd!
75 Bedealf us man on deopan seaþe.   Hwæðre me þær dryhtnes þegnas,
freondas gefrunon,
ond gyredon me   golde ond seolfre.
Nu ðu miht gehyran,   hæleð min se leofa,
þæt ic bealuwara weorc   gebiden hæbbe,
80 sarra sorga.   Is nu sæl cumen
þæt me weorðiað   wide ond side
menn ofer moldan,   ond eall þeos mære gesceaft,
gebiddaþ him to þyssum beacne.   On me bearn godes
þrowode hwile.   Forþan ic þrymfæst nu
85 hlifige under heofenum,   ond ic hælan mæg
æghwylcne anra,   þara þe him bið egesa to me.
Iu ic wæs geworden   wita heardost,

370

For all that, men hastened to the side
of that brave prince. I saw it all.
My heart was heavy, yet I bowed at their command
with humble courage. Then they took Almighty God,
they raised him from his rack. The brave ones
left me bloodied, riddled through and through
with spikes. They laid him down heavy-limbed.
Stood at his head. Gazed on the Lord
as he lay battle-weary. They began to build a tomb
for him before his killers' eyes. They carved it from bright stone.
Therein they placed the Conqueror. Bereft, they sang
a hymn of sorrow until worn out with grief
by eventide. He lay at rest among that small band.

For all that, we stayed rooted to the spot,
weeping on long after the outcry of the warriors
had died away. The corpse, the vessel
of the soul, grew cold. Then they began to cut
us down. That was fate indeed.
They dug a deep pit and buried us therein.
For all that, the Lord's followers dug me up again
and covered me in gold and silver gear.

Now you can know, dear warrior,
what work of criminals have I endured,
what deep distress. The time has come
that men throughout this grand creation
honor me and bow their heads
before this beacon. On me, God's son
suffered for a time. And that is why I am exalted
under Heaven and can heal all those
who look to me and hold this Cross in awe.
For I was once an instrument of torture,

leodum laðost,   ærþan ic him lifes weg
rihtne gerymde,   reordberendum.
90 Hwæt, me þa geweorðode   wuldres ealdor
ofer holmwudu,   heofonrices weard!
Swylce swa he his modor eac,   Marian sylfe,
ælmihtig god   for ealle menn
geweorðode   ofer eall wifa cynn.
95 Nu ic þe hate,   hæleð min se leofa,
þæt ðu þas gesyhðe   secge mannum,
onwreoh wordum   þæt hit is wuldres beam,
se ðe ælmihtig god   on þrowode
for mancynnes   manegum synnum
100 ond Adomes   ealdgewyrhtum.
Deað he þær byrigde,   hwæðere eft dryhten aras
mid his miclan mihte   mannum to helpe.
He ða on heofenas astag.   Hider eft fundaþ
on þysne middangeard   mancynn secan
105 on domdæge   dryhten sylfa,
ælmihtig god,   ond his englas mid,
þæt he þonne wile deman,   se ah domes geweald,
anra gehwylcum   swa he him ærur her
on þyssum lænum   life geearnaþ.
110 Ne mæg þær ænig   unforht wesan
for þam worde   þe se wealdend cwyð.
Frineð he for þære mænige   hwær se man sie,
se ðe for dryhtnes naman   deaðes wolde
biteres onbyrigan,   swa he ær on ðam beame dyde.
115 Ac hie þonne forhtiað,   ond fea þencaþ
hwæt hie to Criste   cweðan onginnen.
Ne þearf ðær þonne ænig   **anforht** wesan
þe him ær in breostum bereð   beacna selest,
ac ðurh ða rode sceal   rice gesecan
120 of eorðwege   æghwylc sawl,

hated by the multitude, until I gave the path
of life to those who have the gift of speech.
Listen: the Prince of Glory, Watchman of the Heavens,
picked me out above all other trees,
just as he did, Almighty God, exalt
his mother, Mary, above all womankind
for all to hold in veneration.
Now, dear warrior, do I command you—
tell the world what I have seen, reveal
with words the secret of the Glory Tree
on which Almighty God was sorely tried
for all the many sins of men
and Adam's ancient deadly deed.

He tasted death there, yet the Lord arose again
to help men with his mighty power.
He then ascended into Heaven, and again
will venture down into this Middle Earth
to seek out humankind on Doomsday,
God Almighty with his throng of angels;
and he, Supreme Judge, will deem us all
according to our deeds in this brief life.
Nor may anyone be unafraid
before the words the Wielder of the Word proclaims.
He will enquire of all of us, where is the man
who in the name of God would savor bitter death
as he did taste it on that bitter tree.
And then they tremble, lost for words
in which to put their case before the Christ.
But none need fear his wrath
who bear upon their breast the brightest emblem:
it is through the Cross that every soul
who hopes to dwell forever with the Lord

seo þe mid wealdende   wunian þenceð."
Gebæd ic me þa to þan beame   bliðe mode,
elne mycle,   þær ic ana wæs
mæte werede.   Wæs modsefa
125 afysed on forðwege,   feala ealra gebad
langunghwila.   Is me nu lifes hyht
þæt ic þone sigebeam   secan mote
ana oftor   þonne ealle men,
well weorþian.   Me is willa to ðam
130 mycel on mode,   ond min mundbyrd is
geriht to þære rode.   Nah ic ricra feala
freonda on foldan,   ac hie forð heonon
gewiton of worulde dreamum,   sohton him wuldres cyning,
lifiaþ nu on heofenum   mid heahfædere,
135 wuniaþ on wuldre,   ond ic wene me
daga gehwylce   hwænne me dryhtnes rod,
þe ic her on eorðan   ær sceawode,
on þysson lænan   life gefetige
ond me þonne gebringe   þær is blis mycel,
140 dream on heofonum,   þær is dryhtnes folc
geseted to symle,   þær is singal blis,
ond **me** þonne asette   þær ic syþþan mot
wunian on wuldre,   well mid þam halgum
dreames brucan.   Si me dryhten freond,
145 se ðe her on eorþan   ær þrowode
on þam gealgtreowe   for guman synnum.
He us onlysde   ond us lif forgeaf,
heofonlicne ham.   Hiht wæs geniwad
mid bledum ond mid blisse   þam þe þær bryne þolodan.
150 Se sunu wæs sigorfæst   on þam siðfate,

must seek the Kingdom from this earthly way.

Uplifted then, I prayed before the Cross
with all my heart, where I was quite alone
with no one near. My soul yearned
for the final journey, having suffered many times
of longing. Now I have this happy aim
in life, to seek the Tree of Victory
more single-mindedly than anyone,
and to uphold it over all. My heart is set
on that, my hope of shelter
is the Cross. My friends upon this earth
are few, for they have long since left
all worldly pleasures, having found the King of Glory;
now they live in Heaven with the Father.
There they dwell in glory;
daily I look forward to the Cross
I once beheld on earth,
that it might lift me from this transitory life
into the realm of happiness, to taste
the joys of Paradise, where all the people
of the Lord are gathered at the everlasting feast.

There shall I be well set up, to dwell
in glory with the saints in sheer delight.
May the Lord be my friend, who suffered
for men's sins upon the gallows tree when here on earth.
Redeeming us, he gave us life,
this heaven-haven: joy made ever new
with blessings and with bliss for all those
who endured the fire below.
The Son was mighty and triumphant
on that expedition, as he led

mihtig ond spedig,   þa he mid manigeo com,

gasta weorode,   on godes rice,

anwealda ælmihtig,   englum to blisse

ond eallum ðam halgum   þam þe on heofonum ær

155   wunedon on wuldre,   þa heora wealdend cwom,

ælmihtig god,   þær his eðel wæs.

those many companies of souls into the kingdom
of the Lord Almighty, to the great delight
of all the angels and the holy ones
who dwelt already there in glory;
whereupon he came, the Wielder of the Word,
into his rightful realm.

The Descent into Hell

Ongunnon him on uhtan   æþelcunde mægð
gierwan to geonge;   wiston gumena gemot
æþelinges lic   eorðærne biþeaht.
Woldan werigu wif   wope bimænan
5 æþelinges deað   ane hwile,
    reonge bereotan.   Ræst wæs acolad,
heard wæs hinsið;   hæleð wæron modge,
þe hy æt þam beorge   **bliðe** fundon.
Cwom seo murnende   Maria on dægred,
10 heht hy oþre mid   eorles dohtor.
Sohton sarigu tu   sigebearn godes
ænne in þæt eorðærn   þær hi ær wiston
þæt hine gehyddan   hæleð Iudea;
wendan þæt he on þam beorge   bidan sceolde,
15 ana in þære easterniht.   Huru þæs oþer þing
wiston þa wifmenn,   þa hy on weg cyrdon!
Ac þær cwom on uhtan   an engla þreat,
behæfde heapa wyn   hælendes burg.
Open wæs þæt eorðærn,   æþelinges lic
20 onfeng feores gæst,   folde beofode,
hlogan helwaran;   hagosteald onwoc

The Descent into Hell

John F. Deane

Before day dawned, some women of true worth
dressed themselves to go; the men, drawn together,
believed, in dread, their Lord's body lay buried in the earth;

the women, wearied from weeping for their
Lord's death, would lament a while
and cry bitterly; His passing cruel; cold the weather

in His grave. Yet though they grieved, they would go, to find
brilliant men already at the tomb, bright and cheerful. And she came,
that Mary, mourning, at daybreak, who had desired

another worthy woman to set out with her; these brave
and sorrowing women sought out the worldwinning Son
of God, solitary in His grave, in that spot that was saved

by some just men of the Jews to hide Him. Alone, alone
He must stay, in death, in the sepulchre, through that drear
dark Easter night. They would know deep gladness, have grown

wiser, those worthy women, on turning home. For there,
at dawn of day, a host of angels drew in joyfulness, round
that sacred citadel. The sepulchre was open, the deathstone bare,

the breath of life reborn in the body of the Lord. Now
Earth quaked, inhabitants of Hell were hoisted quickly
into joy, for the young Jewish warrior awoke, walked out

modig from moldan,   mægenþrym aras
sigefæst ond snottor.   Sægde Iohannis,
hæleð helwarum,   hlyhhende spræc
25 modig to þære mengo   ymb his mæges . . . :
"Hæfde me gehaten   hælend user,
þa he me on þisne sið   sendan wolde,
þæt he me gesoht . . .   siex monað,
ealles folces fruma.   Nu . . . . . . sceacen.
30 Wene ic ful swiþe   ond witod
. . . . . . to dæge   dryhten wille
. . . . . . gesecan,   sigebearn godes."
Fysde hine þa to fore   frea moncynnes;
wolde heofona helm   helle weallas
35 forbrecan ond forbygan,   þære burge þrym
onginnan reafian,   reþust ealra cyninga.
Ne rohte he to þære hilde   helmberendra,
ne he byrnwigend   to þam burggeatum
lædan ne wolde,   ac þa locu feollan,
40 clustor of þam ceastrum;   cyning in oþrad,
ealles folces fruma   forð onette,
weoruda wuldorgiefa.   Wræccan þrungon,
hwylc hyra þæt sygebearn   geseon moste,
Adam ond Abraham,   Isac ond Iacob,
45 monig modig eorl,   Moyses ond Dauid,
Esaias   ond Sacharias,
heahfædra fela,   swylce eac hæleþa gemot,
witgena weorod,   wifmonna þreat,
fela fæmnena,   folces unrim.
50 Geseah þa Iohannis   sigebearn godes
mid þy cyneþrymme   cuman to helle,
ongeat þa geomormod   godes sylfes sið.

proudly from that place, a Prince in majesty, in victory,
and in wisdom. Then John the Baptist spoke, puffed up with pride,
to Hell's inhabitants, of his kinsman's coming: "When He called me,

when He sent me on this long journey, the Savior had not lied
that He would seek me out, six months being over, He
the sweet savor of all peoples. That season's passed. So now in bright

certainty, I trust today the Lord Himself, will be
a visitor amongst us, victorious Son of God." And straight the Lord
of humankind came hastening on His way, in Heaven's mercy

intending to destroy that kingdom's walls, His sword
most powerful, a king plundering Hell's people. He gave
no thought to helmet-wearing warriors, nor to a horde

of weapon-carriers to crush that city's gates, for they caved
in, the locks broke off, the bolts slipped from the citadel.
The King rode in, the keeper of all people, for He craved

to offer the hosts salvation. They hurried through the halls of Hell
who wished to stand forward first to see God's wondrous Son—
Adam and Abraham, Isaac and Jacob, fearless lords as well,

Moses and David, Isaiah, Zacharias, many long-gone
patriarchs, a mighty host, a meeting-hall of prophets, a throng
of holy women, a mighty multitude that His death had won.

Now came into view the victorious Son of God who rode along
in regal majesty into Hell; then, rising out of sadness, John, late
learning at long last what God alone had done,

Geseah he helle duru   hædre scinan,

þa þe longe ær   bilocen wæron,

55   beþeahte mid þystre;   se þegn wæs on wynne.

Abead þa bealdlice   burgwarena ord

modig fore þære mengo   ond to his mæge spræc

ond þa wilcuman   wordum grette:

"þe þæs þonc sie,   þeoden user,

60   þæt þu us . . . . . . ige   secan woldest,

nu we on þissum bendum   bidan . . . . . .

þonne monige bindeð   broþorleasne

wræccan . . . . . .   (he bið wide fah),

ne bið he no þæs nearwe   under niðloc . . .

65   þæs bitre gebunden   under bealuclommum,

þæt he þy yð ne mæge   ellen habban,

þonne he his hlafordes   hyldo gelyfeð,

þæt hine of þam bendum   bicgan wille.

Swa we ealle to þe   an gelyfað,

70   dryhten min se dyra.   Ic adreag fela

siþþan þu end to me   in siþadest,

þa þu me gesealdest   sweord ond byrnan,

helm ond heorosceorp,   (a ic þæt heold nu giet),

ond þu me gecyðdest,   cyneþrymma wyn,

75   þæt þu mundbora   minum wære.

Eala Gabrihel,   hu þu eart gleaw ond scearp,

milde ond gemyndig   ond monþwære,

wis on þinum gewitte   ond on þinum worde snottor!

þæt þu **gecyðdest**   þa þu þone cnyht to us

80   brohtest in Bethlem.   Bidan we þæs longe,

saw the gateway of Hell gleam brightly, that bitter gate
so long locked and dimmed in darkness. Now at last
the servant of the Lord stood cheered after that lengthy wait

and, leader of those who lived in that fortress and who held fast
for ages, spoke, boldest among the multitude, greeting before the throng
his kingly kinsman thus: "Be thanks to You, kind Lord, from us outcast,

that You willed to seek us out, we who have suffered long
writhing in our bonds. When he who is brotherless is bound and barred
into exile and left to suffer in excess of sorrow and a strong

sense of shame, though he be so strongly held in hard
chains or caught so cruelly in fearful fetters, he may yet find
great hope in the good faith of his long lost Lord

that He will ransom him from his bondage. Thus in my mind
had I deep faith in You, dear Lord. For myself I have endured
great trouble since that time You first traveled to me to bind

my soul in the armor of faith, helmet and battle-dress and sword
kept until now—and You made known to me, majestic King,
that You were guide and keeper, forever good as Your word.

And you, O angel Gabriel, how pure, how all-perceiving,
how sharp and keen in vision, how clear and wise,
how mild, humane and holy, how merciful and all-receiving,

how wondrous in your words. All came clear before my eyes
when you brought the boy to us in our long night in Bethlehem.

setan on sorgum,   sibbe oflyste,
wynnum ond wenum,   hwonne we word godes
þurh his sylfes muð   secgan hyrde.
Eala Maria,   hu þu us modigne
85 cyning acendest,   þa þu þæt cild to us
brohtest in Bethlem.   We þæs beofiende
under helle **dorum**   hearde sceoldon
bidan in bendum.   Bona weorces gefeah;
wæron ure ealdfind   ealle on wynnum
90 þonne hy gehyrdon   hu we hreowen . . .
. . . on murnende   mægburg usse,
oþþæt . . . . . .   sigedryhten god,
bimengdes . . . . . . gust ealra cyninga.
. . . . . . nu us mon modge þe
95 ageaf from usse geogoðe.   We þurh gifre mod
beswican us sylfe;   we þa synne forþon
berað in urum breostum   to bonan honda,
sculon eac to ussum feondum   freoþo wilnian.
Eala Hierusalem   in Iudeum,
100 hu þu in þære stowe   stille gewunadest!
Ne mostan þe geondferan   foldbuende
ealle lifgende,   þa þe lof singað.
Eala Iordane   in Iudeum,
hu þu in þære stowe   stille gewunadest!
105 Nales þu geondflowan   foldbuende;
mostan hy þynes wætres   wynnum brucan.
Nu ic þe halsie,   hælend user,
deope in gedyrstum,   (þu eart dryhten Crist),
þæt þu us gemiltsie,   monna scyppend.
110 þu fore monna lufan   þinre modor bosm
sylfa gesohtes,   sigedryhten god,
nales fore þinre þearfe,   þeoda waldend,
ac for þam miltsum   þe þu moncynne

For so long we had waited, living in grief, watching the skies,

longing for peace, praying and hoping for the time
we would hear God's words from His own mouth. And you, Mary,
how brave a king you bore in that boy, for men and women

of Bethlehem. Behind the doors of Hell, in bondage, we
waited in misery. The murderer took wild delight
enslaving us, and our old enemies knew such ecstasy

in our distress as we, doing penance, imprisoned day and night,
lamented for our kinsmen, until You, our Lord and King,
bravest of all, brought hope amongst us. Hence, with all our might,

in pride, we place ourselves before You, pleading;
through sin and greed, we bear great sorrow in our heart
before our slaughterer, and must sue for peace, seeking

judgment from our foes. Jerusalem of the Jews, set apart
by staying steadfast in your place, not all of those who know
how to pronounce your praise and who dwell here on this earth

may move amongst you. Jordan of the Jews, set apart
by staying steadfast in your place, you may not flow
peacefully around all those people who have known no dearth

of joy from your dear waters. I would, out of our depths, O Word
of life, that You, Savior of us all, look mercifully down
on us in our miseries, You, mankind's Maker. You, Lord,

for the benefit of humankind, sought Your mother's breast, O Crown
of Victory, not out of Your own need, *Verbum nostrum,*
but from mercy, a mercy You have poured out on men who have drowned

oft ætywdest,   þonne him wæs are þearf.
115 þu meaht ymbfon   eal folca gesetu,
swylce þu meaht geriman,   rice dryhten,
sæs sondgrotu,   selast ealra cyninga.
Swylce ic þe halsige,   hælend user,
fore . . . inum cildhade,   cyninga selast,
120 ond fore þære wunde,   weoruda dry . . .
þinum æriste,   æþelinga wyn,
ond fore þinre me . . .   . . . ian nama,
þa ealle hellwara   hergað ond lof . . .
. . . lum   þe þe ymb stondað,
125 þa þu þe lete sittan   . . . . . . hond,
þa þu us on þisne wræcsið,   weoroda dryhten,
þurh þines sylfes geweald   secan woldest,
ond **fore** Hierusalem   in Iudeum,
(sceal seo burg nu þa   bidan efne swa **þeah**,
130 þeoden leofa,   þines eftcymes),
ond for Iordane   in Iudeum,
(wit unc in þære burnan   baþodan ætgædre).
Oferwurpe þu mid þy wætre,   weoruda dryhten,
bliþe mode   ealle burgwaran,
135 swylce git Iohannis   in Iordane
mid þy fullwihte   fægre onbryrdon
ealne þisne middangeard.   Sie þæs symle meotude þonc!"

in the greatest need of grace. In You there will be blest
all places and all peoples, You have power to number, too,
Lord of all strength, the grains of sand in the sea. Best

of Kings, I call You, too, Savior of us all, and Counselor, through
memory of Your childhood, O Most Powerful, through Your pains,
O Richest in Glory, through Your rising, greatest of Kings, You

and Your mother, whose name is Mary, who reigns
with You, whom the inhabitants of Hell all hold in honor and praise,
and through Your angels ranged about You, who, with royal trains

of glory are set at Your right hand, when You, Lord God, raise
us here out of our exile, You have abandoned Your excellent place,
through Your own will and power, and by Jerusalem of the Jews, please

(city that yet, beloved Lord, believes in Your coming in blessed grace)
and by Jordan of the Jews, (both of us bathed together
in the one stream) wash from us with such sacred water all trace

of sin, bind the inhabitants of this city blithely into one, whether
with Judah or with John, in Jordan waters, and send Your spirit then
on all this world, this middle-earth, in baptism, in the blessed weather

of Your presence, to be praised, for ever, and for evermore." Amen.

from Andreas

Gesæt him þa se halga   helmwearde neah,
360 æðele be æðelum.   æfre ic ne hyrde
þon cymlicor   ceol gehladenne
heahgestreonum.   Hæleð in sæton,
þeodnas þrymfulle,   þegnas wlitige.
ða reordode   rice þeoden,
365 ece ælmihtig,   heht his engel gan,
mærne maguþegn,   ond mete syllan,
frefran feasceafte   ofer flodes wylm,
þæt hie þe eað mihton   ofer yða geþring
drohtaþ adreogan.   þa gedrefed wearð,
370 onhrered hwælmere.   Hornfisc plegode,
glad geond garsecg,   ond se græga mæw
wælgifre wand.   Wedercandel swearc,
windas weoxon,   wægas grundon,
streamas styredon,   strengas gurron,
375 wædo gewætte.   Wæteregsa stod
þreata þryðum.   þegnas wurdon
acolmode.   ænig ne wende
þæt he lifgende   land begete,
þara þe mid Andreas   on eagorstream
380 ceol gesohte.   Næs him cuð þa gyt
hwa þam sæflotan   sund wisode.
Him þa se halga   on holmwege
ofer argeblond,   Andreas þa git,

from **Andreas**

Eamon Grennan

The apostle Matthew has been imprisoned by a cannibal people, the
Mermedonians. Instructed by God, the apostle Andrew travels by sea to
their land to save him. With his band of followers, he boards a ship that is,
unknown to him, captained by God Himself.

Then the saint sat down by the ship's captain—
two noble men together. I've never heard tell
of a finer vessel, brim-full with treasure.
A crew of heroes came aboard her—
highborn men all, and all handsome.
Then the almighty, everlasting Lord
ordered his angel, his illustrious servant,
to bring food and comfort to those cast out
on the surging sea, so they'd survive
that salty tumult. Sea-rage increased then:
spear-fish rearing up, springing between billows,
while a gray seagull savage with hunger
circles and circles. The sun-candle's quenched:
storm winds howl, waves crash and heave:
ocean roaring, ship's tackle groaning,
everything sea-sodden. Then the surging deep
rose up like an army rigged for battle,
so the heroes' hearts heaved with terror.
Not one of those who'd set sail with Andrew
believed they'd reach land again alive.
Still no one knew who was steering the ship
on that rolling sea-road. Yet even then
on this tide-way of troubled water
the holy Andrew, loyal to his lord,

þegn þeodenhold,   þanc gesægde,
385 ricum ræsboran,   þa he gereordod wæs:
"ðe þissa swæsenda   soðfæst meotud,
lifes leohtfruma,   lean forgilde,
weoruda waldend,   ond þe wist gife,
heofonlicne hlaf,   swa ðu hyldo wið me
390 ofer firigendstream   freode gecyðdest!
Nu synt geþreade   þegnas mine,
geonge guðrincas.   Garsecg hlymmeð,
geofon geotende.   Grund is onhrered,
deope gedrefed,   **duguð** is geswenced,
395 modigra mægen   myclum gebysgod."
Him of **helman** oncwæð   hæleða scyppend:
"Læt nu geferian   flotan userne,
lid to lande   ofer lagufæsten,
ond þonne gebidan   beornas þine,
400 aras on earde,   hwænne ðu eft cyme."
Edre him þa eorlas   agefan ondsware,
þegnas þrohthearde,   þafigan ne woldon
ðæt hie forleton   æt lides stefnan
leofne lareow   ond him land curon:
405 "Hwider hweorfað we   hlafordlease,
geomormode,   gode orfeorme,
synnum wunde,   gif we swicað þe?
We bioð laðe   on landa gehwam,
folcum fracoðe,   þonne fira bearn,
410 ellenrofe,   æht besittaþ,
hwylc hira selost   symle gelæste
hlaforde æt hilde,   þonne hand ond rond
on beaduwange   billum **forgrunden**
æt niðplegan   nearu þrowedon."

refreshed after eating, found the words
to give thanks to that great Captain:
"For this meal may almighty God—
Author of light and life, Lord of hosts—
reward you with food, with the bread of heaven,
since you showed on this high-shouldering ocean
such loving-kindness to me and my men!
Now my young band of battle-tough warriors
are all grief-stricken. In great surges
the sea roars around them; the ocean's roused,
its depths shaken: my troop of soldiers,
a brave battalion, is sorrow-broken."
From the helm the Creator answered him:
"Let this vessel of ours voyage on
over the tossing sea till it touches land,
where these men of yours can make camp
and be safe, so, till you sail back to them."
But right away the warriors responded,
those young soldiers steady in adversity: ·
they'd never abandon their beloved teacher,
leaving him at sea while they chose land.
"Where should we look then, lacking our leader—
heavy-hearted, nothing good about us,
and sin-blighted if we betrayed you?
We'd be loathed in every land:
people will despise us when daring men
come together to say in council
who's always best at backing up his lord
in any heavy struggle—where hands
are severed, shields sword-splintered
in the cut and thrust of terrible battle."

Wæs þæs halgan lic

sarbennum soden,   swate bestemed,

1240 banhus abrocen.   Blod yðum weoll,

hatan heolfre.   Hæfde him on innan

ellen untweonde,   wæs þæt æðele mod

asundrad fram synnum,   þeah he sares swa feala

deopum dolgslegum   dreogan sceolde.

1245 Swa wæs ealne dæg   oððæt æfen com

sigetorht swungen.   Sar eft gewod

ymb þæs beornes breost,   oðþæt beorht gewat

sunne swegeltorht   to sete glidan.

Læddan þa leode   laðne gewinnan

1250 to carcerne.   He wæs Criste swa þeah

leof on mode.   Him wæs leoht sefa

halig heortan neh,   hige untyddre.

þa se halga wæs   under heolstorscuwan,

eorl ellenheard,   ondlange niht

1255 searoþancum beseted.   Snaw eorðan band

wintergeworpum.   Weder coledon

heardum hægelscurum,   swylce hrim ond forst,

hare hildstapan,   hæleða eðel

lucon, leoda gesetu.   Land wæron freorig

1260 cealdum cylegicelum,   clang wæteres þrym

ofer eastreamas,   is brycgade

*Having reached shore, and recognized at last who the ship's captain was,
Andrew (God having departed) enters the city and releases Matthew, who
leaves in safety. Andrew then reenters the city, where he is taken by the
Mermedonians, imprisoned and tortured.*

                    Then the saint's body
was blood-sodden, soaked in its wounds—
his house of bone bruised beyond measure
so blood gushed out, a pulsing gore.
Still his soul was never shaken.
His saintly mind was free of sin
though he had to endure desperate torments:
grief-giving blows and bloody gashes.
So all day till evening descended
this sun-bright man was scourged:
bitter pains laid siege to his body
till the radiant sun had left the sky—
that field of light—and found its rest.
Then those people hauled to prison
their loathed foe. Still Christ was his friend
and held him in His heart; high-minded,
that saintly spirit was never shaken.
Then the dear man lay in darkness
all night long, this soldier of the Lord,
full of wise thoughts. Snow bound the world
in wintry drifts, the weather grew chill:
hail hammered down, hoar frost
came marching like a rime-gray militia
and locked up the land wherever folk lodged,
manacling fields and people, snapping shackles
on their dwelling-places. Icicles, dead cold,
froze everything in sight. The river-spate
hardened: a bridge of black ice

blæce brimrade.   Bliðheort wunode
eorl unforcuð,   elnes gemyndig,
þrist ond þrohtheard   in þreanedum
1265 wintercealdan niht.   No on gewitte blon,
acol for þy egesan,   þæs þe he ær ongann,
þæt he a domlicost   dryhten herede,
weorðade wordum,   oððæt wuldres gim
heofontorht onhlad.   ða com hæleða þreat
1270 to ðære dimman ding,   duguð unlytel,
wadan wælgifre   weorodes brehtme.
Heton ut hræðe   æðeling lædan
in wraðra geweald,   wærfæstne hæleð.
ða wæs eft swa ær   ondlangne dæg
1275 swungen sarslegum.   Swat yðum weoll
þurh bancofan,   ˙blodlifrum swealg,
hatan heolfre.   Hra weorces ne sann,
wundum werig.

þæt is fyrnsægen,
1490 hu he weorna feala   wita geðolode,
heardra hilda,   in þære hæðenan byrig.
He be wealle geseah   wundrum **fæste**
under **sælwage**   sweras unlytle,
stapulas standan,   storme bedrifene,
1495 eald enta geweorc.   He wið anne þæra,
mihtig ond **modrof,**   mæðel gehede,
wis, wundrum gleaw,   word stunde ahof:

braced itself over the ocean. Blameless,
the hero remained heart-happy, his mind
full of courage, enduring all calmly
through the winter-frigid night; his words
praising God till heaven's precious jewel
appeared, blazing in the blue.
Then the mob, a mighty rabble,
descended into that grim dungeon—
carrion-hungry, a clamorous gang.
They gave orders, then, that the good man,
the loyal hero, should be led out
and hurried into the hands of his enemies.
Then, as before, for the livelong day
he was beaten and battered: his blood
spurted from every pore, smothering him
in its hot gobbets. Wound-weary as he was,
still he paid no heed to his pain.

The sufferings of Andrew continue, which he endures until, by the divine intervention of a miracle, he overcomes his captors.

                    Tradition tells us
the many brutalities and beastly torments
he had to bear in that heathen city. But then
he saw by the side of a certain building,
fixed to the wall, fantastic columns:
weather-worn, storm-beaten standing pillars
giant-built in times gone by. Brave of heart,
uncowed, he right away confronted one of them;
wise, far-seeing, he spoke these words:

"Geher ðu, marmanstan,   meotudes rædum,
fore þæs onsyne   ealle gesceafte
1500 forhte geweorðað,   þonne hie fæder geseoð
heofonas ond eorðan   herigea mæste
on middangeard   mancynn secan.
Læt nu of þinum staþole   streamas weallan,
ea inflede,   nu ðe ælmihtig
1505 hateð, heofona cyning,   þæt ðu hrædlice
on þis fræte folc   forð onsende
wæter widrynig   to wera cwealme,
geofon geotende.   Hwæt, ðu golde eart,
sincgife, sylla!   On ðe sylf cyning
1510 wrat, wuldres god,   wordum cyðde
recene geryno,   ond ryhte æ
getacnode   on tyn wordum,
meotud mihtum swið.   Moyse sealde,
swa hit soðfæste   syðþan heoldon,
1515 modige magoþegnas,   magas sine,
godfyrhte guman,   **Iosua** ond Tobias.
Nu ðu miht gecnawan   þæt þe cyning engla
gefrætwode   furður mycle
giofum geardagum   þonne eall gimma cynn.
1520 þurh his halige hæs   þu scealt hræðe cyðan
gif ðu his ondgitan   ænige hæbbe."
Næs þa wordlatu   wihte þon mare
þæt se stan togan.   Stream ut aweoll,
fleow ofer foldan.   Famige walcan
1525 mid ærdæge   eorðan þehton,
myclade mereflod.   Meoduscerwen wearð
æfter symbeldæge,   slæpe tobrugdon
searuhæbbende.   Sund grunde onfeng,
deope gedrefed.   Duguð wearð afyrhted
1530 þurh þæs flodes fær.   Fæge swulton,

"Listen, carved stone of marble, to our Lord's decree,
in whose terrible sight all creatures will tremble,
seeing the high Creator of heaven and earth
entering with his enormous army
the world he made, seeking mankind.
Let streams now flood from your foundations,
a river rush out of them, for this very instant
the almighty King of heaven commands you
to spew at once on this stiff-necked people
a great spate of water to wipe them out,
smother them in wild sea surges. Don't you see
you're nobler than gold or any rich gift!
On stone like you the invincible King of heaven
has written words that at once revealed
the terrible mysteries and true law
carved into his Ten Commandments. . . .
Now you can show, hearing his holy edict,
if you've understood any of this at all."
In the blink of an eye the order was obeyed:
the stone in an instant split asunder
and a fierce flood-rush overflowed the land.
By daybreak the springtide had drowned the earth
in frothing surf. After the day's feasting
came a bitter drink: those armed men
started from sleep: stirred from its depths,
water overwhelmed the world.
Trained soldiers were terrified
by the flood's fury: doomed to die,

geonge on geofene   guðræs fornam
þurh **sealtne weg**.   þæt wæs sorgbyrþen,
biter beorþegu.   Byrlas ne gældon,
ombehtþegnas.   þær wæs ælcum genog
1535 fram dæges orde   drync sona gearu.
Weox wæteres þrym.   Weras cwanedon,
ealde æscberend.   Wæs him ut myne
fleon fealone stream,   woldon feore beorgan,
to dunscræfum   drohtað secan,
1540 eorðan ondwist.   Him þæt engel forstod,
se ða burh oferbrægd   blacan lige,
hatan heaðowælme.   Hreoh wæs þær inne
beatende brim.   Ne mihte beorna hloð
of þam fæstenne   fleame spowan.
1545 Wægas weoxon,   wadu hlynsodon,
flugon fyrgnastas,   flod yðum weoll.
ðær wæs yðfynde   innan burgum
geomorgidd wrecen.   Gehðo mændan
forhtferð manig,   fusleoð **golon**.
1550 Egeslic æled   eagsyne wearð,
heardlic hereteam,   hleoðor gryrelic.
þurh lyftgelac   leges blæstas
weallas ymbwurpon,   wæter mycladon.
þær wæs wop wera   wide gehyred,
1555 earmlic ylda gedræg.   þa þær an ongann,
feasceaft hæleð,   folc gadorigean,
hean, hygegeomor,   heofende spræc:
"Nu ge magon sylfe   soð gecnawan,
þæt we mid unrihte   ellþeodigne
1560 on carcerne   clommum belegdon,
witebendum.   Us seo wyrd scyðeð,
heard ond hetegrim.   þæt is her swa cuð,
is hit mycle selre,   þæs þe ic soð talige,

young men were swept into the salty abyss
as in the tide of battle. A sorrowful brew
it was, a draft of bitter beer: servants, cupbearers
went diligently to work: from dawn of day
the drink was ready—enough for everyone.
The flood increased: men cried out,
old spear-carriers craving escape: to flee
the gleaming water, be safe far away
among high mountain caves, housed there
in any earth-refuge. But an angel stayed them,
shrouding the city in sheets of fire,
in a swirl of scald-mist. Inside, the sea
battered everything, so those battalions
closed in their stronghold couldn't escape.
The torrent grew rougher: waves roared,
sparks went flying, the flood surging,
and in the city it was easy to come on
a dirge being sung: many a scared man
moaning over his sorrow, singing a song of death.
Sight-blasting fires burned brighter:
catastrophe, devastation, deafening clamor;
whirlwinds whipping flames to a frenzy;
walls enveloped; waters rising higher;
and the sound, widespread, of people wailing,
wretched men crying out. Then one man—
old, forlorn, grief-stricken—began to gather
the people together, speaking through tears:
"Now you see the truth for yourselves:
without justice we punished this stranger,
flinging him in prison, putting fetters on him
of cruel bondage. So we're being crushed
by this stone-pitiless fate. Can't you see
it's best—I believe this; it's true surely—

þæt we hine alysan   of leoðobendum,
1565 ealle anmode,   (ofost is selost),
ond us þone halgan   helpe biddan,
geoce ond frofre.   Us bið gearu sona
sybb æfter sorge,   gif we secaþ to him."
þa þær Andrea   orgete wearð
1570 on fyrhðlocan   folces gebæro,
þær wæs modigra   **mægen** forbeged,
wigendra þrym.   Wæter fæðmedon,
fleow firgendstream,   flod wæs on luste,
oþþæt breost oferstag,   brim weallende,
1575 eorlum oð exle.   þa se æðeling het
streamfare stillan,   stormas restan
ymbe stanhleoðu.   Stop ut hræðe
cene collenferð,   carcern ageaf,
gleawmod, gode leof.   Him wæs gearu sona
1580 þurh streamræce   stræt gerymed.
Smeolt wæs se sigewang,   symble wæs dryge
folde fram flode,   swa his fot gestop.
Wurdon burgware   bliðe on mode,
ferhðgefeonde.   þa wæs forð cumen
1585 geoc æfter gyrne.   Geofon swaðrode
þurh haliges hæs,   hlyst yst forgeaf,
brimrad gebad.   þa se beorg tohlad,
eorðscræf egeslic,   ond þær in forlet
flod fæðmian,   fealewe wægas,
1590 geotende gegrind   grund eall forswealg.
Nalas he þær yðe   ane bisencte,
ach þæs weorodes eac   ða wyrrestan,
faa folcsceaðan,   feowertyne
gewiton mid þy wæge   in forwyrd sceacan
1595 under eorþan grund.   þa wearð acolmod,
forhtferð manig   folces on laste.

that we agree to release him right now,
and ask this holy man to help us,
to settle and comfort us. Solace after sorrow
we'll find soon enough, and we turn to him."
There and then Andrew knew full well
in his inmost heart how it was with the people:
that here the pride of the mighty was humbled,
their force subdued. Then the waters kept spreading:
that tumble-flood raged in a rushing torrent
till it rose, a buffeting ocean, above men's breasts,
even to their shoulders. Then the noble man shouted
to the waters to subside, the storm to be still
around those sloped stones. Then, with all speed,
that man of courage quit the prison:
wise-minded he was, dear to the Lord. With haste
a way was made for him through all that water.
Serene was the site of his victory: wherever
he laid foot the flood receded, the ground dried up.
Then the townspeople tasted true happiness,
their hearts jumped with joy. For help had come,
comfort after calamity: the sea stilled
and the storm silenced by the saint's command.
So the flood subsided. Then the holy one split open
a deep pit in the earth, let the waters pour in
in a swirling surge: the ground swallowed all up.
Not only did he cause the cataract to sink there,
but a slew of the city's most vicious criminals—
fourteen unrepentant enemies of the people—
were rushed to destruction in that raging torrent,
dashed into the depths of the earth. Full of dread,
terror-stricken, were all those still in the city:

Wendan hie wifa   ond wera cwealmes,
þearlra geþinga   ðrage hnagran,
syððan mane faa,   morðorscyldige,
1600 guðgelacan   under grund hruron.

they expected a slaughter of men and women,
some terrible fate, a time utterly wretched,
seeing those blood-guilty killers—
wicked warriors all—perish in the abyss.

*But, after this, Andrew brings back to life all the young men who—though
not guilty—had been drowned in the flood. This leads to the conversion of a
great multitude of the defeated but now reconciled citizens, whose spirits he
restores. His mission accomplished, the saint leaves Mermedonia in triumph.*

Fifth
Riddle-Hoard

Riddle 50

Wiga is on eorþan   wundrum acenned
dryhtum to nytte,   of dumbum twam
torht atyhted,   þone on teon wigeð
feond his feonde.   **Forstrangne** oft
5 wif hine wrið;   he him wel hereð,
þeowaþ him geþwære,   gif him þegniað
mægeð ond mæcgas   mid gemete ryhte,
fedað hine fægre;   he him fremum stepeð
life on lissum.   Leanað grimme
10 þam þe hine wloncne   weorþan læteð.

Riddle 51

Ic seah wrætlice   wuhte feower
samed siþian;   swearte wæran lastas,
swaþu swiþe blacu.   Swift wæs on fore,
fuglum framra;   **fleag on** lyfte,
5 deaf under yþe.   Dreag unstille
winnende wiga   se him **wegas** tæcneþ
ofer fæted gold   feower eallum.

Fighter across the Earth

Peter Campion

Fighter across the earth:
two speechless creatures birth
him
        glimmering.
                Then
he rides to war with men
though tended by their wives.

If carefully held
                he lives
to please, brings warm reward.
But if he goes ignored

he puffs with proud disdain:
his only gift is pain.

I Saw Four Beings

Jane Hirshfield

I saw four beings
traveling strangely as one.
That creature took dark steps,
left tracks of surprising blackness.
It moved more quickly when as a bird flock
it climbed now in clear air,
plunged now beneath black waves.
It seemed a ceaseless laboring
when a noble warrior drove those four
to mark one road across the painted gold.

Riddle 52

Ic seah ræpingas   in ræced fergan
under hrof sales   hearde twegen,
þa wæron **genamnan**,   nearwum bendum
gefeterade   fæste togædre;
5   þara oþrum wæs   an getenge
wonfah Wale,   seo weold hyra
bega siþe   bendum fæstra.

Riddle 53

Ic seah on bearwe   beam hlifian,
tanum torhtne.   þæt treow wæs on wynne,
wudu weaxende.   Wæter hine ond eorþe
feddan fægre,   oþþæt he frod dagum
5   on oþrum wearð   aglachade
deope gedolgod,   dumb in bendum,
wriþen ofer wunda,   wonnum hyrstum
foran gefrætwed.   Nu he fæcnum **weg**
þurh his heafdes **mægen**   hildegieste
10   oþrum rymeð.   Oft hy an **yste** strudon
hord ætgædre;   hræd wæs ond unlæt
se æftera,   gif se ærra fær
genamnan in nearowe   neþan moste.

I Saw the Captives Carried In

Macdara Woods

I saw the captives carried in,
Under the rafters, two hard men
Tethered at the neck
In fierce and harsh constraint.
At hand, a dark-skinned Welsh girl,
Given the bossing of them,
Who directed their halting
Hobble-gait course together.

I Saw a Tree Tinseled with Light

James Harpur

I saw a tree tinseled with light,
towering from the forest, full of heart,
rich in sap. With its soil and rain
it was doing so well, until in its dotage
it fell into wretchedness—riven deep,
silent in chains wrapped round its scars,
a dark sheath adorning its forehead.

Now his strong skull smashes a path
clearing the way for another sly warrior.
In the hurricane of battle, they'll plunder the hoard,
and if the first is boxed in, needs to be freed,
his friend must react, with energy and speed.

Riddle 54

Hyse cwom gangan,   þær he hie wisse
stondan in wincsele,   stop feorran to,
hror hægstealdmon,   hof his agen
hrægl hondum up,   **hrand** under gyrdels
5 hyre stondendre   stiþes nathwæt,
worhte his willan;   wagedan buta.
þegn onnette,   wæs þragum nyt
tillic esne,   teorode hwæþre
æt stunda gehwam   strong ær þon **hio**,
10 werig þæs weorces.   Hyre weaxan ongon
under gyrdelse   þæt oft gode men
ferðþum freogað   ond mid feo bicgað.

A Boy Came Walking to Where He Knew
Marcia Karp

A boy came walking to where he knew
she would stand for what he would do.
He stepped from afar to her in that corner.
      His hand raised his shirt.
      He pushed under her skirt
his stiff I-know-not-what and he horned her.

That boy worked his will; they waggled together.
His good servant bestirred him and sometimes did help.
That strong handyman stopped, bedraggled, who'd wet her
      who'd only begun,
      though he'd come undone.

      Then there did grow
      in her below
what good men might hold dear and get by their wealth.

Riddle 56

Ic wæs þær inne   þær ic ane geseah
 winnende wiht   wido bennegean,
holt hweorfende;   heaþoglemma feng,
deopra dolga.   Daroþas wæron
5   weo þære wihte,   ond se wudu searwum
fæste gebunden.   Hyre fota wæs
biidfæst oþer,   oþer bisgo dreag,
leolc on lyfte,   hwilum londe neah.
Treow wæs getenge   þam þær torhtan stod
10 leafum bihongen.   Ic lafe geseah
minum hlaforde,   þær hæleð druncon,
þara **flana geweorc**,   on flet beran.

Riddle 57

ðeos lyft byreð   lytle wihte
ofer beorghleoþa.   þa sind blace swiþe,
swearte salopade.   Sanges rope
heapum ferað,   hlude cirmað,
5   tredað bearonæssas,   hwilum burgsalo
niþþa bearna.   Nemnað hy sylfe.

I Was in There Where I Saw a Turning

Phillis Levin

I was in there where I saw a turning
wood-beam injure
a striving creature enduring battle-wounds,
deep wounds. Darts
were a woe to that creature, and with craft
was the wood bound fast. One foot
was fixed securely, the other worked busily,
jumping into the air, close at times
to the ground. Nearby was a tree, brightly
standing there, draped all around
with leaves. I saw the unleavings, the work
of those darts, carried off
to my lord, into a hall of warriors drinking.

The Wind Sends Small Creatures

Gary Soto

The wind sends small creatures
From the other side of the headlands:
Feathery as grain, fine as smoke,
They arrive dark but brighten to chirm and clamor.
They are many, an army to themselves,
Angling for the green pond but not touching down.
We folks know them from a distance,
Salute them with hands over our furrowed brows.
As they toot the language of trees,
We recognize a common song.

Riddle 60

Ic wæs be sonde,   sæwealle neah,
æt merefaroþe,   minum gewunade
frumstaþole fæst;   fea ænig wæs
monna cynnes,   þæt minne þær
5   on anæde   eard beheolde,
ac mec uhtna gehwam   yð sio brune
lagufæðme beleolc.   Lyt ic wende
þæt ic ær oþþe sið   æfre sceolde
ofer **meodubence**   muðleas sprecan,
10   wordum wrixlan.   þæt is wundres dæl,
on sefan searolic   þam þe swylc ne conn,
hu mec **seaxes** ord   ond seo swiþre hond,
eorles ingeþonc   ond ord somod,
þingum geþydan,   þæt ic wiþ þe sceolde
15   for unc anum **twam**   ærendspræce
abeodan bealdlice,   swa hit beorna ma
uncre wordcwidas   widdor ne mænden.

I Stood Once by Sand, Near the Sea-Surge
Jane Hirshfield

I stood once by sand, near the sea-surge
close by the shore, fast-rooted in my first life.
Few, almost none among men,
saw my solitude and dwelling-place there,
though each dawn small waves would come to play,
covering me in the dark embraces of water.
I little guessed I would ever, early or late,
speak mouthless across the bench of a mead hall,
exchanging voiceless words. It is a wonder
quite inconceivable to any mind that does not know
how a knife-tip held by a strong right hand,
a man's cleverness and a sharp point come together,
might work on me such ardent change
that I might with confidence carry a message,
tell you what we two alone might hear,
that no one else could spread our conversation further.

Riddle 61

Oft mec fæste bileac   freolicu meowle,
ides on earce,   hwilum up ateah
folmum sinum   ond frean sealde,
holdum þeodne,   swa hio haten wæs.
5 Siðþan me on hreþre   heafod sticade,
nioþan upweardne,   on nearo fegde.
Gif þæs ondfengan   ellen dohte,
mec frætwedne   fyllan sceolde
ruwes nathwæt.   Ræd hwæt ic mæne.

Riddle 62

Ic eom heard ond scearp,   **hingonges** strong,
forðsiþes from,   frean unforcuð,
wade under wambe   ond me weg sylfa
ryhtne geryme.   Rinc bið on ofeste,
5 se mec on þyð   æftanweardne,
hæleð mid hrægle;   hwilum ut tyhð
of hole hatne,   hwilum eft fareð
on nearo nathwær,   nydeþ swiþe
suþerne secg.   Saga hwæt ic hatte.

She Has Me Under Lock and Key
Neil Rollinson

She has me under lock and key
this lass—until he wants to play,
and then she takes me out
and holds me up and begs her master
kneel for her: the hairy nut.
He shoves his greasy loaf in
nice and tight, a hearty thrust
that leaves him proud and fired up.
I take the noble head. I'm full of it.
What do you make of that?

I Am the Hard, Headstrong Push and Pull
Gail Holst-Warhaft

I am the hard, headstrong push and pull
of power forcing forward, coming keen in
as I serve my lord. I burrow
a tight tunnel under the belly
while my lord heaves hasty from behind.
Cloth catching, he drags me hot from the hole
or thrusts me through a tight passage
urging me on, the southern thruster.
Say who I am.

Prayers, Admonitions, and Allegories

Cædmon's Hymn: West Saxon Version

Nu sculon herigean   heofonrices weard,
meotodes meahte   and his modgeþanc,
weorc wuldorfæder,   swa he wundra gehwæs,
ece drihten,   or onstealde.
5   He ærest sceop   eorðan bearnum
heofon to hrofe,   halig scyppend;
þa middangeard   moncynnes weard,
ece drihten,   æfter teode
firum foldan,   frea ælmihtig.

Cædmon's Hymn

Harvey Shapiro

Guardian of heaven   whom we come to praise
who mapped creation   in His thought's sinews
Glory-Father   who worked out each wonder
began with broad earth   a gift for His children
first roofed it with heaven   the Holy Shaper
established it forever   as in the beginning
called it middle kingdom   fenced it with angels
created a habitation   for man to praise His splendor

The Kentish Hymn

Wuton wuldrian   weorada dryhten
halgan hlioðorcwidum,   hiofenrices weard,
lufian liofwendum,   lifæs agend,
and him simle sio   sigefæst wuldor
5 uppe mid **ænglum**,   and on eorðan sibb
gumena gehwilcum   goodes willan.
We ðe heriað   halgum stefnum
and þe blætsiað,   **bilewit** fæder,
and ðe þanciað,   þioda walden,
10 ðines weorðlican   wuldordreames
and **ðinra** miclan   mægena gerena,
ðe ðu, god dryhten,   gastes mæhtum
hafest on gewealdum   hiofen and eorðan,
an ece fæder,   ælmehtig god.
15 ðu eart cyninga cyningc   cwicera gehwilces,
ðu eart sigefest sunu   and soð hælend
ofer ealle gescæft   angla and manna.
ðu, dryhten god,   on dreamum wunast
on ðære upplican   æðelan ceastre,
20 frea folca gehwæs,   swa ðu æt fruman wære
efeneadig bearn   agenum fæder.
ðu eart heofenlic lioht   and ðæt halige lamb,
ðe **ðu** manscilde   middangeardes
for þinre arfæstnesse   ealle towurpe,
25 fiond geflæmdest,   follc generedes,
blode gebohtest   bearn Israela,
ða ðu ahofe   ðurh ðæt halige triow

The Kentish Hymn

Derek Mahon

Lord, we praise you with pious voices,
Guardian of the godly kingdom,
love loudly the Lord of Life
and grant you gladly your great glory.

We bless you, Lord, above with angels,
for peace on Earth, eternal Father,
goodwill to men, with grateful voices,
and give thanks, Author of nations,

for all your great glories on high,
you who through spirit-strength for ever
hold in your hand Heaven and Earth,
merciful Father, far-seeing God.

You are the Creator, King of all kings,
triumphant Son and true Savior
of men and angels, all creation,
in your supreme palace above.

As in the beginning, beloved by all,
holy Lamb and light of Heaven,
the many sins of middle Earth
you overthrew through your virtue,

put the fiend to flight for us,
preserved the people of Israel
when you hung on that holy tree

ðinre ðrowunga   ðriostre senna,
þæt ðu on hæahsetle   heafena rices
30 sitest sigehræmig   on ða swiðran hand
ðinum godfæder,   gasta gemyndig.
Mildsa nu, meahtig,   manna cynne,
and of leahtrum ales   ðine ða liofan gescæft,
and us hale gedo,   heleða sceppend,
35 niða nergend,   for ðines naman are.
ðu eart soðlice   simle halig,
and ðu eart ana   æce dryhten,
and ðu ana bist   eallra dema
cwucra ge deadra,   Crist **nergende**,
40 forðan ðu on ðrymme ricsast   and on ðrinesse
and on annesse,   ealles waldend,
hiofena heahcyninc,   haliges gastes
fegere gefelled   in fæder wuldre.

by dying for our deadly sins.

Now on your high heavenly throne
you sit glorious at God's right hand.
Show mercy to mankind, O Lord,
absolve your belovèd world of sin.

Grant us health, holy Creator.
You are our one undying Lord
and you alone will know us all,
quick and dead, Christ our Savior.

Our help in trouble, triumphant Name,
over the whole you rule as a Trinity,
High King of Heaven, Holy Ghost
and gracious Son, one with the Father.

Metrical Epilogue to the Pastoral Care

ðis is nu se wæterscipe   ðe us wereda god
to frofre gehet   foldbuendum.
He cwæð ðæt he wolde   ðæt on worulde forð
of ðæm innoðum   a libbendu
5 wætru fleowen,   ðe wel on hine
gelifden under lyfte.   Is hit lytel tweo
ðæt ðæs wæterscipes   welsprynge is
on hefonrice,   ðæt is halig gæst.
ðonan hine hlodan   halge and gecorene,
10 siððan hine gierdon   ða ðe gode herdon
ðurh halga bec   hider on eorðan
geond manna mod   missenlice.
Sume hine weriað   on gewitlocan,
wisdomes stream,   welerum gehæftað,
15 ðæt he on unnyt   ut ne tofloweð.
Ac se wæl wunað   on weres breostum
ðurh dryhtnes giefe   diop and stille.
Sume hine lætað   ofer landscare
riðum torinnan;   nis ðæt rædlic ðing,
20 gif swa hlutor wæter,   hlud and undiop,
tofloweð æfter feldum   oð hit to fenne werð.
Ac hladað iow nu drincan,   nu iow dryhten geaf
ðæt iow Gregorius   gegiered hafað
to durum iowrum   dryhtnes welle.
25 Fylle nu his fætels,   se ðe fæstne hider
kylle brohte,   cume eft hræðe.
Gif her ðegna hwelc   ðyrelne kylle
brohte to ðys burnan,   bete hine georne,
ðy læs he forsceade   scirost wætra,
30 oððe him lifes drync   forloren weorðe.

King Alfred's Epilogue to the Pastoral Care of Gregory the Great

Maurice Riordan

Here is the water which the Lord of all
Pledged for the well-being of His people.
He said it was His wish that water
Should flow forever into this world
Out of the minds of generous men,
Those who serve Him beneath the sky.
But none should doubt the water's source
In Heaven, the home of the Holy Ghost.
It is drawn from there by a chosen few
Who make sacred books their study.
They seek out the tidings they contain,
Then spread the word among mankind.
But some retain it in their hearts.
They never let it pass their lips
Lest it should go to waste in the world.
By this means it stays pure and clear,
A pool within each man's breast.
Others pour it freely over all the land,
Though care must be taken lest it flow
Too loud and fast across the fields,
Transforming them to bogs and fens.
Gather round now with your drinking cups,
Gregory has brought the water to your door.
Fill up, and return again for refills.
If you have come with cups that leak
You must hurry to repair and patch them,
Or else you'll squander the rarest gift,
And the drink of life will be lost to you.

from Phoenix

60 þær ne hægl ne hrim   hreosað to foldan,
    ne windig wolcen,   ne þær wæter fealleþ,
    lyfte gebysgad,   ac þær lagustreamas,
    wundrum wrætlice,   wyllan onspringað
    fægrum **flodwylmum**.   Foldan leccaþ
65 wæter wynsumu   of þæs wuda midle;
    þa monþa gehwam   of þære moldan tyrf
    brimcald brecað,   bearo ealne geondfarað,
    þragum þrymlice.   Is þæt þeodnes gebod,
    þætte twelf siþum   þæt tirfæste
70 lond geondlace   lagufloda wynn.

         þonne feor ond neah
    þa swetestan   somnað ond gædrað
    wyrta wynsume   ond wudubleda
195 to þam eardstede,   æþelstenca gehwone,
    wyrta wynsumra,   þe wuldorcyning,
    fæder frymða gehwæs,   ofer foldan gescop
    to indryhtum   ælda cynne,
    swetes under swegle.   þær he sylf biereð
200 in þæt treow innan   torhte frætwe;
    þær se wilda fugel   in þam westenne
    ofer heanne beam   hus getimbreð,
    wlitig ond wynsum,   ond gewicað þær

from The Phoenix

Robert Anthony Welch

1 THE PHOENIX'S EDEN

Neither frost nor hail fall there to earth
nor do clouds descend, nor sleet get driven
by lashing winds. No, clear streams,
wondrous and strange, are here, sweet waters
that spring, freely, in the middle of the wood
to enrich the soil. Every month, through the grass
and leaf-mould, these waters pulse, cold
as the sea, and flow steadily throughout
the grove: it is God's will that twelve
times a year these delightful waters
should flow out over this marvelous ground.

2 THE PHOENIX'S DEATH AND
REBIRTH IN THE SYRIAN FOREST

Far and near it gathers up
fragrant spoils, the sweetest herbs
and foliage of the forest for its steading in the wood.
Every plant and flower with the choicest scent,
created for us by the King of Glory,
the Father of all, it brings together.
The most delicate herbs that grow in the sun
it carries itself to a hollow of a tree
that flourishes in a Syrian wildwood,
and there it stores its vernal treasures.
And now the phoenix builds a nest

sylf in þam solere, ond ymbseteð utan
205 in þam leafsceade lic ond feþre
on healfa gehware halgum stencum
ond þam æþelestum eorþan bledum.
Siteð siþes fus. þonne swegles gim
on sumeres tid, sunne hatost,
210 ofer sceadu scineð ond gesceapu dreogeð,
woruld geondwliteð, þonne weorðeð his
hus onhæted þurh hador swegl.
Wyrta wearmiað, willsele stymeð
swetum swæccum, þonne on swole byrneð
215 þurh fyres feng fugel mid neste.
    Bæl bið onæled. þonne brond þeceð
heorodreorges hus, hreoh onetteð,
fealo lig feormað ond fenix byrneð,
fyrngearum frod. þonne fyr þigeð
220 lænne lichoman; lif bið on siðe,
fæges feorhhord, þonne flæsc ond ban
adleg æleð. Hwæþre him eft cymeð
æfter fyrstmearce feorh edniwe,
siþþan þa yslan eft onginnað
225 æfter ligþræce lucan togædre,
geclungne to cleowenne. þonne clæne bið
beorhtast nesta, bæle forgrunden
heaþorofes hof; hra bið acolad,
banfæt gebrocen, ond se bryne sweþrað.
230 þonne of þam ade æples gelicnes
on þære ascan bið eft gemeted,
of þam weaxeð wyrm, wundrum fæger,

in the lofty branches, and dwells alone
in that sun-filled enclosure. In a leafy shade
it spreads about its body and feathers
on every side the exquisite fragrances
from the blossoms of the earth as it sits and awaits
its journey thence. In the summer time
when the sun shines hottest over that shade,
as it surveys all with its tremendous glare
it accomplishes what it is given to do:
the phoenix's nest grows incandescent
with this powerful heat from serenest heaven.
The herbs grow hot and the bird's nest steams
with the sweetest fragrance. With that glow of heat
the bird and its nest are together consumed,
in a fiery blaze, a shock of flame.
Fire engulfs the hour-weary creature,
and, hastening fiercely, yellow flames
lick and devour the timeworn frame
of the phoenix's body. Its life, its destined spirit
now goes forth on its fated journey
as fire scorches flesh and bone.
But, after a time, life returns
to where it was, and the ashes begin
to draw together in the wake of that
fierce ignition, and start to coagulate
into a compacted sphere. The fragrant nest
is now burnt clean, purified by fire,
while the bird itself has grown cold,
its skeleton pulverized. The conflagration past,
a little ball, like an apple, reveals itself
amongst the ashes, and from it waxes
a tiny creature, a flexing thing
lustrous and fair. It's a strange little worm,

swylce he of ægerum   ut alæde,
scir of scylle.   þonne on sceade weaxeð,
235 þæt he ærest bið   swylce earnes brid,
fæger fugeltimber;   ðonne furþor gin
wridað on wynnum,   þæt he bið wæstmum gelic
ealdum earne,   and æfter þon
feþrum gefrætwad,   swylc he æt frymðe wæs,
240 beorht geblowen.   þonne bræd weorþeð
eal edniwe   eft acenned,
synnum asundrad.

like something you'd see breaking out of an egg,
sheer from the shell. In the shade it grows
to a fledgling eagle until it thrives
to a majestic specimen of that tribe;
but then it is covered with the gorgeous feathers
it had before, adorned in radiance.
Its flesh is renewed, is born again,
and, sundered from sin, is utterly
transformed to what it was.

The Panther

Monge sindon   geond middangeard
unrimu cynn,   þe we æþelu ne magon
ryhte areccan   ne rim witan;
þæs wide sind   geond **world** innan
5   fugla ond deora   foldhrerendra
wornas widsceope,   swa wæter bibugeð
þisne beorhtan bosm,   brim grymetende,
sealtyþa geswing.   We bi sumum hyrdon
wrætlice gecynd   wildra secgan
10   firum freamærne   feorlondum on
eard weardian,   eðles neotan
æfter dunscrafum.   Is þæt deor pandher
bi noman haten,   þæs þe niþþa **bearn**,
wisfæste weras   on gewritum **cyþað**
15   bi þam anstapan.   Se is **æghwam** freond,
duguða estig,   butan dracan anum,
þam he in ealle tid   ondwrað leofaþ
þurh yfla gehwylc   þe he geæfnan mæg.
ðæt is wrætlic deor,   wundrum scyne
20   hiwa gehwylces;   swa hæleð secgað,
gæsthalge guman,   þætte Iosephes
tunece wære   telga gehwylces
bleom bregdende,   þara beorhtra gehwylc
æghwæs ænlicra   oþrum lixte
25   dryhta bearnum,   swa þæs deores hiw,
blæc brigda gehwæs,   beorhtra ond scynra
wundrum lixeð,   þætte wrætlicra
æghwylc oþrum,   ænlicra gien

The Panther

Brad Leithauser

Creatures of all kinds are found on earth,
In numbers and natures beyond our reckoning;
Birds of the sky, beasts of the land
Venture to the very limits
Of the seas that enfold the valleyed earth
In roaring breakers.
                  We have heard tell
Of a famed and faraway country where
A wondrous animal lives within
A mountain cave.
              This is the Panther—
For so he is called, and so we have learned
From men of wisdom, whose writings speak
Of this lone rover. Friend to all,
He's generous to all, except the Dragon,
With whom he struggles endlessly,
Seeking always to work him harm.

The Panther is a wondrous beast,
Bravely bright; just as Joseph's coat—
As holy men have told us—shone
With hues of every shade, bedazzling
Its beholders, so the Panther's
Coat is surpassingly various,
Each fair color appearing to glow

ond fægerra   frætwum bliceð,

30 symle sellicra.   He hafað sundorgecynd,

milde, gemetfæst.   He is monþwære,

lufsum ond leoftæl,   nele laþes wiht

ængum geæfnan   butan þam attorsceaþan,

his fyrngeflitan,   þe ic ær fore sægde.

35 Symle fylle fægen,   þonne foddor þigeð,

æfter þam gereordum   ræste seceð

dygle stowe   under dunscrafum;

ðær se **þeodwiga**   þreonihta fæc

swifeð on swefote,   slæpe **gebiesgad**.

40 þonne ellenrof   up astondeð,

þrymme **gewelgad**,   on þone þriddan dæg,

sneome of slæpe.   Sweghleoþor cymeð,

woþa wynsumast   þurh þæs wildres muð.

æfter þære stefne   stenc ut cymeð

45 of þam wongstede,   wynsumra steam,

swettra ond swiþra   swæcca gehwylcum,

wyrta blostmum   ond wudubledum,

eallum æþelicra   eorþan **frætwum**.

þonne of ceastrum   ond cynestolum

50 ond of burgsalum   beornþreat monig

farað foldwegum   folca þryþum,

eoredcystum,   ofestum gefysde,

dareðlacende;   deor efne swa some

æfter þære stefne   on þone stenc farað.

55 Swa is dryhten god,   dreama rædend,

eallum eaðmede   oþrum gesceaftum,

duguða gehwylcre,   butan dracan anum,

attres ordfruman.   þæt is se ealda feond,

þone he gesælde   in susla grund,

Brighter and rarer than the rest.
He is a solitary spirit—
Mild, slow to anger; he's kindly,
Loving and good-natured. He wishes
No harm to any creature except
His enemy, the venomous
Dragon, as I have said before.

Pleased amid plenty, he feasts fully,
Later finding rest and shelter
Hidden in his mountain cave;
There, for three whole nights, wrapped
In slumber, the great warrior reposes;
Then, on the third day, renewed,
Invigorated, he rises straightway
From the depths of sleep; and from his mouth—
Purest of sounds—a melody issues.

Once the music fades, he releases a breath—
A lovely, irresistible scent,
Sweeter than the perfumes of fruits or flowers,
Better than all the goods of earth.
And then from towns, as well as palaces
And castle-halls, throngs of men
Emerge, and animals too, hastening
In search—the music having faded—
For some pathway to that holy incense.

In just this manner the Lord our God,
The Joy-Giver, is generous
To every creature but the Dragon,
That spring of poison—that ancient enemy
Whom He cast in the abyss of torments,

60 ond gefetrade   fyrnum teagum,
    biþeahte þreanydum,   ond þy þriddan dæge
    of digle aras,   þæs þe he deað fore us
    þreo niht þolade,   þeoden engla,
    sigora sellend.   þæt wæs swete stenc,
65 wlitig ond wynsum   geond woruld ealle.
    Siþþan to þam swicce   soðfæste men
    on healfa gehwone   heapum þrungon
    geond ealne ymbhwyrft   eorþan **sceata**.
    Swa se snottra gecwæð   sanctus Paulus:
70 "Monigfealde sind   geond middangeard
    god **ungnyðe**   þe us to giefe dæleð
    ond to feorhnere   fæder ælmihtig,
    ond se anga hyht   ealra gesceafta,
    uppe ge niþre."   þæt is æþele stenc.

Bound in fire, weighted with misery.
And on the third day, He too rose
From his secret place, the Prince of Angels,
The Granter of Victories, who suffered
Death for us.

    That was a sweet scent,
Fair and beckoning on every breeze.
And afterward, steadfast men
Came thronging, drawn to that perfume
From the far reaches of the earth.
So spoke Saint Paul in all his wisdom:
"Manifold throughout the world
Are the lavish bounties granted us
By the Father Almighty, in hope
Of the salvation of all creatures, above
And below."

    That is a goodly scent.

The Whale

Nu ic fitte gen   ymb fisca cynn
wille woðcræfte   wordum cyþan
þurh modgemynd   bi þam miclan hwale.
Se bið unwillum   oft gemeted,
5   frecne ond ferðgrim,   fareðlacendum,
niþþa gehwylcum;   þam is noma cenned,
fyrnstreama geflotan,   Fastitocalon.
Is þæs hiw gelic   hreofum stane,
swylce worie   bi wædes ofre,
10 sondbeorgum ymbseald,   særyrica mæst,
swa þæt wenaþ   wægliþende
þæt hy on ealond sum   eagum wliten,
ond þonne gehydað   heahstefn scipu
to þam unlonde   oncyrrapum,
15 setlaþ sæmearas   sundes æt ende,
ond þonne in þæt eglond   up gewitað
collenferþe;   ceolas stondað
bi staþe fæste,   streame biwunden.
ðonne gewiciað   werigferðe,
20 faroðlacende,   frecnes ne wenað,
on þam ealonde   æled weccað,
heahfyr ælað;   hæleþ beoþ on wynnum,
reonigmode,   ræste geliste.
þonne gefeleð   facnes cræftig
25 þæt him þa ferend on   fæste wuniaþ,
wic weardiað   wedres on luste,
ðonne semninga   on sealtne wæg
mid þa noþe   niþer gewiteþ

Whale

Robert Pinsky

Now, some words fit for a strange kin of fish:
Finned but no fish, and well worth attention,
The mighty Whale, called Phasti-Tokalon.

As he floats at his ease in ocean, seafarers
Mistake him for an island with dark beaches
Where they anchor their boats and climb ashore.

They encamp on the island, they light their fires,
Glad to be back on solid land, weary—then
Whale dives to the bottom, and all the men drown.

garsecges gæst,   grund geseceð,
30 ond þonne in deaðsele   drence bifæsteð
scipu mid scealcum.   Swa bið scinna þeaw,
deofla wise,   þæt hi drohtende
þurh dyrne meaht   duguðe beswicað,
ond on teosu tyhtaþ   tilra dæda,
35 wemað on willan,   þæt hy wraþe secen,
frofre to feondum,   oþþæt hy fæste ðær
æt þam wærlogan   wic geceosað.
þonne þæt gecnaweð   of cwicsusle
flah feond gemah,   þætte fira gehwylc
40 hæleþa cynnes   on his hringe biþ
fæste gefeged,   he him feorgbona
þurh sliþen searo   siþþan weorþeð,
wloncum ond heanum,   þe his willan her
firenum fremmað,   mid þam he færinga,
45 heoloþhelme biþeaht,   helle seceð,
goda geasne,   grundleasne wylm
under mistglome,   swa se micla hwæl,
se þe bisenceð   sæliþende
eorlas ond yðmearas.   He hafað oþre gecynd,
50 wæterþisa wlonc,   wrætlicran gien.
þonne hine on holme   hungor bysgað
ond þone aglæcan   ætes lysteþ,
ðonne se mereweard   muð ontyneð,
wide weleras;   cymeð wynsum stenc
55 of his innoþe,   þætte oþre þurh þone,
sæfisca cynn,   beswicen weorðaþ,
swimmað sundhwate   þær se sweta stenc
ut **gewiteð**.   Hi þær in farað
unware weorude,   oþþæt se wida ceafl
60 gefylled bið;   þonne færinga
ymbe þa herehuþe   hlemmeð togædre

He pulls down the ships by their ropes to the bottom.
The Devil himself doles exactly like that,
Tricking any who think he has given them haven.

He murders them all, yes he pulls them all down
With his helm of deception and his grappling ropes.
When they think they are safe he hauls them to Hell.

There's another trick the great Whale plays:
When he's hungry he gapes the cave of his mouth,
And from it he issues a luscious perfume

grimme goman.   Swa biþ gumena gehwam,
se þe oftost his   unwærlice
on þas lænan tid   lif bisceawað,
65   læteð hine beswican   þurh swetne stenc,
leasne willan,   þæt he biþ leahtrum fah
wið wuldorcyning.   Him se awyrgda ongean
æfter hinsiþe   helle ontyneð,
þam þe leaslice   lices wynne
70   ofer ferhtgereaht   fremedon on unræd.
þonne se fæcna   in þam fæstenne
gebroht hafað,   bealwes cræftig,
æt þam edwylme   þa þe him on cleofiað,
gyltum gehrodene,   ond ær georne his
75   in hira lifdagum   larum hyrdon,
þonne he þa grimman   goman bihlemmeð
æfter feorhcwale   fæste togædre,
helle hlinduru;   nagon hwyrft ne swice,
utsiþ æfre,   þa þær in cumað,
80   þon ma þe þa fiscas   faraðlacende
of þæs hwæles fenge   hweorfan motan.
Forþon is eallinga
dryhtna **dryhtne**,   ond a deoflum wiðsace
wordum ond weorcum,   þæt we wuldorcyning
85   geseon moton.   Uton a sibbe to him
on þas hwilnan tid   hælu secan,
þæt we mid swa leofne   in lofe motan
to widan feore   wuldres neotan.

That fools the poor fish that rush in to be eaten.
Like the wave-making Whale the Devil entices
Complicit souls with ambergris and comfort,

Then in his salt mouth spirits them away
From pleasant sunlight down to the dark, where
Hell's gates close like the jaws of the Whale.

Sixth
Riddle-Hoard

Riddle 65

Cwico wæs ic, ne cwæð ic wiht,   cwele ic efne seþeah.
ær ic wæs, eft ic cwom.   æghwa mec reafað,
hafað mec on headre,   ond min heafod scireþ,
biteð mec on bær lic,   briceð mine wisan.
5 Monnan ic ne bite,   nymþe he me bite;
sindan þara monige   þe mec bitað.

Riddle 66

Ic eom mare   þonne þes **middangeard**,
læsse þonne hondwyrm,   leohtre þonne mona,
swiftre þonne sunne.   Sæs me sind ealle
flodas on fæðmum   ond **þes** foldan bearm,
5 grene wongas.   Grundum ic hrine,
helle underhnige,   heofonas oferstige,
wuldres eþel,   wide ræce
ofer engla eard,   eorþan gefylle,
ealne middangeard   ond merestreamas
10 side mid **me** sylfum.   Saga hwæt ic hatte.

Alive I Was—I Didn't Speak a Bit
Phillis Levin

Alive I was—I didn't speak a bit; even so, I die.
Once I was, I came again: everyone ravages me,
holds me tight and shears my head,
tears into my bare body, breaks my neck.
I wouldn't bite a man unless he bit me;
so many of them bite me.

Up Beyond the Universe and Back
Edwin Morgan

Up beyond the universe and back
Down to the tiniest chigger in the finger—
I outstrip the moon in brightness,
I outrun midsummer suns.
I embrace the seas and other waters,
I am fresh and green as the fields I form.
I walk under hell, I fly over the heavens.
I am the land, I am the ocean.
I claim this honor, I claim its worth.
I am what I claim. So, what is my name?

Riddle 68–69

1 Ic þa wiht geseah   on weg feran;
1 heo wæs wrætlice   wundrum gegierwed.
2 Wundor wearð on wege;   wæter wearð to bane.

Riddle 70, lines 1–4

1 Wiht is wrætlic   þam þe hyre wisan ne conn.
2 Singeð þurh sidan.   Is se sweora woh,
3 orþoncum geworht;   hafaþ eaxle tua
4 scearp on gescyldrum.   His gesceapo **dreogeð**

Riddle 70, lines 5–6

5 þe swa wrætlice   be wege stonde
6 heah ond hleortorht   hæleþum to nytte.

I Saw That Creature Wander on the Way
Jennifer Grotz

I saw that creature wander on the way,
wonderfully adorned. A wonder floating on a wave:
she was water turned to bone.

For the Hearing Ear She Shapes Her Sound
Gail Holst–Warhaft

For the hearing ear she shapes her sound,
singing through her sides. Her slender neck
is round and round her shoulders lie
lovely jewels. Uncanny, her song.

High on This Headland Day and Night I Stand
Robert B. Shaw

High on this headland day and night I stand
and show a blushing cheek, but feel no shame.
Men out cruising ogle me, weigh my worth.
Hear my solicitation: what's my name?

Riddle 72

Ic wæs lytel . . . . . .
fo . . . . . .
. . . te geaf . . . . . .
. . . pe   þe unc gemæne . . .
5   . . . . . . sweostor min,
fedde mec . . . . . .   oft ic feower teah
swæse broþor,   þara onsundran gehwylc
dægtidum me   drincan sealde
þurh þyrel þearle.   Ic þæh on lust,
10   oþþæt ic wæs yldra   ond þæt an forlet
sweartum hyrde,   siþade widdor,
mearcpaþas Walas træd,   moras pæðde,
bunden under beame,   beag hæfde on healse,
wean on laste   weorc þrowade,
15   earfoða dæl.   Oft mec isern scod
sare on sidan;   ic swigade,
næfre meldade   monna ængum
gif me ordstæpe   egle wæron.

I Was Little (Little Did I Know)

David Barber

I was little (little did I know)
With others like me (look at me now)
And my sister . . . alongside me . . . feasting . . .
O to be that golden again—tugging away
On four sweet brothers, who one by one
Let me lap up my fill all day long
From blissful holes that bubbled with their brew.
And then I was older and that was all over:
The hard dark herdsmen hauled me off
To wander with them far and wide
Over country lanes and muddy lowlands—
A beam on my back, a ring round my neck—
Plodding along from place to place
In a world of hurt, weighed down with woes,
My backside scored by stabs of iron
On that trail of tears. I bit my tongue:
Never groaning, grumbling to no one,
Even when the goads made me gasp.

Riddle 74

Ic wæs fæmne geong,   feaxhar cwene,
ond ænlic rinc   on ane tid;
fleah mid fuglum   ond on flode swom,
deaf under yþe   dead mid fiscum,
5   ond on foldan stop,   hæfde **ferð** cwicu.

Riddle 75–76

Ic swiftne geseah   on swaþe feran
ᛗ ᛏᚱᚾ.
Ic ane geseah   idese sittan.

Riddle 77

Sæ mec fedde,   sundhelm þeahte,
ond mec yþa wrugon   eorþan getenge
feþelease.   Oft ic flode ongean
muð ontynde.   Nu wile monna sum
5   min flæsc fretan,   felles ne recceð,
siþþan he me of sidan   seaxes orde
hyd arypeð, . . . ec hr . . . . . . þe siþþan
iteð unsodene   ea . . . . . . d.

I Was a Girl, a Gray Queen

Molly Peacock

I was a girl,   a gray queen,
and a man, solo,   all in a single hour.
I flew with the birds   swam in the seas
dove under waves   died with the fishes
and stepped out on earth   —alive, all in a single soul.

I Saw Her—Quick—She Slipped Behind

Molly Peacock

I saw her—quick—she slipped behind—
I saw that woman squat alone.

Sea Fed, Shore Sheltered

Gail Holst-Warhaft

Sea fed, shore sheltered,
I rocked with sea wrack.
Footless yet fixed I often opened
my mouth wide to the tide's wax.
Now some man will slide a knife
down my sides, strip skin
from bone, a quick snack he slurps
raw, delighting as he sucks me in.

Riddle 79–80

1 Ic eom æþelinges   æht ond willa.

1 Ic eom æþelinges   eaxlgestealla,
 fyrdrinces gefara,   frean minum leof,
 cyninges geselda.   Cwen mec hwilum
 hwitloccedu   hond on legeð,
5 eorles dohtor,   þeah hio æþelu sy.
 Hæbbe me on bosme   þæt on bearwe geweox.
 Hwilum ic on wloncum   wicge ride
 herges on ende;   heard is min tunge.
 Oft ic woðboran   wordleana sum
10 agyfe æfter giedde.   Good is min wise
 ond ic sylfa salo.   Saga hwæt ic hatte.

I Am a Prince's Property and Joy

Macdara Woods

I am a prince's property and joy,
His dearest shoulder-companion,
The veteran's comrade, my lord's favorite,
A king's retainer. Even my bright-haired queen
Will sometimes lay her hand on me,
Noble as she is, an earl's daughter.
I hold in my belly sweet fire from the woods.
Sometimes too on a proud horse I ride
At the head of the host with my harsh voice.
Often and again I grant the poet reward for song
After singing. My nature is good
And my self dark. Say what I am called.

Remedies
and Charms

Metrical Charm 1: For Unfruitful Land

Her ys seo bot, hu ðu meaht þine æceras betan gif hi
nellaþ wel wexan oþþe þær hwilc ungedefe þing on gedon bið
on dry oððe on lyblace. Genim þonne on niht, ær hyt
dagige, feower tyrf on feower healfa þæs landes, and gemearca
5   hu hy ær stodon. Nim þonne ele and hunig and beorman,
and ælces feos meolc þe on þæm lande sy, and ælces treow-
cynnes dæl þe on þæm lande sy gewexen, butan heardan
beaman, and ælcre namcuþre wyrte dæl, butan glappan anon,
and do þonne haligwæter ðær on, and drype þonne þriwa on
10 þone staðol þara turfa, and cweþe ðonne ðas word: *Crescite*,
wexe, *et multiplicamini,* and gemænigfealda, *et replete,* and
gefylle, *terre,* þas eorðan. *In nomine patris et filii et spiritus
sancti sit benedicti.* And Pater Noster swa oft swa þæt oðer.
And bere siþþan ða turf to circean, and mæssepreost asinge
15 feower mæssan ofer þan turfon, and wende man þæt grene to

Field Remedy
Nick Laird

Here's the thing:
                 your lands will spring to life again
if blight or curse is set on them through poisoning
or witchery or worse—but only if
you follow me faithfully in this.
         At night, before the dawn, rise and spade
four turfs from the edges of your acreage
and mind precisely whence you take them.
         Then obtain some honey, oil and barm
and a drop from every milch that pastures on your fields,
and a splinter from the trunk of every species of the trees
that grow upon your holding—except for hardwood beams—
and scratchings from the plants you have which have a name,
apart from buckbean.
                 Then add a stir of holy water
to the crock and drip, drip, drip the mixture
carefully upon the belly of the sods, and say,

                 Widen, heighten, multiply,
                 and fill this earth onto its limit.
                 Be blessèd in the trinity
                 of father, son and sacred spirit.

Recite the Paternoster, and afterward
transport the sodden turfs to church,
and pay the priests to say four masses
and let the clods' green surfaces
be turned toward the altarpiece,

ðan weofode, and siþþan gebringe man þa turf þær hi ær
wæron ær sunnan setlgange. And hæbbe him gæworht of
cwicbeame feower Cristes mælo and awrite on ælcon ende:
Matheus and Marcus, Lucas and Iohannes. Lege þæt
20 Cristes mæl on þone pyt neoþeweardne, cweðe ðonne: *Crux
Matheus, crux Marcus, crux Lucas, crux sanctus Iohannes.*
Nim ðonne þa turf and sete ðær ufon on and cweþe ðonne
nigon siþon þas word, *Crescite*, and swa oft Pater Noster,
and wende þe þonne eastweard, and onlut nigon siðon
25 eadmodlice, and cweð þonne þas word:
Eastweard ic stande,   arena ic me bidde,
bidde ic þone mæran domine,   bidde ðone miclan drihten,
bidde ic ðone haligan   heofonrices weard,
eorðan ic bidde   and upheofon
30 and ða soþan   sancta Marian
and heofones meaht   and heahreced,
þæt ic mote þis gealdor   mid gife drihtnes
toðum ontynan   þurh trumne geþanc,
aweccan þas wæstmas   us to woruldnytte,
35 **gefyllan** þas foldan   mid fæste geleafan,
wlitigigan þas wancgturf,   swa se witega cwæð
þæt se hæfde are on eorþrice,   se þe ælmyssan

and let them then be carried to your acres—

but before you rest the turfs back in their scars,
have four crosses carved from rowan, to represent our Savior,
and on the first score *Matthew's*, the second *Mark's*, the third *Luke's*,
the fourth *John's*, and set each crucifix
down gently in its divot, saying,

> *Matthew's Cross and Mark's and Luke's and the cross of Holy John.*

Then take the turfs and settle them
before sunset and say at least nine times,
Widen, heighten . . . as before, and so on,
and repeat the Paternoster just as often,
and turn against the west, and bow nine times and say

> *Eastward I stand, and favors entreat.*
> *I call the illustrious ones to yield;*
> *the earth I beseech and each*
> *of her keepers I summon to this field;*

> *Mary, Christ, the blessèd Lord.*
> *Into your ears this glamour I pour.*
> *From my teeth I speak each word*
> *and will not fail: the blooms are sure*

> *to bloom once more, the fruits*
> *to fruit, the earth grow whole*
> *and full again, for worldly use,*
> *for us again, still plentiful—*

> *even as the prophet tells*
> *lack of favor on the realm*
> *till, following His fearful will,*

dælde domlice   drihtnes þances.

Wende þe þonne III sunganges, astrece þonne on andlang

40 and arim þær letanias and cweð þonne: Sanctus, sanctus,
sanctus oþ ende. Sing þonne Benedicite aþenedon earmon
and Magnificat and Pater Noster III, and bebeod hit Criste
and sancta Marian and þære halgan rode to lofe and to
weorþinga and **to** are **þam** þe þæt land age and eallon þam þe

45 him underðeodde synt. ðonne þæt eall sie gedon, þonne
nime man uncuþ sæd æt ælmesmannum and selle him twa
swylc, swylce man æt him nime, and gegaderie ealle his
sulhgeteogo togædere; borige þonne on þam beame stor and
finol and gehalgode sapan and gehalgod sealt. Nim þonne

50 þæt sæd, sete on þæs sules bodig, cweð þonne:
Erce, Erce, Erce,   eorþan modor,
geunne þe se alwalda,   ece drihten,
æcera wexendra   and wridendra,
eacniendra   and elniendra,

55 sceafta **hehra**,   **scirra** wæstma,
and **þæra** bradan   berewæstma,
and **þæra** hwitan   hwætewæstma,
and ealra   eorþan wæstma.
Geunne him   ece drihten

60 and his halige,   þe on **heofonum** synt,
þæt hys yrþ si gefriþod   wið ealra feonda gehwæne,
and heo si geborgen   wið ealra bealwa gehwylc,

they re-allot the alms.

Then turn yourself three times in line with the running sun
and stretch out on the ground and speak the litanies again,
saying *Holy, holy, holy* to the end: then chant
the *Benedicte* with your arms out wide, and the *Magnificat*,
and offer to the sainted Mary, the Holy Cross, to Jesus Christ,
the Paternoster, twice,
in adoration, reverence, flattery and praise;
and for yourself, the tenantry, persuade;
and for the churls who work the soil
beneath your soles, prevail.
  When all of that has been discharged,
take seeds from the almsmen in the churchyard,
and give them double what you took, then gather
all your ploughing gear in the one place together
and drill a hole, deep, in the crossroad of the plough beams
and pour in hallowed salve and salt, frankincense and fennel seeds.
Then set the beggar's seeds out along the body of the plough, and say

> *Erce! Erce! Our earth-mother,*
>
> *let your barley and your spelt*
> *emerge in some new splendor.*
> *Let your emmer and your wheat*
> *rise up straight-backed forever.*
>
> *Let crops crop, and seeds seed,*
> *and the yield yield to me. Let God*
> *and every saint in heaven grant*
> *my acres fortified against all slant*
>
> *adversaries, their foul goetic means,*

þara lyblaca   geond land sawen.
Nu ic bidde ðone waldend,   se ðe ðas woruld gesceop,
65 þæt ne sy nan to þæs cwidol wif   ne to þæs cræftig man
þæt awendan ne mæge   **word** þus gecwedene.
þonne man þa sulh forð drife and þa forman furh onsceote,
cweð þonne:
Hal wes þu, folde,   fira modor!
70 Beo þu growende   on godes fæþme,
fodre gefylled   firum to nytte.
Nim þonne ælces cynnes melo and abacæ man **innewerdre**
handa bradnæ hlaf and gecned hine mid meolce and mid
haligwætere and lecge under þa forman furh. Cweþe þonne:
75 Ful æcer fodres   fira cinne,
beorhtblowende,   þu gebletsod weorþ

> their demonry, their one-eyed spite,
>> the sortilege and jealousy
> abroad like torches in the night.

> I pray to Him who made this place
>> no woman deft in conjuration
> or man adept in talk and cunning
> may halt the words I here unloose.

Then plough the plough, and break the furrow, saying

>> I praise the earth, the turf I hail,
>>> the silt I stirred up I applaud;
>> the sod, the clod, the dirt, the soil,
>> the loam and clay I dig I laud.

>> I praise the use we put its fruits to,
>> commend provender, vittles, vivers,
>> whatever's lowered in on hooks to
>> hang and blacken in the smokehouse,

>> whatever's threshed or dried or milled,
>> whatever's plucked or picked or caught,
>> whatever's raw or boiled or killed,
>>> I consecrate, I celebrate, I eat.

Then take flour of every make and bake a loaf to fit
your hands, kneading it with sacred water and a little milk
before you stow it in the furrow, saying

>> Let vines incline and salmon churn
>>> the surface of the lough.
>> Let wheat-fields sway in sun-warmed

þæs haligan noman   þe ðas heofon gesceop
and ðas eorþan   þe we on lifiaþ;
se god, se þas grundas geworhte,   geunne us growende gife,
þæt us corna gehwylc   cume to nytte.
80 Cweð þonne III *Crescite in nomine patris, sit benedicti.*
Amen and Pater Noster þriwa.

breezes bearing seeds aloft.

Ours is the earth, and consecrated
in the name of Him who loved so much
He made the land on which we stand
and skies to turn above us.

May He forgive enough to grant
what's inside the clay comes good.
May He rain, and may He shine,
and may He send forth shoots.

Then say thrice,
Widen, heighten, multiply . . . and remember
to do all this in the name of our Father
and the Son etc., Amen,
and then repeat the Paternoster another three times again.

Metrical Charm 2: The Nine Herbs Charm

Gemyne ðu, mucgwyrt,   hwæt þu ameldodest,
hwæt þu renadest   æt Regenmelde.
Una þu hattest,   yldost wyrta.
ðu miht wið III   and wið XXX,
5   þu miht wiþ attre   and wið onflyge,
þu miht wiþ **þam** laþan   ðe geond lond færð.
Ond þu, wegbrade,   wyrta modor,
eastan **openo,**   innan mihtigu;
ofer **ðe crætu** curran,   ofer **ðe** cwene reodan,
10 ofer **ðe** bryde bryodedon,   ofer **þe** fearras fnærdon.
Eallum þu þon wiðstode   and wiðstunedest;
swa ðu wiðstonde   attre and onflyge

The Nine Herbs Charm

Tom Sleigh

Mugwort, don't forget
                 what you forged in your roots,
the rites you ruled over
                 at Regenmeld.
Oldest of herbs,
                 we named you Una:
Against three and against thirty,
                 you work your wonders,
your power against poison
                 bites back venom,
you block the road against the fiend
                 faring through the fields.

And you, Way-Broad,
                 mighty mother of herbs,
you make roadside wheel ruts
                 and cart tracks home,
you open to the sun-wheel
                 rolling from the east:
crushing your leaves, over you
                 queens trampled, carts creaked,
brides cried out, bulls bellowed—
                 but inside your green stalk
you grow tougher, stronger,
                 spring back whole:
and in just that way you withstand
                 pestilence and poison,

and þæm laðan   þe geond lond fereð.
Stune hætte þeos wyrt,   heo on stane geweox;
15   stond heo wið attre,   stunað heo wærce.
Stiðe heo hatte,   wiðstunað heo attre,
wreceð heo wraðan,   weorþeð ut attor.
þis is seo wyrt   seo wiþ wyrm gefeaht,
þeos mæg wið attre,   heo mæg wið onflyge,
20   heo mæg wið **ðam** laþan   ðe geond lond fereþ.
Fleoh þu nu, attorlaðe,   seo læsse ða maran,
seo mare þa læssan,   oððæt him beigra bot sy.
Gemyne þu, mægðe,   hwæt þu ameldodest,
hwæt ðu geændadest   æt Alorforda;
25   þæt næfre for gefloge   feorh ne gesealde

the fiend wandering
>
> far and wide.

And you whom we call Stune,

> you grow in stony ground

and like a stone hold out

> against pain, hurl yourself at poison.

And as for you, Nettle,

> you're nicknamed

"Harsh" for how you treat the malice

> of the malignant one,

your fangs bared

> against the serpent's fangs

until poison and pestilence

> pass over,

the fiend driven

> from the fields.

Now Woundwort, against the greater poison

> you're the mighty runt

who cuts giants down to size;

> and against the lesser poison

you're the wise giant holding back

> your might until he's cured of both.

Remember, Chamomile, what your roots

> revealed at Alorford?

So sick with infection

syþðan him mon mægðan   to mete gegyrede.

þis is seo wyrt   ðe wergulu hatte;

ðas onsænde seolh   ofer sæs hrygc

ondan attres   oþres to bote.

30 ðas VIIII magon   wið nygon attrum.

Wyrm com snican,   toslat he man;

ða genam Woden   VIIII wuldortanas,

sloh ða þa næddran,   þæt heo on VIIII tofleah.

þær geændade   æppel and attor,

35 þæt heo næfre ne wolde   on hus bugan.

Fille and finule,   felamihtigu twa,

þa wyrte gesceop   witig drihten,

infection ruled over him,
but once they ground you up
                                    and cooked you in his food
you raised him up,
                    overruled infection.

Now look at this herb
                        called Crab Apple—
the seal sent it
                    over the sea's broad back
for its power against harm
                            and hatefulness of poisons.

Nine in all, nine herbs
                        against nine poisons.

Then Malice-Striker sneaking like a serpent
                                            struck a man—
Wodin grasped
                nine Glory Sticks and struck
the writher into wriggling pieces,
                                    nine in all.
So apple and the wood of apple
                                worked an end to poison—
no longer would that snake
                            come sneaking through the house.

Chervil, Fennel, fierce companions,
                            your wise lord

halig on heofonum, þa he hongode;
sette and sænde on VII worulde
40 earmum and eadigum eallum to bote.
Stond heo wið wærce, stunað heo wið attre,
seo mæg wið III and wið XXX,
wið feondes hond and wið **færbregde**,
wið malscrunge **manra** wihta.
45 Nu magon þas VIIII wyrta wið nygon wuldorgeflogenum,
wið VIIII attrum and wið nygon onflygnum,
wið ðy readan attre, wið **ðy** runlan attre,
wið ðy hwitan attre, wið ðy wedenan attre,
wið ðy geolwan attre, wið ðy grenan attre,
50 wið ðy wonnan attre, wið ðy wedenan attre,
wið ðy brunan attre, wið ðy basewan attre,
wið wyrmgeblæd, wið wætergeblæd,
wið þorngeblæd, wið **þystelgeblæd**,

shaped you leaf and stalk
                    as he hung on heavens' crosstrees.
Down to each of the seven worlds
                        he sent your roots
to rich and poor,
               a remedy to all.
Pain can't withstand you,
                  poison drains away,
against three and against thirty
                    you stand your ground.
Fiend's hand or dirty trick,
               spells spat
in heart's hate,
            all such bane you vanquish.

So these nine herbs drive out
                  nine glory-haters,
stand strong against
              nine poisons, nine contagions:
against red poison,
             against rust-running poison,
against white poison,
              against pale blue poison,
against yellow poison,
              against green poison,
against black poison,
              against dark blue poison,
against brown poison,
              against crimson poison,
against blasting worm,
            blot of water,
against thorn prick,

wið ysgeblæd,   wið attorgeblæd,

55 gif ænig attor cume   eastan fleogan

oððe ænig norðan   cume

oððe ænig westan   ofer werðeode.

Crist stod ofer **adle**   ængan cundes.

Ic ana wat   ea rinnende

60 **þær** þa nygon nædran   **nean** behealdað;

motan ealle weoda nu   wyrtum aspringan,

sæs toslupan,   eal sealt wæter,

ðonne ic þis attor   of ðe geblawe.

Mugcwyrt, wegbrade þe eastan open sy, lombescyrse,

65 attorlaðan, mageðan, netelan, wudusuræppel, fille and finul,

ealde sapan. Gewyrc ða wyrta to duste, mængc wiþ þa

sapan and wiþ þæs æpples gor. Wyrc slypan of wætere

and of axsan, genim finol, wyl on þære slyppan and beþe mid

æggemongc, þonne he þa sealfe on **do**, ge ær ge æfter. Sing

70 þæt galdor on ælcre þara wyrta, III ær he hy wyrce and

on þone æppel ealswa; ond singe þon men in þone muð and

in þa earan buta and on ða wunde þæt ilce gealdor, ær he

þa sealfe on **do**.

                    thrust of thistle,
against ice's bitter breath,
                    venom's bloody blister,
against any poison
                    that comes flying from the east,
flying from the north,
                    flying from the west
to make trial against the tribe,
                    work woe on woman and man.

Cruelly slow, ravagingly quick,
                    disease and death face Christ down.

I alone know the running rivers
                    and the nine serpents they enfold.
May all weeds everywhere
                    spring up into healing herbs,
may all salty waters
                    of all seas part
when my breath blows away from you
                    the blast of poison.

Now, take Mugwort, Way-Broad that opens east, take Stune called lamb's
cress, Woundwort, Chamomile, Nettle, Crab Apple, Chervil and Fennel,
and some old soap. Grind the herbs into powder, mix them with the soap
and some apple juice. Make a paste from ash and water, take fennel, boil it
in the paste and soak it in a beaten egg when you apply the salve, both
before and after. Then sing this charm three times over each herb, then
three times over the mixture before you grind it all together, and over the
apple too. And just before you rub on the salve, sing this charm into the
sick man's mouth, into both of his ears, and into his wound.

Metrical Charm 3: Against a Dwarf

Wið dweorh man sceal niman VII lytle oflætan, swylce
man mid ofrað, and **writan** þas naman on ælcre oflætan:
Maximianus, Malchus, Iohannes, Martimianus, Dioni-
sius, Constantinus, Serafion. þænne eft þæt galdor, þæt
5 her æfter cweð, man sceal singan, ærest on þæt wynstre
eare, þænne on þæt swiðre eare, þænne **bufan** þæs mannes
moldan. And ga þænne an mædenman to and ho hit on
his sweoran, and do man swa þry dagas; him bið sona sel.
Her com in gangan,   in **spiderwiht**,
10 hæfde him his haman on handa,   cwæð þæt þu his hæncgest wære,
legde þe his teage an sweoran.   Ongunnan him of þæm lande liþan;
sona swa hy of þæm lande coman,   þa ongunnan him ða liþu colian.
þa com in gangan   **dweores** sweostar;
þa geændade heo   and aðas swor
15 ðæt næfre þis ðæm adlegan   derian ne moste,
ne þæm þe þis galdor   begytan mihte,
oððe þe þis galdor   ongalan cuþe.
Amen. Fiað.

Against a Dwarf

Thomas McCarthy

You scald this dwarfish outpour, you score
such names as these on seven wafers from the paten:
Maximianus,
Malchus,
Iohannes,
Martimianus,
Dionisius,
Constantinus,
Serafion

And pray this paean afterward, sing to the left ear, pray likewise
to the right: crown of the head, with words manipulate. This time
a maiden hangs prayer upon your neck; a pendant for three days.
All shall be well.

And come upon you   this spiderlight
With cloak at hand   making you his horse-beast
His rope upon your neck   goading you 'til airborne
For soon as lightened thus   fevers begin to cool
Companion of grief   this dwarfish sister
To degrade such heat   to swear such oaths
Never to harm the stricken   never do worse
Nor any follower   who breathing recites
Who gains such words   such gallant myths

It is written.
Amen.

Metrical Charm 4: For a Sudden Stitch

Wið færstice feferfuige and seo reade netele, ðe þurh
ærn inwyxð, and wegbrade; wyll in buteran.
Hlude wæran hy, la, hlude,   ða hy ofer þone hlæw ridan,
wæran anmode,   ða hy ofer land ridan.
5 Scyld ðu ðe nu, þu ðysne nið   genesan mote.
Ut, lytel spere,   gif her inne sie!
Stod under linde,   under leohtum scylde,
þær ða mihtigan wif   hyra mægen beræddon
and hy gyllende   garas sændan;
10 ic him oðerne   eft wille sændan,
fleogende flane   forane togeanes.
Ut, **lytel** spere,   gif hit her inne sy!
Sæt smið,   sloh seax lytel,
iserna,   **wundrum** swiðe.
15 Ut, lytel spere,   gif her inne sy!
Syx smiðas sætan,   wælspera worhtan.
Ut, spere,   næs in, spere!
Gif her inne sy   **isernes** dæl,
hægtessan geweorc,   hit sceal gemyltan.
20 Gif ðu wære on fell scoten   oððe wære on flæsc scoten
oððe wære on blod scoten
oððe wære on lið scoten,   næfre ne sy ðin lif atæsed;
gif hit wære esa gescot   oððe hit wære ylfa gescot
oððe hit wære hægtessan gescot,   nu ic wille ðin helpan.
25 þis ðe to bote esa gescotes,   ðis ðe to bote ylfa gescotes,
ðis ðe to bote hægtessan gescotes;   ic ðin wille helpan.
Fleoh þær   on **fyrgenheafde**.
Hal westu,   helpe ðin drihten!
Nim þonne þæt seax, ado on wætan.

Against a Sudden Stitch

Michael Collier

Against a sudden stitch boil waybread in butter,
Add feverfew and then the red nettle that threads through homes.

Lo, loud did they come! Loud   over the hills as they rode,
Unstoppable   over the land as they rode.
Quickly, up with your shield   fend off their threat   seek safety.
Be gone, little spear,   don't pierce me!
Under linden I stood   under a light-wood shield
Where blond furies circled   brayed their strength
Brash battle cries   before they flung spears
Or I aimed mine   one and then more
Arrow fast   against them.
Be gone, little spear,   don't pierce me!
Once a smithy forged a short sword:
Small blade   murderous wounds.
Be gone, little spear,   don't pierce me!
Six blacksmiths   hammered six warrior spears.
Don't pierce me, be gone,   little spear!
But if its iron tip   lodges,
A fury's work,   it will weaken.
And if the shot grazes your skin   or the shot pierces flesh
Or the shot taints blood
Or the shot writhes limbs   may your life force be unharmed;
And no matter if the gods shoot   or the elves shoot
Or the furies shoot   now I can help you.
This cures the god's shot,   this the elves'
And this the furies';   I will help you.
Lo, they have flown,   fled to the mountains.
Be whole again!   Trust the Lord's help!

Now, take the short sword and dip it in the potion.

Metrical Charm 6: For Delayed Birth

Se wifman, se hire cild afedan ne mæg, gange to gewitenes
mannes birgenne and stæppe þonne þriwa ofer þa byrgenne
and cweþe þonne þriwa þas word:
þis me to bote   þære laþan lætbyrde,
5 þis me to bote   þære swæran **swærbyrde**,
þis me to bote   þære laðan lambyrde.
And þonne þæt wif seo mid bearne and heo to hyre hlaforde
on reste ga, þonne cweþe heo:
Up ic gonge,   ofer þe stæppe
10 mid cwican cilde,   nalæs mid cwellendum,
mid fulborenum,   nalæs mid fægan.
And þonne seo modor gefele þæt þæt bearn si cwic, ga
þonne to cyrican, and þonne heo toforan þan weofode cume,
cweþe þonne:
15 Criste, ic sæde,   þis gecyþed!
Se wifmon, se hyre bearn afedan ne mæge, genime heo
sylf hyre agenes cildes gebyrgenne dæl, **wry** æfter þonne on
blace wulle and bebicge to cepemannum and cweþe þonne:
Ic hit bebicge,   ge hit bebicgan,
20 þas sweartan wulle   and þysse sorge corn.
Se **wifman**, se **ne** mæge bearn afedan, nime þonne anes
bleos cu meoluc on hyre handæ and gesupe þonne mid hyre
muþe and gange þonne to yrnendum wætere and spiwe þær
in þa meolc and hlade þonne mid þære ylcan hand þæs
25 wæteres muð fulne and forswelge. Cweþe þonne þas word:
Gehwer ferde ic me þone mæran   maga þihtan,
mid þysse mæran   mete þihtan;
þonne ic me wille habban   and ham gan.

Charm for Bearing a Full-Term Baby

Carol Muske–Dukes

A woman who wants   to birth a strong babe
Must go to the graveyard   dream-step over the dead
Three times—and thrice   walk within these words:

Help me harbor   safe against still-birth
Help as I hinder   the dark dismal birth
Help me hold   against the lame lost one.

Big with the unborn   she steps over her spouse
In bed—calling back   Up I go, unadorned
But active and able   to bear a live babe

Not dead or doomed   my babe, full-born.
Quiet, feeling quickening,   carries herself to church
Cries out: O Christ   I announce at the altar.

To carry to childbirth—   Go to the grave of one gone
Early in the earth   Wrap dirt in dark wool
Market it to merchants   "I sell, you sell!"

Black wool, weeping   Green seeds of grief.
She who can't carry   must milk a mild cow
Sip sweet sustaining   milk in her mouth

Then spit, not swallow   with water, these words:
I carry a strong child   to have and take home.

þonne heo to þan broce ga, þonne ne beseo heo, no ne eft
30 þonne heo þanan ga, and þonne ga heo in oþer hus oþer heo
ut ofeode and þær gebyrge metes.

Metrical Charm 7: For the Water-Elf Disease

Gif mon biþ on wæterælfadle, þonne beoþ him þa hand-
næglas wonne and þa eagan tearige and wile locian niþer.
Do him þis to læcedome: eoforþrote, cassuc, fone nioþo-
weard, eowberge, elehtre, eolone, merscmealwan crop,
5 fenminte, dile, lilie, attorlaþe, polleie, marubie, docce, ellen,
felterre, wermod, streawbergean leaf, consolde; ofgeot mid
ealaþ, do hæligwæter to, sing þis gealdor ofer þriwa:
Ic **benne** awrat   betest beadowræda,
swa benne ne burnon,   ne burston,
10 ne fundian,   ne feologan,
ne hoppettan,   ne wund waxsian,
ne dolh diopian;   ac him self healde halewæge,
ne ace þe þon ma,   þe eorþan on eare ace.
Sing þis manegum siþum: Eorþe þe onbere eallum hire
15 mihtum and mægenum. þas galdor mon mæg singan on
wunde.

Stopping at the stream   she refuses to look round.

Depart for a dwelling.   Not home, but home halfway.

Against Water–Elf Disease

Michael Collier

When the water-elf infects you, fingernails turn bloodless, eyes tear
And all you do is stare at your feet.

To drive out the disease grind hassock, horehound and dill;
        Leaf of strawberry, horse-heal, and pennyroyal;
Lupine, cockspur, and yew;
        Wormwood, mallow, and elder;
Dill, dock, and fern-mint;
        Comfrey, stock of iris, and lily.

Once this is done steep it in beer
And bless it with sanctified water,
Then charm the poultice three times with this song:

Take care to field dress the sword gash
So neither rent-flesh burns   nor blood bursts
Nor rots gangrenous   nor goes green with pus
Nor needs salve to soothe   nor is slow to scab
Nor reddens with fever: then the scar is health's sign,
And the welt disfigures skin no more than waves tumult shore.

Sing this again and again and the Earth's magnificence
Will make you well.

Any wound from sword gash to hangnail this charm cures.

Metrical Charm 8: For a Swarm of Bees

Wið ymbe nim eorþan, oferweorp mid þinre swiþran
handa under þinum swiþran fet, and cwet:
 Fo ic under fot,   funde ic hit.
 Hwæt, eorðe mæg   wið ealra wihta gehwilce
5 and wið andan   and wið æminde
and wið þa micelan   mannes tungan.
And **wiððon** forweorp ofer greot, þonne hi swirman, and cweð:
 Sitte ge, sigewif,   sigað to eorþan!
 Næfre ge wilde   to wuda fleogan.
10 Beo ge swa gemindige   mines godes,
swa bið manna gehwilc   metes and eþeles.

Charm for a Swarm of Bees

David Barber

When the bees begin to stir, scoop up some earth
With your right hand, sling it under your right foot, and say:

> Here where I stand I will stake my claim.
> Listen to the land speak, lord of us all:
> Mightier than malice, mightier than spite,
> The master of every man's mother tongue.

When the bees begin to swarm, sift some sand in your palm,
Scatter it over them like a soft cloud, and say:

> Stay put on this plot, proud sisters in arms!
> Never turn wild and take to the woods.
> What is good for you is good for me,
> As any man will tell you who tends the land.

Metrical Charm 9: For Loss of Cattle

Ne forstolen ne forholen nanuht, þæs ðe ic age, þe ma ðe
mihte Herod urne drihten. Ic geþohte sancte Eadelenan
and ic geþohte Crist on rode ahangen; swa ic þence þis feoh
to findanne, næs to oðfeorrganne, and to witanne, næs to
5   oðwyrceanne, and to lufianne, næs to oðlædanne.
Garmund,   godes ðegen,
find þæt feoh   and fere þæt feoh
and hafa þæt feoh   and heald þæt feoh
and fere ham þæt feoh.
10 þæt he næfre næbbe landes,   þæt he hit oðlæde,
ne foldan,   þæt hit oðferie,
ne husa,   þæt he hit **oðhealde**.
Gif hyt hwa gedo,   ne gedige hit him næfre!
Binnan þrym nihtum   cunne ic his mihta,
15 his mægen and his mihta   and his mundcræftas.
Eall he weornige,   swa **syre** wudu weornie,
swa breðel **seo** swa þystel,
se ðe ðis feoh   oðfergean þence
oððe ðis orf   oðehtian ðence.
20 Amen.

Charm for Stolen Cattle

Jennifer Grotz

May nothing I own be stolen or lost
anymore than Herod could take Our Lord.
In the name of St. Helen and of Christ hanged on the cross,
so I claim these cattle will be found, that I will not allow them to be
    taken,
that I will keep them, that they will not be harmed,
that I will cherish them, that they will not be snatched away.

Garmund, servant of the Lord:
find the cattle and make the cattle move
and take possession of the cattle and guard the cattle
and bring the cattle back home!
See that he who took them will never have any land,
nor fields for him who snatched them,
nor house for him that hid them.
And if he obtain any of these, let it never work out for him!

Within three days I shall know of his powers,
his strength and his powers and his protections.
Like dust-dry wood that begins to crumble, he shall wear them all out,
he shall be as brittle as a thistle,
he that hopes to get away with this cattle,
and hopes to drive my livestock away!

Metrical Charm 10: For Loss of Cattle

ðis man sceal cweðan ðonne his ceapa hwilcne man for-
stolenne. **Cwyð** ær he ænyg oþer word cweðe:
Bethlem hattæ seo burh   ðe Crist on geboren wes,
seo is gemærsod   ofer ealne middangeard;
5 swa ðeos dæd wyrþe   for monnum mære,
per crucem Christi! And gebide þe ðonne þriwa east and
cweð þriwa: *Crux Christi ab oriente reducat.* And **III**
west and cweð: *Crux Christi ab occidente reducat.* And
III suð and cweð: *Crux Christi a meridie reducant.* And
III norð and cweð: *Crux Christi abscondita sunt et inuenta
est.* Iudeas Crist ahengon, gedidon him dæda þa wyrstan;
hælon þæt hi forhelan ne mihton. Swa næfre ðeos dæd
forholen ne wyrðe *per crucem Christi.*

For Loss of Cattle

Kathryn Maris

If you've been robbed, this is what you say. Say it immediately:

Just as it's well known to men
that Christ was born in Bethlehem,
make it known to all you see
a grievous wrong was done to me.
Per crucem Christi!

Then turn to the east, bow three times and say three times:
Crux Christi ab oriente reducat.

Then turn to the west, bow three times and say three times:
Crux Christi ab occidente reducat.

Then turn to the south, bow three times and say three times:
Crux Christi a meridie reducat.

Then turn to the north, bow three times and say three times:
Crux Christi abscondita sunt et inuenta est. Then:

Christ was tortured, crucified,
a truth his killers tried to hide.
Reveal this, then, to all you see:
a grievous crime was done to me.
Per crucem Christi.

Metrical Charm 11: A Journey Charm

Ic me on þisse gyrde beluce   and on godes helde bebeode
wið þane sara **stice**,   wið þane sara slege,
wið þane grymma gryre,
wið ðane micela egsa   þe bið eghwam lað,
5   and wið eal þæt lað   þe in to land fare.
Sygegealdor ic begale,   sigegyrd ic me wege,
wordsige and worcsige.   Se me dege;
ne me **mere** ne gemyrre,   ne me maga ne geswence,
ne me næfre minum feore   forht ne gewurþe,
10   ac gehæle me **ælmihtig** and sunu   **and** frofre gast,
ealles wuldres   **wyrðig** dryhten,
swa swa ic gehyrde   heofna scyppende.
Abrame and Isace
and swilce men,   Moyses and Iacob,
15   and Dauit and Iosep
and Evan and Annan   and Elizabet,
Saharie and ec Marie,   modur Cristes,
and eac þæ gebroþru,   Petrus and Paulus,
and eac þusend   **þinra** engla
20   clipige ic me to are   wið eallum feondum.

Charm for a Journey

Peter Sirr

With this rod I inscribe a circle
and trust to the grace of God
against the sore ache, the raw bite.
the sinking fear,
against the swarming horror none can bear
and evil slinking into the land.

I sing a victory chant, lift a victory rod,
word-victory, victory of deeds
let them help me now.
Let no lake hinder me, or hated enemy
beat me down.

Let fear not hover above my life
but keep me safe
Almighty Father, Son and Holy Ghost,
Lord of all the marvelous
and maker, I have heard, of heaven itself.

Abraham and Isaac,
Moses and Jacob I call on
and David and Joseph
and Eve and Anna and Elizabeth
and Sarah and Mary, mother of Christ,

and the brothers, Peter and Paul,
and the thousands of your angels I call on
to guard me from my enemies

Hi me ferion and friþion   and mine fore nerion,
eal me gehealdon,   **me** gewealdon,
worces stirende;   si me wuldres hyht,
hand ofer heafod,   haligra rof,

25 sigerofra **sceolu**,   soðfæstra engla.
Biddu ealle   bliðu mode
þæt me beo **Matheus** helm,   Marcus byrne,
leoht, lifes rof,   Lucos min swurd,
scearp and scirecg,   scyld Iohannes,

30 wuldre gewlitegod   **wælgar** Serafhin.
Forð ic gefare,   frind ic gemete,
eall engla blæd,   eadiges lare.
Bidde ic nu sigeres god   godes miltse,
siðfæt godne,   smylte and lihte

35 **windas on waroþum.**   Windas gefran,
circinde wæter   **simble gehælede**
wið eallum feondum.   Freond ic gemete wið,
þæt ic on þæs ælmihtgian **frið**   wunian mote,
belocun wið **þam** laþan,   se me lyfes eht,

40 on engla **blæd**   gestaþelod,
and inna halre hand   **heofna rices,**
þa hwile þe ic on þis life   wunian mote.
Amen.

and go before me on the path.
Let them bear me up and rule me
and guide my work,

may that holy host,
triumphant, true,
bring glory, and touch my head;
Matthew be my helmet, Mark my armor,
light and strength, Luke my sword,
sharp and quick. Let John be my shield,
richly ornamented, angel of the narrow path.

And now I go. I will meet friends,
I will be in the company of angels,
the good will learn of me.
I pray to the God of victory
for mercy, a safe passage, a light
wind from the shore.

I know there are storms
flinging up the angry waters.
Keep me safe against all enemies,
let me find friends
and live in the peace of the Lord
hidden from the evil that stalks me
and would have my life,
raised up in the arms of angels
and in the hand of the king of heaven
as long as I am alive.
Amen.

Metrical Charm 12: Against a Wen

Wenne, wenne,   wenchichenne,
her ne scealt þu timbrien,   ne nenne tun habben,
ac þu scealt north eonene   to þan nihgan berhge,
þer þu hauest, ermig,   enne broþer.
5   He þe sceal legge   leaf et heafde.
Under fot **wolues**,   under ueþer earnes,
under earnes clea,   a þu geweornie.
Clinge þu   alswa col on heorþe,
scring þu   alswa **scerne** awage,
10 and weorne   alswa weter on anbre.
Swa litel þu gewurþe   alswa linsetcorn,
and miccli lesse   alswa anes handwurmes hupeban,
and alswa litel þu gewurþe   þet þu nawiht gewurþe.

Against a Wen

Maurice Riordan

Pip, pip, nay   small pippin
Here you have no home   no welcome
Out you go   to the cold hillside
There you'll find   an older brother
Who'll place the herb   upon your head
Then under wolf's foot   eagle's wing
In the claw's grip   you'll wilt and wizen
Contract like   charcoal in the fire
Wear off like   dirt from the wall
Evaporate like   water from the pail
Grow small as   grain of linseed
Smaller than   bone of earwig
Thus will you   be gone for good

Final
Riddle-Hoard

Riddle 80

Ic eom æþelinges   eaxlgestealla,
fyrdrinces gefara,   frean minum leof,
cyninges geselda.   Cwen mec hwilum
hwitloccedu   hond on legeð,
5 eorles dohtor,   þeah hio æþelu sy.
Hæbbe me on bosme   þæt on bearwe geweox.
Hwilum ic on wloncum   wicge ride
herges on ende;   heard is min tunge.
Oft ic woðboran   wordleana sum
10 agyfe æfter giedde.   Good is min wise
ond ic sylfa salo.   Saga hwæt ic hatte.

Riddle 81

Ic eom byledbreost,   belcedsweora,
heafod hæbbe   ond heane steort,
eagan ond earan   ond ænne foot,
hrycg ond heardnebb,   hneccan steapne
5 ond sidan twa,   sag on middum,
eard ofer ældum.   Aglac dreoge,
þær mec wegeð   se þe wudu hrereð,
ond mec stondende   streamas beatað,
hægl se hearda,   ond hrim þeceð,
10 . . . orst . . . eoseð,   ond fealleð snaw
on þyrelwombne,   ond ic þæt . . . ol . . .
. . . mæ . . .   wonsceaft mine.

I Stand at the Noble's Shoulder

Jon Stallworthy

I stand at the noble's shoulder,
bound to him, his brother-in-arms,
the king's companion, while the queen—
a lord's blond daughter, no less—
lays a light hand on me. I hold
in my body what grew on the bough.
Sometimes I set off on a proud steed
at the head of the host, giving tongue harshly.
Poets I often reward for their words.
I may be swarthy, but everyone says
I'm open-natured. Now, what's my name?

Look at My Puffed-Up Breast

Patricia McCarthy

Look at my puffed-up breast.
I'm blessed with a noble head, swaying tail.
I've such ears and eyes. I balance on one leg.
I've a grand long neck, sharp beak, a back,
two sides and a rod through my middle.
My home's far above men. When he who stirs
the trees stirs me I am tortured.
Caught out in sheets of rain, hard hail,
frost coats me, snow buries me. I must hold up,
refrain from cockadoodledo-ing my misery.

Riddle 83

Frod wæs min **fromcynn** . . . . . .
biden in burgum,   siþþan bæles weard
. . . . . . wera   life bewunden,
fyre gefælsad.   Nu me fah warað
5 eorþan broþor,   se me ærest wearð
gumena to gyrne.   Ic ful gearwe gemon
hwa min fromcynn   fruman agette
eall of earde;   ic him yfle ne mot,
ac ic **hæftnyd**   hwilum aræe
10 wide geond wongas.   Hæbbe ic **wundra** fela,
middangeardes   mægen unlytel,
ac ic miþan sceal   monna gehwylcum
degolfulne dom   dyran cræftes,
siðfæt minne.   Saga hwæt ic hatte.

Old Was My Race, Steady and Gaining

Jacqueline Jones LaMon

Old was my race, steady and gaining.
I lived in towns, since fire's protector
spun fast for me, told of men wound in flame,
purified by fire. Now a hostile slice
of mankind holds me, those men who first became
my misfortune. I remember it all,
those who, from the beginning, ravaged my kin
from the homeland; I may not treat them with evil
but I am the reason the enslaved are captured and kept
around the world. I have pierced and dazzled
with great strength beneath smooth surfaces
but I must conceal from all the secret power
of my precious craft, my journey. Tell me what I am.

Riddle 84

An wiht is **on eorþan** wundrum **acenned,**
hreoh ond reþe, hafað ryne strongne,
grimme grymetað ond be grunde fareð.
Modor is monigra mærra wihta.
5 Fæger ferende fundað æfre;
neol is nearograp. Nænig oþrum mæg
wlite ond wisan wordum gecyþan,
hu mislic biþ mægen þara cynna,
fyrn forðgesceaft; fæder ealle bewat
10 or ond ende, swylce an sunu,
mære meotudes bearn, þurh . . . ed,
ond þæt hyhste mæge . . . . . . es gæ . . .
. . . . . . dyre cræft . . .
. . . . . .
15 . . . onne hy aweorp . . . . . .
. . . þe ænig þara . . . . . .
. . . fter ne mæg . . . . . .
. . . oþer cynn eorþan . . . . . .
. . . . . . þon ær wæs
20 wlitig ond wynsum, ...
Biþ sio moddor mægene eacen,
wundrum bewreþed, wistum gehladen,
hordum gehroden, hæleþum dyre.
Mægen bið gemiclad, meaht gesweotlad,
25 wlite biþ geweorþad wuldornyttingum,
wynsum wuldorgimm wloncum getenge,
clængeorn bið ond cystig, cræfte eacen;
hio biþ eadgum leof, earmum getæse,

On Earth There's a Creature Sprung from a Wonder

David Constantine

On earth there's a creature sprung from a wonder
Savage, wayward, an unkempt runner
Fierce in her shouting she courses the ground
Teeming with offspring, lovely as their mother.
She is quick in her beauty, she is always eager,
She closes, she keeps. No one has found
Words to convey her various looks
Her myriad spawn, nor reach any way
Back to her start, the birth of the father
Of all the beginnings and all their endings
Back to the spirit of a father brooding
Over a mother for his marvelous son
The fish . . .
   . . . when she cast them . . .
      . . . kin on the earth . . .
               . . . once
In beauty and grace . . .
Bearing, forbearing, this mother can nurture
All always, she stores and restores
She gives and forgives and wherever she shows
However adorned her children on the earth
Rich and poor know her and love her.
Nothing they ever set eyes on is deeper

freolic, sellic;   fromast ond swiþost,

30 gifrost ond grædgost   grundbedd trideþ,
þæs þe under lyfte   aloden wurde
ond ælda bearn   eagum sawe,
swa þæt wuldor wifeð,   worldbearna **mægen**,
þeah þe ferþum gleaw

35 mon mode snottor   mengo wundra.
Hrusan bið heardra,   hæleþum frodra,
geofum bið gearora,   gimmum deorra;
worulde wlitigað,   wæstmum tydreð,
firene dwæsceð,

40 oft utan beweorpeð   anre þecene,
wundrum gewlitegad,   geond werþeode,
þæt wafiað   weras ofer eorþan,
þæt magon micle . . . sceafte.
Biþ stanum bestreþed,   stormum

45 . . . len . . . timbred weall,
þrym . . .   . . . ed,
hrusan hrineð,   h . . .
. . . . . . etenge,
oft searwum biþ . . . . . .

50 . . . . . . deaðe ne feleð,
þeah þe . . . . . .
. . . du hreren,   hrif wundigen,
. . . . . . risse.
Hordword onhlid,   hæleþum ge . . .

55 . . . wreoh,   wordum geopena,
hu mislic sy   mægen þara cy. . . .

Wider, higher, she is a traveler,
She may be a bead, she may be the sum
And compass of all you could spy from a midpoint.
She is hungry, she swallows. Man and woman
Are one of her fabrics, warp and weft
We are woven of her threads. Out of her
The solid ground surfaced, a platform for heroes
But what they bestow, she has bestowed.
Pearls are hers, amber and narwhal
And nothing on earth or under the earth
Is beautiful but by her doing. Life
Respires where she goes and even our wrongs
Our bad wrongdoings, she has swaled away
Till now. Look up, on the invisible air
Those are her shapings, her drifts and unshapings.
We pray for her teeming over our labors
Kindly . . .
Strewn with stones, storms . . .
                          . . . timber walls
. . . our pride . . .
earthward . . .
                          . . . and not feel death
. . . though hurt in the womb
The hoard of words, the best of our people
. . . uncover, open with words
Her zest, how mixed and many her kin. . . .

Riddle 85

Nis min sele swige,   ne ic sylfa hlud
ymb . . . . . .   unc **dryhten** scop
siþ ætsomne.   Ic eom **swiftre** þonne he,
þragum strengra,   he þreohtigra.
5 Hwilum ic me reste;   he sceal yrnan forð.
Ic him in wunige   a þenden ic lifge;
gif wit unc gedælað,   me bið dead witod.

My Home Harps On as I Hold My Tongue

David Barber

My home harps on as I hold my tongue—
The Maker has matched us, so we must
Stick together. I'm the swifter,
Sometimes stronger; he outlasts me.
Whenever I rest, he rolls right along.
I'll dwell in his din for all my days:
If I go it alone, I'll be a ghost.

Riddle 86

Wiht cwom gongan   þær weras sæton
monige on mæðle,   mode snottre;
hæfde an eage   ond earan twa,
ond II fet,   XII hund heafda,
5 **hrycg** ond wombe   ond honda twa,
earmas ond eaxle,   anne sweoran
ond sidan twa.   Saga hwæt ic hatte.

Many Men Were Sitting

Marcia Karp

Many men were sitting
Wise and deep in thought
A thing came in to where they sat
Here are the things this thing has got

    One eye for its seeing
    Two ears for its sounds
    Two feet to walk round on around on its rounds

    Twelve wise men each counted
    Up ten heads times ten
    The heads are enough heads for twelve hundred men

    Two hands for its doings
    Two arms as is custom
    Attached to two shoulders from which it can thrust them

    One back and one front
    To hold it together
    One neck and two sides that keep out the weather

Tell me truly tell me do
The name I shall be called by you

Riddle 92

Ic wæs brunra beot,   beam on holte,
freolic feorhbora   ond foldan wæstm,
weres wynnstaþol   ond wifes sond,
gold on geardum.   Nu eom guðwigan
hyhtlic hildewæpen,   hringe beg . . .
e . . . .   byreð,
oþrum. . . .

When I Was a Tree in the Wood the Creatures

Eiléan Ní Chuilleanáin

When I was a tree in the wood the creatures
Bounced in my shade, brown as my bark,
I flourished in the ground, there was gold on the earth
Joy and joking, women whispering;
When I wear the ring that binds,
The soldier rejoices and I . . .
What I am passes into another. . . .

Riddle 93

Frea min . . . . . .

. . . de   willum sinum,

. . . . . .

heah ond hyht . . . . . .

5   . . . rpne,   hwilum . . .

. . . . . . wilum sohte

frea . . .   . . . s wod,

dægrime frod,   deo . . . . . . s,

hwilum stealc hliþo   stigan sceolde

10 up in eþel,   hwilum eft gewat

in deop dalu   duguþe secan

strong on stæpe,   stanwongas grof

hrimighearde,   hwilum hara scoc

forst of **feaxe**.   Ic **on** fusum rad

15 oþþæt him þone gleawstol   **gingra** broþor

min agnade   ond mec of earde adraf.

Siþþan mec isern   innanweardne

brun bennade;   blod ut ne com,

heolfor of hreþre,   þeah mec heard bite

20 stiðecg style.   No ic þa stunde bemearn,

ne for wunde weop,   ne wrecan meahte

on wigan feore   wonnsceaft mine,

ac ic aglæca   ealle þolige,

þæt . . . e bord biton.   Nu ic blace swelge

25 wuda ond wætre,   w . . . . . . b . . . befæðme

þæt mec on fealleð   ufan þær ic stonde,

eorpes nathwæt;   hæbbe anne fot.

Nu min hord warað   hiþende feond,

He Had His Way, His Pleasure

Eiléan Ní Chuilleanáin

He had his way, his pleasure . . .
I was his, sharp, and those times
I went with him, old master, across deep water
Climbed high cliffs and another day
Off down into the valleys to find safety
Leaving our tracks in the stony places
He shook the frost from his hair. He bore me running
Till my little brother grew and took over
The house he kept his wits in. I was gone.
Then iron tore into me though I could not bleed
When steel was biting. I did not cry,
Weep, plan revenge. Now I must hold
Whatever pours down into me, I must stand,
Let the dark stuff rain down. I have one foot,
I am snatched and robbed by the enemy,

se þe ær wide bær   wulfes gehleþan;
30 oft me of wombe   bewaden fereð,
steppeð on stið bord, ...
deaþes d . . .   þonne dægcondel,
sunne . . . . . .
. . . eorc   eagum wliteð
35 ond spe. . . .

Riddle 94

Smeþr . . .   . . . ad,
hyrre þonne heofon . . .
. . . . . . glædre þonne sunne,
. . . . . . style,
5 smeare þonne sealtry . . .
leofre þonne þis leoht eall,   leohtre þon w. . . .

The wolf's companion, and when he leaves me
It's often then his . . . death is dealing.
The candle of the day, the sun . . . looks on.

Smoother, Than, Smoother Than . . . *Where?*

Eiléan Ní Chuilleanáin

Smoother, than, smoother than . . . *where?*
Higher than sky
Brighter than sun, *more,*
Say it, *where?* than steel,
Sharper than salt . . . *say more,*
Dearer than all this light, lighter than wisps of wind.

Riddle 95

Ic eom indryhten   ond eorlum cuð,
ond reste oft;   ricum ond heanum,
folcum gefræge   **fere** wide,
ond me fremdes ær   freondum stondeð
5 hiþendra hyht,   gif ic habban sceal
blæd in burgum   oþþe beorhtne god.
Nu snottre men   swiþast lufiaþ
midwist mine;   ic monigum sceal
wisdom cyþan;   no þær word sprecað
10 ænig ofer eorðan.   þeah nu ælda bearn
londbuendra   lastas mine
swiþe secað,   ic swaþe hwilum
mine bemiþe   monna gehwylcum.

I Am Noble, Known to Earls

Jane Hirshfield

I am noble, known to earls,
at home with high-born and humble,
famed among men. Traveling far,
leaving behind old friends,
the bright joy of plunderers stamps my body,
whether I honor wealthy cities or shining God.
Now wise men love my company most strongly:
I carry wisdom to multitudes
without speaking one word on this earth.
And though the children of men hunt
now through all lands for my footprints,
at times I keep my tracks concealed from all.

ON TRANSLATING OLD ENGLISH POETRY

WE THOUGHT ASKING A SELECTION OF POETS TO WRITE A SHORT, informal piece about why and how they approached translating Anglo-Saxon poems would provide an instructive dimension to the book. We chose poets who knew Old English (such as Bernard O'Donoghue) along with poets who were not as familiar with it (such as David Slavitt). This section gives some insight into how the various poets undertook their task.

DAVID BARBER (*Charm for a Swarm of Bees* and miscellaneous riddles)

Hwaet! Here's one of the touchstone locutions in the Anglo-Saxon word-hoard, and just try to spit it out, much less transliterate it to save your life. Forget about saying it trippingly on the tongue. Good luck making much sense of its sound. Philology isn't much help, when all is said and done. Proto-Germanic: cognates in Old Frisian and Old Norse. Grammatically promiscuous: alternatively an interjection, an adverb, a pronoun. A shadow of itself in all the trots: Hark, What, Listen, Now, Indeed. *Hwaet! Beowulf* begins with it, and just about every translator takes a different swipe at sweeping away the cobwebs: a few years back, Seamus Heaney's radically resourceful solution was simply to go with "So."

So where does that leave us? The readiest answer is the gloomiest: we'd better abandon all hope of doing any rough justice to the ghostly vestiges of Anglo-Saxon poetry at this late date. We can brush up on the metric with all due diligence, and still feel like we're gargling with gravel. We can hark till we croak and still get nowhere near the pulse of memorable speech—its pitch and its bite, its piths and its gists. Bede, begging our pardon for his Latin crib of Cædmon's eponymous hymn, said it best: "This is the sense but not the order of the words as he sang them in his sleep; for verses, though never so well composed, cannot be literally translated out of one language into another without loss of their beauty and loftiness."

But wait. That *hwaet* is still trying to tell us something. It can't be literally translated and that's precisely the beauty of it. We have it on good authority that it's a nettle best grasped not as a word to parse so much as a call to attention, a shock to the system that bypasses verbal muddle in a visceral whoosh of breath. And taken on those terms, it comes through loud and clear. That primal yelp might be the strongest ancestral claim Anglo-Saxon poetry still has on us, far outstripping any fitful bonds of linguistic kinship. Even when it's not there in the text at hand, you can begin to sense its reverberations crackling above the page—an implicit imperative that's part exhortation, part admonition, and all business.

For my own part, I'd say that goes double for the riddle, that homegrown form of gnomic gamesmanship that in the hands of the scops was the furthest thing from child's play. *Hwaet!* Here comes another dark saying, an enigma wrapped in a mystery and bound up in the muscle memory of metaphor: lend it your ears and it will throttle any reflexive twinges of condescension you might feel about this alliterative artifact as poor man's poetry or the fossil remains of savage jabber. *Hwaet!* Here's one so fiendishly cunning and concentrating the mind so wonderfully that it must have been conjured up as a neck riddle—no mere brainteaser, but the last best hope of making sure you didn't get your head handed to you. Many's the slip between cup and lip, but that *hwaet* is here to tell us that as long as we keep our ear to the groundbeat all is not lost, not even in translation.

EAVAN BOLAND (*The Wife's Lament*)

I studied Anglo-Saxon literature as a student, and continued to read it, in translation, as a poet. My student image was of a poetry barnacled with historical and grammatical mysteries. But in time a second impression replaced the first. As I read more and struggled to write, I found myself turning more often to Anglo-Saxon translations. In Pound's words, in Auden's, I found a new excitement. Their sense that this poetry was an archive of lost values and treasurable energies captivated and persuaded me.

From then on, Anglo-Saxon poetry ceased to be stored in a magic attic of my mind, hoarded rather than held; inherited rather than used. The historic shadows fell away. Texts like *The Seafarer* and *The Wanderer* and *The Battle of Maldon* now seemed urgent, contemporary, and necessary. As does *The Wife's Lament,* which I translated for this book.

These fifty-three lines from the Exeter book are alive with music, protest, and feeling. The backdrop seems both ancient and up to date. This is, essentially, the account of an abandoned wife. Her husband has fled the land. She is left behind. The poem has a complex layering of anger and elegy, and a reliable one. It helped to know this is one of the relatively intact Anglo-Saxon texts.

The speaker in *The Wife's Lament* mourns a lost leader and a treacherous friend, all at the same time. But there are other delights here. The landscape of dark water, briars, and sharp cliffs is lonely and invigorating: a metaphor for desolation. But undoubtedly the poem's true achievement is the construction of a portrait of a woman alone, caught in a hostile environment. If its main depth and texture is psychological, it is also rich in history and political nuance. The reader can see the woman at the center here as being abandoned to and by history.

As a translator, I wanted to hear this poem as incantation. I wanted to emphasize the hypnosis of music, protest, and lament. In its existence, the poem seems to me heraldic—not just a speaking voice but a symbolic one. I used close rhymes and half-lines to bring out the acoustic of complaint. I used them for another reason as well: no matter how this speaker paints her time and condition in a fresh, compelling way, this is not a realistic poem. It has the heft and shadow of allegory and parable. I wanted a sound system to go with that; hence the blunt rhythms, the chorus of end rhymes.

This is an immensely rewarding text. I felt close to it from the start. That said, I am grateful to the editors for their clarification of some of this syntax, which locks in place the mystery and complication of this speaker, which in turn is one of the poem's lasting charms.

MICHAEL COLLIER (*Against a Sudden Stitch; Against Water-Elf Disease*)
   "Translating Anglo-Saxon Charms: Trouble, Corruption, and Disagreement"

One of the pleasures of creating a contemporary version of Anglo-Saxon metrical charms is the pleasure of dwelling in a realm of superstition and magic, in which words, chants, and incantations in conjunction with potions and elixirs are powerful enough to cure physical and spiritual wounds or to revitalize and integrate one's being, a world in which water elves wait to invade unguarded bathers and washerwomen or a cramp or sudden stitch is the sign of a battle with ethereal furies. This realm of magic and superstition, although not much recognized by "modern" cultures, reminds us of the mystery that is at the root of all human utterance and illustrates as well the fluid relationship between imagination, dream, and reality.

Another pleasure was working with Anglo-Saxon texts that by their cousin-twice-removed relationship to English had a ghostly and magically vaporous quality to them. If you don't know Old English, you can almost pronounce the words and almost understand what they mean. I found that I was immensely influenced by Ezra Pound's approach to *The Seafarer,* in which he created a pseudo alliterative-accentual verse, with emphasis on alliteration. At times, it felt as if I had to fight against something like stage Old English, but ultimately I found it satisfactory to the task at hand.

My overall goal was to create translations that made sense by filling in gaps or lacunae. I was aided and abetted in this procedure by Michael Matto, the coeditor of the anthology, who was apt to answer my queries thusly: "The line that is giving you trouble is troublesome—in the manuscript it seems corrupt, and editors do not agree at all about what's going on." Trouble, corruption, disagreement, and uncertainty were the anti-muses—the demons, dybbuks, and furies—that riddled my two texts, and it was these contending forces I tried as best I could to charm into readable versions.

DAVID CURZON (*Maxims I-A; Exodus;* "I Am a Monad Gashed by Iron")
"The Anglo-Saxon Meter and Me"

My attraction to a meter of alliteration, assonance, and bunched strong stresses started in childhood when my mother read me Alliteration's Artful Aid:

> An Austrian army awfully arrayed,
> Boldly by battery besieged Belgrade.
> Cossack commanders cannonading come,
> Dealing destruction's devastating doom.

and so on. What Cossack commanders were doing in an Austrian army became a puzzle in later life but the child and his mother were not pedants, and were just listening to the sound it made, as Ezra Pound advised poets to do in the last sentence of his "Treatise on Metre": "LISTEN to the sound that it makes."

This attraction to alliteration was reinforced by the Strine spoken by me and me mates as I grew up in Melbourne in the 1950s. I sang the old songs all adolescent boys -sang:

> There's a girl on 'er back
> in the middle of the track
> along the road to Gundagai.
> There's a swaggie there beside 'er
> you can bet your balls he'll ride 'er
> beneath a clear blue sky

The phrase "bet your balls" stuck in my mind as the unit and epitome of modern poetic diction. And of course a few years later we boasted of doing adolescent things on the backseats of (at least for the kids of wealthy parents who could afford spacious American cars) Yank Tanks, which became, by our actions, Sin Bins, and, if things really progressed, Fuck Trucks. Hence love of bunched stress.

I had a bar mitzvah and so learned enough Hebrew to become, some time later, interested in ancient biblical poetry. This was compressed in expression, heavy with alliteration and assonance and lacking in rhyme but with a strong break in the middle of the poetic unit due to parallelism. As I wrote in an essay on translating the Psalms, the English poetic form closest to ancient Hebrew prosody is the old Anglo-Saxon alliterative meter, which draws on the curt Anglo-Saxon word-hoard, not the Latinate multisyllabic words introduced later, and has a strong caesura in the middle of the line.

When Katherine Washburn asked me to translate some biblical poetry for her celebrated anthology *World Poetry* I chose Ezekiel's vision of the Valley of Dry Bones. In the King James translation of Ezekiel 37:1–11 this is rendered, accurately, as "The hand of the Lord was upon me and carried me out in the spirit of the Lord and set me down in the midst of the valley which was full of bones." This came out in four stress alliterative meter as:

> The hand of the Lord   held me transported
> and spirited my spirit   and set me down
> in the fell of a valley   filled with bones.

This is the background I brought to translating the portion of the Anglo-Saxon Exodus telling of the crossing of the Red Sea by the Israelites that, as a retelling, with the omissions and changed emphases of all retellings, is for me an example of the rabbinic genre of midrash:

> [N]ow God, who owns them,   has banked red waters,
> a shield to protect you.   These retaining walls
> are piled as high   as the sky's ceiling,
> a wonderful walkway   between waves.

DAVID FERRY (*Genesis A: Offering of Isaac*)

When Greg Delanty and Michael Matto asked me to try my hand at translating an Anglo-Saxon poem for this volume I immediately thought of the *Genesis A: Offering of Isaac*. Ever since I first read it, in graduate school, I had found it powerful and deeply upsetting, just as the King James version of the story as told in the first book of the Bible is powerful and deeply upsetting, and so is Robert Alter's wonderful translation of it. I know that it is the intention of the story, in whatever version, that this should be the case.

James Wood, in a brilliant essay about Alter's translation of the Pentateuch says, "The best example of the incomprehensible in the Pentateuch is God's command to Abraham that he sacrifice his son Isaac. The brevity of the account is searing, as if the text itself flinches from the unreason, is shocked into wordlessness." The opening of the Hebrew text, in Robert Alter's translation, is a devastatingly simple marching order: "Take, pray, your son, your only one, whom you love, Isaac, and go forth to the land of Moriah and offer him up as a burnt offering on one of the mountains which I shall say to you." It is true that the brevity of the account is searing, and the telling of the story is shocked into wordlessness; and this is true also of the King James version of the story. I certainly have no way of arguing that the Anglo-Saxon version is superior and no desire to do so. But it has its own power, its own way of telling this story so that the scandalous terms of God's trial of Abraham's faith are made unbearably vivid. The Anglo-Saxon marching order is devastating in a different way:

> þu scealt Isaac me
>
> onsecgan, sunu ðinne,   sylf to tibre.
>
> Siððan þu gestigest   steape dune,
>
> hrincg þæs hean landes,   þe ic þe heonon getæce,
>
> up þinum agnum fotum,   þær þu scealt ad gegærwan,
>
> bælfyr bearne þinum,   and blotan sylf
>
> sunu mid sweordes ecge,   and þonne sweartan lige
>
> leofes lic forbærnan   and me lac bebeodan

These appalling lines are appalled at what they are saying: that he must go up there on his own two feet, nobody but the mountains witnessing, and himself, himself, sacrifice his son (*sylf to tibre, blotan sylf*); it tells him how, exactly how, with the sword's edge, and how to build the pyre, and cook his dear body black till it is the burnt offering. To my mind the prosody of the Anglo-Saxon lines, "two half-lines with four major stresses, and two or three of the first three, but never the fourth, bearing alliteration," with its insistent shocked overstressed alliterating and its insistent rhythmical pairing of half-lines marching forward toward the anticipated deed, intensifies every effect of the meaning of the things being said, delineating so graphically the unspeakable terms of the test Abraham's faith is to be put to.

I could not attempt to replicate this prosody, especially its degree of alliteration, in modern English without the artificiality of the attempt being its dominant characteristic. The verse form I used (pairs of short trimeter lines) has some characteristics of the original (in the pairings, in the shortness of the paired lines, marching forward, and maybe with some of the overstressing that occurs in such short lines), but these are only referential to the characteristic movement and stressing of the Anglo-Saxon lines.

EAMON GRENNAN (*Andreas*)

What I loved about the great Anglo-Saxon poems, about *Beowulf* and *Dream of the Rood* and *The Wanderer, The Seafarer, The Battle of Maldon*—the poems I studied as an undergraduate in the 1960s in University College Dublin, was their powerful rhythmic sense of a narrative (or a big-limbed emotional outburst) proceeding inexorably down the page in line after line of solidly balanced verse, punctuated by the director's baton or the drumbeat of the great caesura pause in each line, and the way the alliterative repetitions orchestrated it all. So silence and stress became for me the mark of the verse, and it was the music these composed between them that took over my ear. (I could hear them surfacing at times in the verse of Ted Hughes that I later grew to love.) Then I loved their concreteness—the extraordinarily palpable sense that language had a physical life equivalent to the world of weather and of hard, unyielding facts. I never became any good at the language, but even in my rudimentary grasp of it I could relish in a physical way the ponder and velocity of lines from *The Seafarer* and *The Wanderer*—the hail that was coldest of corn; the emotional immediacy of the image of the wanderer, at a loss, forsaken, alone; the unabashed power of the epic or historical hero; the extraordinary image of the dead king laid out in his boat, floating off. My teachers then, Fr. Tom Dunning and Alan Bliss, both had a scholarly relish for what was going on in the poems, and for how it was going on, for the way the poems were put together. And this, since they didn't dry the whole enterprise out with an excess of scholarship, though they could have, was a stimulant to enter into the spirit of the poems, to feel their power and enjoy their ways of proceeding. I liked that.

Something of what I've tried to catch, so, in my own attempt at the few passages of the *Andreas* is that sense of a caesura in the line—but cross-pollinating it with the normative run of a line more or less the length of an iambic pentameter. I didn't want too decisive a break for the caesura, but to find some hint at least of natural speech and the natural flow of a sentence, and the more or less idiomatic accumulation of sentences as they are shaped acoustically into lines. And I wanted to find an alliterative presence that wouldn't shout at the reader but would, on inspection (by ear and eye), be found in the lines. (It is this naturalness of rhythmic ongoingness and idiomatic fluency, while maintaining a clear but not intrusive presence of the original form, that I most admire in Seamus Heaney's translation of the *Beowulf*.)

A latecomer to the picking order, I chose the *Andreas* because, though it hasn't got the unmistakable authority of the great art that inhabits and fashions poems such as those I've already mentioned, yet the excerpted passages have their own (heroic) vigor, and suggest the presence of an artist who can at his best bring his Christian matter and his knowledge of the (pagan) epic manner together in a way that suggests the transforming of the raw material (from whatever Christian story text) into convincing poetry. This happens in the storm at sea, in the flooding city, and in the feel of the characters as participating in an epic struggle informed by genuine human feeling. I've tried to follow him in that, by attempting to achieve some decisive pace in narrative manner, and some physical immediacy and conviction in the various descriptions—whether in word-painting a wintry landscape or a storm-beaten sea, whether dramatizing the plight of a character, or a miraculous happening.

RACHEL HADAS (*Maxims II*)

Before I revisited the drafts of my translation of *Maxims II*, my recollection was that here was one translation that had practically written itself. And although this turned out not to be quite true, I didn't find in my worksheets the frantic scribblings and crossings out that had marked my work, two summers earlier, on a very different poetic text, Racine's *Iphigénie*.

Like much of Anglo-Saxon poetry, I believe, *Maxims II* is marked by a simplicity of diction that still leaves plenty of room for a range of tones. (Sometimes, as with much wisdom literature, it can be hard to gauge the precise tone.) This surface simplicity was something I wanted to retain. Also indispensable was the sense of chanting repetition that informs *Maxims II* at both the thematic and formal levels; the poem is both a series of statements and an accumulation of patterned lines. Almost instinctively, I settled on predominantly four-beat lines occasionally punctuated by briefer couplets ("Christ's power is great; / Strongest is Fate."). I rhymed my lines, often so loosely that assonance is probably a better term than rhyme ("realm"/"loom"; "learn"/"alone"), in couplets. Whenever I'm translating poetry, I find that rhyme, even at this technically undemanding level, keeps the work from running into the prosaic sands of boredom.

The muffled drumbeat of repetition drives home the proverb-like points of these maxims. Yet this is a poem, not merely a set of isolated pronouncements; the lines do have a forward momentum, and the whole does have a shape. I have tried to bring across the terse, packed authority of the original—an authority I hear as at once percussive and syncopated. This poem uses great economy of means to express a broad-ranging vision that encompasses both earth and heaven, the human and natural worlds, the known and the unknown. Are these maxims descriptive or prescriptive? Do they depict things as they are or issue a set of instructions? I think the answer is both. I was happy to try to meet the challenge of bringing this poem, in all its forcefulness and strangeness, its familiarity and its unfamiliarity, over into a version of our contemporary idiom.

BERNARD O'DONOGHUE (*Widsith*)

I have been teaching Old English poetry since 1971, so the most studied texts are deeply embedded in my head. By now I can translate *The Wanderer* and *The Seafarer,* as well as *The Wife's Lament* and *Wulf and Eadwacer* without having the text before me. These poems, and some passages in *Beowulf* I know better than anything in English, except maybe Yeats and Heaney. Both formally and thematically I take the elegies as the model of the lyric poem, maybe because of what has been called their blend of "experience and wisdom": the outlining of a personal narrative with an earnest moral conclusion, a conclusion that may or may not be found consolatory.

It is different with the longer poems of course: *Beowulf* summons up a series of half encounters between different worlds—Christian, pagan, mythical, legendary. We are not sure whether we are in a world of ethical responsibility and metaphysical gravity, as Tolkien argued, or in a "wild folktale" told for diversion and excitement. Who are the people in the poem? Do they belong to a society like ours?

All this is even more true of *Widsith.* We recognize some of these strange places and people either as real or as paralleled in other texts like *Beowulf.* What are we to make of this Universal Soldier whose name means Wide-Travel? Like Chaucer's Knight but more so, he could not have been in all those places and times. Like the *Beowulf*-poet, he knows many names and has a half grasp of history and legend: "Theodoric ruled the Franks . . . Caesar ruled the Greeks"; he has been "with the Scots and with the Picts," "with the Assyrians, with the Hebrews and the Jews and with the Egyptians." So how do we take this seriously at all? This sweeping roll call's claim on our serious attention is maybe founded in its conclusion, which is a remarkable ars poetica or minstrel's job description:

> So the minstrels of men go wandering
> by the dictates of fate through many lands.
> They express what is needed and compose thanks.
> Always, south or north, they find someone
> with wise taste for poems, generous with gifts
> who wants his name raised before the people,
> to achieve valor, before everything fails,

This is what poetry is for, and how it relates to reality and history. This is something that means the same for us as it meant in the seventh century, or whenever this wanderer claims to live. And it is the fountainhead in English of a stream that runs from *Mandeville's Travels* to *Gulliver's Travels* to Salman Rushdie.

FIONA SAMPSON (*Solomon and Saturn*)
"Anglo-Saxon Attitudes"

Anglo-Saxon introduced me to both my resistances to, and subsequent passion for, translation. Like many undergraduates, I kicked against the then-compulsory course on Oxford's first-year English syllabus. Bad enough, I thought, that I had to read about tedious battles: worse still that I should have to translate what had already *been* translated and was available to us in cribs, or textbooks.

It wasn't till the summer that the penny dropped. By then I'd had a year of brilliant teaching, and understood that Anglo-Saxon poetry was about more than heroes and honor codes. It formed, I discovered, a threshold between pre-Christian and Christian cultures, animated by the symbolism of both—and by glamorous archetypes. It was frequently Gnostic, always codified and brilliantly compacted, as symbol is. I found myself especially drawn to the wisdom poetry, in which religious doctrine and empirical natural philosophy seemed insepa- rable. Following its logic felt like entering the Anglo-Saxon mind and "having" its thoughts.

So it's no surprise that I've jumped at the chance to work on *Solomon and Saturn*. The very title juxtaposes Christian and classical "pan- theons" in a way that sums up the fertile cultural fragmentation of the Anglo-Saxon era. Although in this Dialogue—one of two, and incomplete—Solomon has most of the answers, there are riffs, such as the opening of the second passage, where both interlocutors seem to pile on the questions. It is possible to read Solomon's interjections here as rhetorical. But even that tests out an imaginative equivalence between Christian and pagan "wisdoms."

When I came to revise my student translations for the exams, I realized that each word I was choosing was the one I believed best understood what the poem was doing. In other words, I suddenly realized that translation was a practice of interpretation, and every bit as sophisticated as the close critical reading I'd already fallen in love with. I recognized how dictionary "finger-work"—with all the humility about the original language it implied—had got me tracing the original poem's actual thought and music. (Poetry's not lost in the translation, but the paraphrase.) This was the most precise, intimate reading I'd done. It set me off, as it turns out, on a continuing com- mitment to poetry in translation.

DAVID R. SLAVITT (*The Battle of Maldon*)

My reason for translating *The Battle of Maldon* is simple enough: I was invited to do it by a fine poet who is a good friend. But my willing- ness to undertake this was informed as well by the echoes of Ezra Pound's rendition of *The Seafarer,* in which the weird mannerisms of much of his own poetry look to be normalized and functional. To a considerable degree, *The Seafarer* opens the door, then, to the rest of his work and illuminates it. The effort seems to be to depart as far as possible from normative English and still be intelligible. And what comes of that is a freshness, a response to his own imperative to "Make it new."

Here are a few lines that I particularly admired when I first encountered them and still do:

> Bosque taketh blossom, cometh beauty of berries,
> Fields to fairness, land fares brisker,
> All this admonisheth man eager of mood,
> The heart turns to travel so that he then thinks
> On flood-ways to be far departing.

A "bosque" is a grove of trees, and my guess is that he chose the word (seized on it delightedly) because it worked with "blossom," "beauty," and "berries" in the alliterative dazzle he wanted.

The question I had in the back of my mind, then, was what this kind of thing would sound like in my voice. And I had never read *The Battle of Maldon,* which was another attractive aspect of the undertaking, much of my work being an enterprise of self-education performed in public.

What reassured me and finally enabled my affirmative answer was the information that I'd have the help of Professor Michael Matto, a literal translation of the Anglo-Saxon, and further explanations about some of the locutions—in other words, just the kind of trot a poet needs in order to undertake such a task. It is comforting to know at least a little of the source language, as I have learned from my versions of Latin, Greek, Hebrew, Italian, and French. But it isn't absolutely essential. What the translator needs is accurate information from a sympathetic guide and a competence in the target language.

My sense, when I'd completed the piece, was that it was appealing, that it stood up well as a poem, and that, accurate or not, it had a certain authority. If this wasn't exactly the original poem, it was clearly a poem. Thinking again of Pound, I am not sure that his *Seafarer* is "accurate." But if the choice is between accurate and wonderful, I'll take 2 or B anytime.

TOM SLEIGH (*The Nine Herbs Charm*)

Wodin and Christ, the serpent before the Fall and after, medicinal plants against nine poisons, a text that withholds as much as it reveals or reveals itself by what it withholds, these contrasts, contradictions, and paradoxes formed my first impression of this charm: but the more I read it, the more I saw that the opposites were mine and not in the Anglo-Saxon, or that the text leaves things tantalizingly obscure.

For example, once I got past my TV childhood image of Wodin as an All Pro linebacker god, wearing a helmet with horns, and Christ as a bearded, sensitive ascetic, as he was depicted in a faded print that hung in the hallway of my family's first real house, they came to seem like near cousins, if not mirror images: Wodin hangs himself from the world tree, Yggdrasil, for nine days and learns the secrets of the runic alphabet, just as Christ gets himself nailed to the Cross and learns the secrets of death and resurrection. As to textual obscurities, whether caused by textual corruptions or interpolations, the snake in the charm might not be my reading of it as Malice-Striker, but simply a poor snake that happens to pass by—and Wodin, in a fit of pique, madness, chiromantic frenzy, strikes the snake into nine pieces: do these by association become the nine poisons? So in one variant the snake seems like a harbinger of the Fall, while in the other, the snake crawls along, minding its own business, until Wodin attacks it with nine Glory Sticks and strikes it into nine pieces.

Inevitably, there were times when I had to commit to one variant or another—but what determines the nature of that commitment? As I read the poem over in Anglo-Saxon and discussed the multiple meanings with Michael Matto, a superbly creative, informed, and subtle scholar, I began to see the charm as not so much a collision of opposing beliefs as an overlap of late pagan and early Christian sensibilities, and of the poem as a kind of staging ground for the intricacies and subtleties of what you could call the poem's spiritual unconscious—an unconscious in which Christian and pagan elements fruitfully intermix.

So while I made my snake writhe under the shadow of the Fall, the apple remains untainted by Christian overtones—in fact, it works "an end to poison." Rather than neaten that up, and make snake and apple conform to Christian iconography and its rap sheet against apples, I let the contradiction stand. And when "your wise lord" shapes "leaf and stalk" of two of the medicinal herbs, chervil and fennel, while hanging on heavens' crosstrees, is it the powerful Wodin of the Glory Sticks or the vulnerable, oh-so-human Christ who, near the end of the poem, finds himself face-to-face with disease and death?

But again, this opposition is a false one: in the sensibility of the speaker, they knit together, Christ's crown of thorns morphing into Wodin's helmet with horns. When with Christlike compassion the speaker envisions a world in which everything that grows will qualify as a healing herb, and then in the next breath asks that the waters of all seas part, Christ's thorns grow into horns. Of course, it's a trick of historical double vision that makes me link up Wodin's power with Yahweh's parting of the Red Sea. Perhaps the composer of the spell knew about this biblical miracle, perhaps not—but in the next line, when his breath blows away from his patient the "blast of poison," you can see how quickly the tone shifts from compassionate concern with the patient to the wild exaggerations of the patent medicine salesman. Rather than sandpaper this smooth, I wanted to preserve the clashing tones of healer and huckster, prophet and egomaniac. It's in this clash that I hear the voice's essential strangeness, its cosmic hopefulness in a world of pain.

A. E. STALLINGS (*The Riming Poem*)

First: I have no Anglo-Saxon, except inasmuch as I speak English. That said, I have spent much of my adult life in the company of dead languages, and thought I would have a go at this with a weather eye on the original, armed with glossary and notes, and some other translations to triangulate from (thanks to Michael Matto—who also aided with some additional puzzles and nudged me toward a better understanding of the piece). So this can only be said to be a version—and maybe in a sense that is more freeing. Being an unrepentant rhymer myself, I was drawn to the added technical challenge of *The Riming Poem*. (Ah, the fascination of what's difficult!) This poem is apparently something of a freak among AS poetry, which is normally unrhymed in a four-beat alliterative accentual meter. *The Riming Poem* adds a dense (claustrophobic?) pattern of rhyme to the mix, internally rhyming the two hemistiches of each line, and sometimes having cadenzas of lines all hammering away at the same rhyme sound. My goal was not to reproduce this system directly, which would have given me too little leeway in my prime goal, to make the poem work in English; but to get across something of the effect of a densely, internally rhymed accentual poem. What seemed to work—give me breathing room as a novice AS translator and yet tightly knit the poem together rhyme-wise—was rhyming the hemistiches in couplets, throwing in other internal rhymes and alliterations where they offered themselves. (Alas, I didn't succeed in any long virtuosic runs of monorhymes!) I enjoyed shifting my own usual Mixolydian mode toward a more Anglo-Saxon register. I went for four strong beats a line, divided into two loose dimeters. I did not hold to a strict line-per-line pattern: where necessary (translatorese for "convenient"), I used more lines or fewer, and occasionally reshuffled details into a slightly different order. I hope the reader can get into the swing of it, and get something of the flavor and texture of the original.

INDEX OF RIDDLE NUMBERS
AND SOLUTIONS

Because there are no riddle answers in the original manuscript, all solutions are conjectural. In cases where scholarly consensus is lacking, the translators have chosen the solutions they like best.

INDEX OF ANGLO-SAXON POETIC RECORDS TITLES

(for Riddles, *see* INDEX OF RIDDLE NUMBERS AND SOLUTIONS)

FOR FURTHER READING ON OLD ENGLISH

Learning Old English

Baker, Peter S. *Introduction to Old English*. Second edition. Oxford: Wiley-Blackwell, 2007. http://faculty.virginia.edu/OldEnglish

Drout, Michael D. C. *King Alfred's Grammar Book*. http://acunix.wheatonma .edu/mdrout/GrammarBook2007/title.html

Hasenfratz, Robert and Thomas Jambeck. *Reading Old English: An Introduction*. Morgantown, WV: West Virginia University Press, 2005.

McGillivray, Murray. *Old English at the University of Calgary*. http://www.ucal gary.ca/UofC/eduweb/eng1401/

Mitchell, Bruce and Fred C. Robinson. *A Guide to Old English*. Seventh edition. Oxford: Wiley-Blackwell, 2007.

Sweet, Henry. *An Anglo-Saxon Primer*. Ninth edition. Oxford, Oxford University Press, 1953.

Dictionaries and Glossaries

Barney, Stephen A. *Word-Hoard: An Introduction to Old English Vocabulary*. Second edition. New Haven, Yale University Press, 1985.

Bosworth, Joseph, T. Northcote Toller and Alistair Campbell. *An Anglo-Saxon Dictionary*. Vol 2: *Supplement* by T. Northcote Toller; Vol 3: *Enlarged Addenda and Corrigenda* by A. Campbell. Oxford: Oxford University Press, 1898, 1921, 1972. http://beowulf.engl.uky.edu/~kiernan/BT/ Bosworth-Toller.htm

Clark Hall, J. R. *A Concise Anglo-Saxon Dictionary*. With a supplement by Herbert D. Meritt. Fourth edition. Cambridge, Cambridge University Press, 1960. Reprinted by Toronto, University of Toronto Press, 1984.

Modern English to Old English Vocabulary. http://www.mun.ca/Ansaxdat/vocab/ wordlist.html

Editions of Poems (a selected list)

Krapp, George Philip, and Elliott Van Kirk Dobbie. *The Anglo-Saxon Poetic Records*. Six volumes. New York: Columbia University Press, 1931–1953.

Muir, Bernard. *The Exeter Anthology of Old English Poetry*. Two volumes. Exeter: University of Exeter Press, 1994.

Pope, John C. and Robert D. Fulk. *Eight Old English Poems*. Third edition. New York: W. W. Norton, 2000. [contains *Cædmon's Hymn, The Battle of Brunanburh, The Dream of the Rood, The Battle of Maldon, The Wanderer, The Seafarer, Deor,* and *The Wife's Lament*]

Williamson, Craig. *The Old English Riddles of the Exeter Book*. Chapel Hill: North Carolina University Press, 1977.

Also useful are the editions of individual poems published by Methuen's Old English Library, which have been reissued by Exeter Medieval English Texts along with a number of new titles.

ACKNOWLEDGMENTS

The editors and translators would like to thank the following for their help, encouragement, and expertise is putting this book together: Mark Amodio, Catherine Barnett, Patricia Dailey, Heide Estes, John Irwin, Paul Keegan, Yvette Kiser, Hugh Magennis, Andrew McNeillie, Hal Momma, Katherine O'Brien O'Keefe, David Parsons, Lahney Preston-Matto, Andrew Scheil, and Meg Tyler. We especially want to thank David Curzon for his expert advice and recommendations on individual translations as well as the book as a whole. The editors thank Peter Simon and Conor Sullivan at W. W. Norton for their patience and faith.

For use of the Old English texts, the editors are grateful to Martin Irvine and Deborah Everhart, keepers of the Labyrinth Web site hosted by Georgetown University. These texts have a long history, and are the products of the labor of many. Their ultimate source is the six-volume *Anglo-Saxon Poetic Records,* edited by George Philip Krapp and Elliott Van Kirk Dobbie, published by Columbia University Press between 1931 and 1953. These editions were typed into machine-readable files by Geraldine Barrett and Marcella Duggan in the 1960s as part of Jess B. Bessinger and Philip H. Smith's work on the *Concordance to the Anglo-Saxon Poetic Records* (Ithaca: Cornell University Press, 1978). According to Murray McGillivray of The University of Calgary, these files were likely used by the Dictionary of Old English project at the University of Toronto as the basis for their texts of the poems. In any case, the DOE texts were edited and collated over time by Greg Hidley, Duncan Macrae-Gibson, and Patricia Bethel, and later Duncan Macrae-Gibson and Tony Jebson. The Labyrinth versions of these texts were further edited by Martin Irvine and Deborah Everhart when hosted on their site.

INDEX OF TITLES, TRANSLATORS, AND FIRST LINES

EDITORS' BIOGRAPHIES

GREG DELANTY'S most recent books are *The Ship of Birth* (Louisiana State University Press 2006), *The Blind Stitch* (Louisiana State University Press, 2003), and *The Hellbox* (Oxford University Press 1998). His *Collected Poems 1986–2006* is out from the Oxford Poet's series of Carcanet Press.

He has received many awards, most recently a Guggenheim for poetry. The magazine *Agenda* has just devoted its latest issue to celebrate Greg Delanty's fiftieth birthday. The National Library of Ireland have recently acquired his papers up to the end of 2010.

Starting in October 2009 he will be the vice president of the Association of Literary Scholars and Critics and will be president of this Association in October 2010.

He teaches at Saint Michael's College, Vermont.

MICHAEL MATTO is associate professor of English at Adelphi University in Garden City, New York, where he teaches medieval literature and the history of the English language. He received a B.A. from the University of California, Berkeley, and a Ph.D. from New York University. He has published articles on Old English poetry in such journals as *Studia Neophilologica* and *Journal of English and Germanic Philology,* and is coeditor (with Haruko Momma) of *A Companion to the History of the English Language* (Wiley-Blackwell, 2008), as well as guest editor of two volumes of *Studies in Medieval and Renaissance Teaching.*